THE SAVIOUR OF THE WORLD

Sermons preached in the Chapel
of Princeton Theological Seminary

BENJAMIN B. WARFIELD

MACK PUBLISHING COMPANY
Cherry Hill, N. J.

*For of him, and through him, and to him, are all things: to whom be glory for
ever. Amen.*   Romans 11:36

Reprinted July, 1972

PRINTED IN THE UNITED STATES OF AMERICA

TABLE OF CONTENTS

Luke xv. 11-32:—And he said, A certain man had two sons: and the younger of them said to his father, Father, give me the portion of thy substance that falleth to me. And he divided unto them his living. And not many days after the younger son gathered all together, and took his journey into a far country; and there he wasted his substance with riotous living. And when he had spent all, there arose a mighty famine in that country; and he began to be in want. And he went and joined himself to one of the citizens of that country; and he sent him into his fields to feed swine. And he would fain have been filled with the husks that the swine did eat: and no man gave unto him. But when he came to himself he said, How many hired servants of my father's have bread enough and to spare, and I perish here with hunger! I will arise and go to my father, and will say unto him, Father, I have sinned against heaven, and in thy sight: I am no more worthy to be called thy son: make me as one of thy hired servants. And he arose, and came to his father. But while he was yet afar off, his father saw him, and was moved with compassion, and ran, and fell on his neck, and kissed him. And the son said unto him, Father, I have sinned against heaven, and in thy sight: I am no more worthy to be called thy son. But the father said to his servants, Bring forth quickly the best robe, and put it on him; and put a ring on his hand, and shoes on his feet: and bring the fatted calf, and kill it, and let us eat, and make merry: for this my son was dead, and is alive again; he was lost, and is found. And they began to be merry. Now his elder son was in the field: and as he came and drew nigh to the house, he heard music and dancing. And he called to him one of the servants, and inquired what these things might be. And he said unto him, Thy brother is come; and thy father hath killed the fatted calf, because he hath received him safe and sound. But he was angry, and would not go in: and his father came out, and intreated him. But he answered and said to his father, Lo, these many years do I serve thee, and I never transgressed a commandment of thine: and yet thou never gavest me a kid, that I might make merry with my friends: but when this thy son came, which hath devoured thy living with harlots, thou killedst for him the fatted calf. And he said unto him, Son, thou art ever with me, and all that is mine is thine. But it was meet to make merry and be glad: for this thy brother was dead, and is alive again; and was lost, and is found.

THE PRODIGAL SON

I wish to speak to you today of the parable of the prodigal son, or, as it is becoming very common to call it, perhaps with greater exactness, the parable of the lost son. I shall not read it to you again. It has already been read in the lesson for the day. And in any event it is too familiar to require that you should be reminded even of the minuter details of the narrative. Probably no passage of the Scriptures is more widely known or more universally admired. The conversation and literature of devotion are full of allusions to it. And in the conversation and literature of the world it has far from an unhonoured place.

It owes the high appreciation it has won, no doubt, in large part to the exquisiteness of its literary form. From this point of view it fully deserves not only the measured praise of a Grotius, but the enthusiastic exclamations of a Trench. It is "the finest of Christ's parables, filled with true feeling, and painted in the most beautiful colours." It is "the pearl and crown of all the parables of Scripture." Nothing could exceed the chaste perfection of the narrative, the picturesque truth of its portraiture, the psychological delicacy of its analysis. Here is a gem of story-telling, which must be pronounced nothing less than artistically perfect, whether viewed in its general impression, or in the elaboration of its details. We must add to its literary beauty, however, the preciousness of the lesson it conveys before we account for the place it has won for itself in the hearts of men. In this setting of fretted gold, a marvel of the artificer, there lies a priceless jewel; and this jewel is displayed to such advantage by its setting that men cannot choose but see and admire.

1

Indeed, we may even say that the universal admiration the parable commands has finished by becoming in some quarters a little excessive. The message which the parable brings us is certainly a great one. To lost sinners like you and me, assuredly few messages could appeal with more over-whelming force. Our hearts are wrung within us as we are made to realize that our Father in heaven will receive our wandering souls back with the joy with which this father in the parable received back his errant son. But it is an exaggera-tion to represent this message as all the Gospel, or even as the core of the Gospel; and to speak of this parable therefore, as it has become widely common to speak of it, as "the Gospel in the Gospel," or even as the summation of the Gospel. It is not that. There are many truths which it has no power to teach us that are essential to the integrity of the Gospel: nay, the very heart of the Gospel is not in it. And, therefore, precious as this parable is to us, and priceless as is its message, there are many other passages of Scripture more precious still, because their message enters more deeply into the sub-stance of the Gospel. Take this passage for example: "For God so loved the world, that He gave His only begotten Son, that whosoever believeth on Him should not perish, but have everlasting life." Or this passage: "God, being rich in mercy, for His great love wherewith He loved us, even when we were dead through our trespasses, quickened us together with Christ (by grace have ye been saved), and raised us up with Him and made us sit with Him in the heavenly places with Christ Jesus." Or even this short passage: "For the Son of Man came to seek and to save that which was lost." All these are more precious passages than the parable of the lost son, not merely because they tell us more fully what is contained in the Gospel, but because they uncover to us, as it does not, what lies at the heart of the Gospel.

It is important that we should recognize this. For the exaggerated estimate which has been put upon this parable has borne bitter fruit in the world. Beginning with an effort to read into it all the Gospel, or at least the essence of the Gospel, it has ended by reading out of the Gospel all that is not in the parable. And thus this parable, the vehicle of a priceless message, has been transformed into the instrument of a great wrong. The worst things are often the corruption of the best: and the attempt to make the parable of the lost son the norm of the Gospel has resulted, I will not say merely in the curtailment of the Gospel,—I will say rather in the evisceration of the Gospel. On this platform there take their stand today a growing multitude the entire tendency and effect of all of whose efforts it is to eliminate from Christianity all that gives it value in the world, all that makes it that religion which has saved the world, and to reduce it to the level of a merely natural religion. "The Christianity of the prodigal son is enough for us," they declare: and they declare this with gusto because, to put it briefly, they do not like the Christianity of the Bible or the Christianity of Christ, and are happy not to find them in the parable of the lost son.

Now, let us recognize frankly at the outset, that the reason why these new teachers of an unchristian Christianity do not find Christianity in the parable of the lost son is, briefly, because this parable does not set forth Christianity, but only a small fragment of Christian teaching. The turn they have given to affairs is therefore merely the nemesis that treads on the heels of the mistaken attempts to read a full Christianity into this parable. The parable was not given to teach us Christianity, in its essence or its sum. It was given to teach us one single truth: a truth of the utmost value, not only full of emotional power, but, when placed in its relation to other truths, of the highest doctrinal significance; but not in itself sufficient to constitute Christianity, or even to embody its essence. How little what this parable teaches us can be conceived as of itself Christianity may easily be made plain by simply enumerating some of the fundamental elements of Christianity which receive no expression in it: and this negative task seems to be made incumbent on us at the outset of any study of the parable by the circumstance of its perversion to the uses of the propaganda of unbelief.

We observe, then, in the first place, that there is no atonement in this parable. And indeed it is precisely because there is no atonement in this parable that it has been seized upon by the modern tendency to which we have alluded, as the norm of the only Christianity it will profess. For nothing is more characteristic of this new type of Christianity than that it knows and will know nothing of an atonement. The old Socinians were quick to perceive this feature of the parable, and to make use of it in their assault upon the doctrine of Christ's satisfaction for sin. See, they cried, the father in the parable asks no satisfaction before he will receive back his son: he rather sees him afar off and runs to meet him and gives him a free and royal welcome. The response is no doubt just that other Scriptures clearly teach the atonement of which no hint is given here; and that we have no "right to expect that every passage in Scripture, and least of all these parables, which exist under necessary limitations in their power of setting forth the truth, shall contain the whole circle of Christian doctrine." This answer is sufficient against the Socinian who appealed to Scripture as a whole and required to be reminded that we "must consider not what one Scripture says, but what all." But it scarcely avails against our modern enthusiast who either professedly or practically would fain make this parable the embodiment of all the Christianity he will profess. For him, Christianity must do without an atonement, because it is quite obvious that there is no atonement in this parable.

Nor is that more than the beginning of the matter. It must do without a Christ as well. For, we must observe, the parable has as little of Christ in it as it has of an atonement. The Socinians neglected to take note of this. In their zeal to point out that there is no trace in the parable of a satisfaction offered to the Father by which alone He might be enabled to receive back the sinner, they failed to note that neither is there trace in it of any mission of a Son at all—even merely to plead with the wanderer, make known the Father's continued love to him, and win him back to his right relation to the Father. That much of a mission of Christ they themselves confessed. But it is as absent from the parable as is the expiating Christ of the Evangelicals. In truth, there is in the parable no trace whatsoever of a Christ, in any form of mission. From all that appears from the narrative, the errant son was left absolutely alone in his sin, until, wholly of his own motion, he conceived the idea of returning to the Father. If its teaching is to be the one exclusive source of our Christianity we must content ourselves therefore with a Christianity without Christ.

Nor is even this by any means all. For, as has no doubt been noted already, there is as little trace of the saving work of the Holy Spirit in the parable as of that of Christ. The old Pelagians were as quick to see this as were the Socinians later to observe the absence of any hint of a sacrificial atonement. See, they said, the prodigal moves wholly of his own power: there is no efficient grace here, no effectual calling, no regeneration of the Spirit. And there is not. If this parable is to constitute our Christianity, then our Christianity must do without these things.

And doing without these things, it must do without a Holy Spirit altogether. For there is not the slightest hint of a Holy Spirit in any conceivable activity he may be thought to employ in the whole parable. Reduce the mode and effect of His operation to the most attenuated possible. Allow Him merely to plead with men from without the penetralium of their personality, to exercise influences upon them only of the nature of persuasion, such as men can exercise upon one another—still there is no hint of such influences here. From all that appears, the prodigal *suo motu* turned to the Father and owed to no one so much as a suggestion, much less assistance, in his resolve or its execution. If our Christianity is to be derived from this parable only, we shall have to get along without any Holy Spirit.

And even this is only the beginning. We shall have to get along also without any God the Father. What! you say,—the whole parable concerns the father! But what a father is this? It is certainly not the Father of the Christian revelation and not the Father of the Christian heart. He permits his son to depart from him without apparent emotion; and so far as appears he endures the absence of his son without a pang,— making not the slightest endeavour to establish or maintain communication with him or to recover him either to good or to himself. If he manifests joy at the happy return of the son after so many days, there is not the least evidence that in all the intervening time he had expended upon him so much as a single message, much less brought to bear upon him the smallest inducement to return. In other words, what we know as the "seeking love of God" is absolutely absent from the dealing of the father with the son as here depicted: that is, the love of God which most nearly concerns you and me as sinners is conspicuous only by its absence. In this respect the parable stands in its suggestions below the companion parables of the lost sheep and the lost coin. When the shepherd lost his sheep, he left the ninety and nine in the wilderness and went after the lost one until he found it. When the woman lost her coin, she lit a candle and swept the house and sought diligently until she found it. But in the parable of the lost son, the father is not pictured as doing anything of the sort. The son leaves him and the son returns to him; and meanwhile the father, so far as appears, goes about his own affairs and leaves the son to go about his. So clear is it that this parable was not intended to embody the whole Gospel and does not contain even its essence. For what is the essence of the Gospel if it is not the seeking love of God?

The commentators, of course, have not left it so. Determined to get the Gospel out of the parable, they diligently go to work first to put it in. Thus one, in depicting the father's state of mind, grows eloquent in his description of his yearning love. "He has not forgotten his son, though he has forgotten him. He has been thinking of him during the long period of his absence. Probably he often cast glances along the road to see if perchance the erring one was returning, thinking he saw him in every stranger who made his appearance. He has continued looking, longing, till hope deferred has made the heart sick and weary to despair." Now no doubt the father felt all this. Only the parable does not tell us so. And it would not have omitted to tell us so, if this state of mind on the father's part entered into the essence of its teaching. The fact is that this commentator is rewriting the parable. He is not expounding the parable we have, but composing another parable, a different parable with different lessons. Our Lord, with His exquisitely nice adjustment of every detail of this parable to His purpose, we may be sure, has omitted nothing needed for the most poignant conveyance of the meaning He intended it to convey. That the expositor feels it necessary to insert all this merely proves that he is bent on making the parable teach something foreign to it as it stands. What he has especially in mind to make it teach proves, as we read on, to be the autonomy of the human will. The lost thing, in the case of this parable, is a man: and because he is a man, and no lifeless thing nor an unthinking beast, we are told, he cannot, like the coin and the sheep, be sought. He must be left alone, to return, if return he ever does, wholly of his own motion and accord. Therefore, forsooth, the father's solicitude can only take the form of a waiting! *Seeking* love can be expended on a coin or a sheep, but not, it seems, on a man. In the case of a man, *waiting* love is all that is in place, or is possible. Is this the Gospel? Is this the Gospel even of these three parables? When we were told of the shepherd seeking his sheep, of the woman searching for her coin, was it of sheep and coins that the Master would have His hearers think? Does God care for oxen, or was it not altogether for our sakes that these parables too were spoken?

Into such self-contradictions, to say nothing of oppositions to the very *cor cordis* of the Gospel, do we fall when we refuse to be led by the text and begin to twist it like a nose of wax to the teaching of our own lessons. The fact is, the parable teaches us none of these things and we must not bend or break it in a vain effort to make it teach them. Even when another commentator more modestly tells us that the two earlier parables—those of the lost sheep and the lost coin—set forth mainly the seeking love of God; while the third—that of the lost son— "describes rather the rise and growth, responsive to that love, of repentance in the heart of man"; he has gone far beyond his warrant. Why say this parable teaches the rise and growth of repentance "responsive to the seeking love of God"? There is no seeking love of God in the parable's picture of the relation of the father to the lost son, as indeed had just been allowed, in the assignment of the teaching as to that to the preceding parables. But why say even that it describes "the rise and growth of repentance"? It does of course describe the path which one repentant sinner's feet trod as he returned to his father: and so far as the case of one may be the case of all, we may therefore be said to have here, so far as the narrative goes, a typical instance. But there is no evidence that this description was intended as normative, and certainly no ground for finding in this the purpose of the parable. That purpose the text itself places elsewhere; and our wisdom certainly lies in refusing to turn the parable into allegory, reading into it all sorts of lessons which we fancy we may see lurking in its language here and there. We are safest in strictly confining ourselves to reading out of it the lesson it was designed to teach. This lesson was certainly not "the growth and course of sin" and "the growth and course of repentance;" but simply that "there is joy in heaven over one sinner that repenteth." The exquisite surety of our Lord's touch as He paints the career of the unhappy man whose fortunes He employs to point His moral may tempt us to look upon the vivid picture He draws as the normative instance of sin and repentance: and surely there is no reason why we should not recognize that the picture thus brought before us corresponds with remarkable closeness to the great drama of human sin and repentance. But one must be on his guard against being led astray here. After all, the descriptions and analyses in the parable are determined directly by the requirements of the story, not by those of the history of the sinful soul over against its God; and we must beware of treating the parable as if its details belonged less to the picture than to something else which it seems to us adapted to illustrate. The only safe course is strictly to confine ourselves to the lesson the parable was framed to teach.

This is not to say, however, that this lesson is so single and simple that we can derive no teaching from the parable beyond what is compressible into a single proposition. It undoubtedly has its main lesson; but it could not well teach that lesson without teaching along with it certain subsidiary ones, closely connected with it as corollaries and supports, or at least implicated in the manner in which it is taught. Only, we must be very wary that we do not either on the one hand confuse these subsidiary things with the main lesson of the parable, or on the other read into it lessons of our own, fancifully derived from its mere forms of expression. We may perhaps illustrate what we mean and at the same time gather the teaching we may legitimately derive from the parable by asking ourselves now seriously what we do really learn from it.

And here, beginning at the extreme circumference of
what we may really affirm we learn from this parable, I think
we may say that we may derive from it, in the first place,—in
its context, in the way it is introduced and in its relation to
the fellow-parables coupled with it—one of those subtle
evidences of the deity of our Lord which are strewn through
the Synoptic Gospels. Although it leads us away from our
main course, it behoves us to pause and take note of this, in
view of the tendency lingering in some quarters to deny to
the Synoptic Gospels a doctrine of the deity of Christ, and
especially to the Jesus of the Synoptics any real divine
consciousness. It would seem impossible for the unprejudiced
reader to glance over these parables in their setting without
feeling that both the evangelist and the Master as reported by
him speak here out of an underlying consciousness of His
divine claims and estate. For, note the occasion out of which
these parables arose and the immediate end to which they are
directed. The publicans and sinners were flocking to the
gracious preaching of Jesus, and Jesus was so far from repelling them, that He welcomed them to Him and mixed in
intimate intercourse with them. This the Pharisees and
Scribes made the subject of unpleasant remark among themselves. And our Lord spoke these parables in defence of
Himself against their attack. But now note how He defends
Himself. By parables of a good shepherd seeking his lost
sheep; of a distressed woman seeking her lost coin; of a
deserted father receiving back his wayward child. We surely
do not need to argue that the good shepherd, the distressed
woman, the deserted father stands in each instance for God.
Jesus Himself tells us this in His application: "I say unto
you" (and we must not miss here the slight but majestic
intimation of the dignity of His person) "that there shall be
joy in heaven;" "Likewise, I say unto you there is joy before
the angels of God." Yet these parables are spoken to vindi-
cate not God's, but Jesus' reception of sinners. The under-

lying assumption that Jesus' action and God's action are one and the same thing is unmistakable: and no reader fails tacitly to recognize Jesus Himself under the good shepherd and the distressed woman and the deserted father. In Him and His action men may see how things are looked upon in heaven. The lost, when they come to Him, are received because this is heaven's way; and since this is heaven's way, how could *He* do otherwise? This is not a mere appeal, as some have supposed, to the sympathy of heaven: as if He would say to the objector, "I have not your sympathy in this, but heaven is on my side!" Nor is it a mere appeal to a future vindication: as if He would say, "Now you condemn, but you wil see it differently after a while." It is a defence of His conduct by reference of it to its true category. These publicans and sinners—why, they are His lost ones: and does not in every sphere of life he who loses what he values welcome its recovery with joy? Throughout the whole discussion there throbs thus the open implication that He bears the same relation to these sinners that the shepherd does to the sheep lost from the flock, the woman does to a coin lost from her store, the father does to a wandering child. And what is this but an equally open implication that He is in some mysterious way that Divine Being against whom all sin is committed, away from whose smile all sinners have turned, and back to whom they come when, repenting of their sin, they are recovered to good and to God?

In these parables, then, we see Jesus teaching with authority. And His divine voice is heard in them also rebuking sin. For the next thing, perhaps, which it behoves us to take notice of is the rebuke that sounds in them of the sin of spiritual pride and jealousy. This rebuke of course culminates in the portrait of the elder son and his unsympathetic attitude towards the rejoicing over his brother's return home, which occupies the latter part of the parable of the lost son. This episode has given the expositors much trouble; but this has been occasioned solely by their failure to apprehend aright the purpose of the parable. It is in truth an integral part of the parable, without which the parable would be incomplete.

In the former two parables—those of the lost sheep and the lost coin— Jesus was directly justifying Himself for "receiving sinners and eating with them." His justification is, shortly, that it is precisely the lost who require His attention: He came to seek and to save the *lost*. But these parables run up into a higher declaration: the declaration that there is joy in heaven over one sinner that repents rather than over ninety and nine just persons who need no repentance. This high note then becomes the dominant note of the discourse: and it is to illustrate it and to give it vividness and force in the consciousness of His hearers that the third parable—that of the lost son—is spoken. This third parable has not precisely the same direct apologetic purpose, therefore, which dominates the other two. It becomes more didactic and as such more of a mirror to reflect the entire situation and to carry home to the questioners the whole involved truth. Its incidents are drawn from a higher plane of experience and the action becomes more complex, by which a more varied play of emotion is allowed and a more complicated series of lessons is suggested. It is, therefore, not content, like the former parables, merely to illustrate the bare fact that joy accompanies the finding of the lost, with the implication that as sinners are what is lost to God, it is their recovery which causes Him joy. It undertakes to take up this fact, already established by the preceding parables, and to fix it in the heart as well as in the mind by summoning to its support the deepest emotions of the human soul, relieving at the same time the free play of these emotions from all interference from the side of a scrupulous sense of justice.

It is this latter function which the episode of the elder brother subserves; and it appears therefore not as an excrescence upon the parable, but as an essential element in it. Its object is to hold up the mirror of fact to the Pharisaic objectors that they may see their conduct and attitude of mind in their true light. Their moving principle was not, as they fancied, a zeal for righteousness which would not have sin condoned, but just a mean-spirited jealousy which was incapable of the natural response of the human spirit in the presence of a great blessing. They are like some crusty elder brother, says our Lord, who, when the long-lost wanderer comes contritely home, is filled with bitter jealousy of the joyful reception he receives rather than with the generous delight that moves all human hearts at the recovery of the lost.

The effect, you see, is to place the Pharisaic objectors themselves in the category of sinners, side by side with the outcasts they had despised; to probe their hard hearts until they recognized their lost estate also; and so to bring them as themselves prodigals back in repentance to the Father's house. That they came back the parable does not say. It leaves them in the midst of bitter controversy with the Father because He is good. And here emerges a wonderful thing. That "seeking iove" which is not signalized in the parable with reference to the lost—the confessedly lost—son, is brought before us in all its beautiful appeal with reference to these yet unrepentant elder brothers. For, you will observe, the father does not wait for the elder brother to come into the house to him; he goes out to him. He speaks soothing words to him in response to his outpouring of bitterness and disrespect. When, in outrageous words, this son celebrates his own righteousness and accuses the father of hardness and neglect, refusing indeed in his wrath to recognize his relationship either with him or his: the father responds with mild entreaties, addressing him tenderly as "child," proffering unbroken intercourse with him, endowing him with all his possessions,—in a word, pleading with him as only a loving father can. Did the elder son hearken to these soft reproofs and yield to this endearing appeal? It was for the Pharisees to answer that question. Our Lord leaves it there. And the effect of the whole is to show them that, contrary to their assumption, the Father in heaven has no righteous children on earth; that His grace is needed for all, and most of all for those who dream they have no need of it. By thus skilfully dissecting, under cover of the sour elder brother, the state of mind of the Pharisaic objectors, our Lord breaks down the artificial distinction by which they had separated themselves from their sinful brethren, and in doing so breaks down also the barriers which held their sympathies back and opens the way to full appreciation by them of the joy He would have them feel in the recovery of the lost. Was there one among them with heart yet open to the appeal of the seeking God, surely he smote his breast as he heard these poignant closing words of the parable and cried, no longer in the voice of a Pharisee, but in the voice of the publican, "God be merciful to me a sinner!" Surely, like one of their own number only a few years later, the scales fell from his eyes and he confessed himself not only a sinner, but even the chief of sinners.

It would not be quite exact perhaps to say that the parable rebukes spiritual pride and jealousy as well as proclaims the joy in heaven over the recovery of the lost. Its lesson is one; and its one lesson is only thrown into a clearer light by the revelation of the dreadfulness of its contrast in jealousy of the good fortune of the saved. When all are in equal need of salvation, where is there room for censorious complaint of the goodness of God? This levelling effect of the parable raises the question whether there is not contained in it some hint of the universalism of the Gospel. Surely through and through its structure sounds the note of, "For there is no difference!" No difference between the publicans and sinners on the one side, and the Pharisees and the Scribes

on the other. The Pharisees themselves being judges, this were
equivalent to no difference between Jew and Gentile. Were
not the publicans to them as heathen men? And was not
"sinners" just the name by which they designated the Gentiles? If their scrupulous attention to the law did not raise
them above all commerce or comparison with sinners, what
profit was there in being a Jew? We certainly do not purpose
to say with some that Jesus was teaching a universal religion
without knowing it: and we certainly do not discover here
the germ of a universal religion in this—that Jesus meant to
teach that nothing lies between the sinner and his recovery to
God but an act of the sinner's own will, an act to which every
sinner is ever competent, at all times and in all circumstances.
And yet it seems not improper to perceive in the levelling
effect of the implied inclusion of the Pharisees themselves in
the one great class of sinners a hint of that universalism
which Jesus gave His Gospel when He proclaimed Himself the
Saviour of all who believe on Him.

But, however this may be, we approach nearer to the
great lesson of the parable when we note that there is
certainly imbedded in its teaching that great and inexpressibly moving truth that there is no depth of degradation,
return from which will not be welcomed by God. A sinner
may be too vile for any and every thing else; but he cannot
be too vile for salvation. We observe at any rate that our Lord
does not hold His hand when He comes to paint the degradation of sinners, through His picture of the degration into
which the lost son had sunk. No depths are left beneath the
depths which He here portrays for us. This man had dealt
with his inheritance with the utmost recklessness. He had
wasted the whole of it until he was left stripped bare of all
that he had brought from his father's house. Nor was there
anything to take its place. The country in which he had
elected to dwell was smitten, throughout its whole extent,
with a biting famine. In all its length and breadth there was

nothing on which a man might live. The prodigal was reduced
to "bend and pray and fawn" at the feet of a certain citizen
of that dread land; and was sent by him out into the barren
fields— to feed swine! To a Jew, degradation could not be
more poignantly depicted. Yes, it could: there was one stage
worse and that stage was reached. The lost son not only
herded the swine; he herded with them. "He was fain to fill
his belly from the husks that the swine did eat." Not with the
same quality of food, observe, but from the swine's own
store—for "no man gave unto him." In this terrible description of extreme degradation there may be a side glance at the
actual state of the publicans, our Lord's reception of and
association with whom was such an offence to the Jewish
consciousness. For did not they not merely serve against their
own people those swines of Gentiles, but actually feed themselves at their trough? But however this may be, it is clear
that our Lord means to paint degradation in its depths. He
does not spare the sinners with whom He consorted. His
defence for receiving them does not turn upon any failure to
recognize or feel their true quality; any representation of
them as not so bad after all; as if they had been painted
blacker than they were, and were nice enough people to
associate with if only we were not so fastidious. He says
rather that they are bad past expression and past belief. His
defence is that they can be saved; and that He is here to save
them. Lost? Yes, they are lost; and there is no reason why we
should not take the word at the top— or rather at the
bottom—of its meaning: this is the parable of the *lost* son.
But Jesus is the Saviour of the lost; and there is none so lost
that he may not be found by Him, and, being found by Him,
be also found in Him. Oh, no! Jesus does not rejoice in
sinners: it is not sin He loves nor sinners as sinners. What He
rejoices in is the rescue of sinners from their sin. And the
deeper the sin the greater the rescue and the greater the joy.
"I say unto you, there is joy before the angels of God over

one sinner that repenteth." "I say unto you, there shall be joy in heaven over one sinner that repenteth, rather than over ninety and nine just persons, such as have no need of repentance."

It is in this great declaration that the real purport of the parable is expressed. This parable was spoken to teach us, to put it briefly, that God in heaven rejoices over the repentance of every sinner that repents. It is a commentary therefore on those great passages which tell us that God would have no man perish, but all to come to Him and live; and it is more than a commentary on these passages, inasmuch as it throws the emphasis upon the positive side and tells us of the joy that God feels at the repentance of every sinner who repents. To the carrying of this great message home to our hearts all the art of the parable is directed, and it is our wisdom to read it simply to this end. We need not puzzle ourselves over the significance, then, of this detail or that, as if we were bound or indeed permitted to discover, allegorically, some spiritual meaning in each turn of the story. The most of these find their account in the demands of the story itself and enter into its lesson only as contributory details, adding vividness and truth to the illustration.

Thus, for instance, if we ask why there are only two sons in the parable, while there were ten pieces of silver in the preceding one, and a hundred sheep in the first one; the answer is that just two sons were needed to serve Jesus' purpose of illustrating the contrast between the Pharisees and Scribes on the one side and the publicans and sinners on the other; his purpose not being at all to indicate proportion of numbers, but difference in status and conduct. In the former parables the suggestion of comparative insignificance was requisite to bring out the full lesson; in this, the contrast of character serves His purpose. If again it is asked why it is the younger son who becomes a prodigal, the answer is that the propriety of the story demands it. It would be inconceivable that the older son, who according to custom was the co-possessor and heir of the fundamental estate, should have asked or received an inheritance apart from it. But the thing was not unnatural, and doubtless not unusual, in a younger son, who was to be portioned off in any event in the end, and was only asking that he might not wait on his father's death, but might be permitted to "set up for himself" at once. We cannot therefore with confidence discover the beginnings of the prodigal's downfall in his request that his inheritance might be told off to him, or wonder overmuch why the father so readily granted this request. It is tempting, no doubt, to see in the wish of the son to "set up for himself" a hint of a heart already little at one with the law and custom of the father's house. But such allegorizing is dangerous, especially when not suggested by any hint in the language of the narrative or necessarily contained in the situation depicted. It is customary to speak of the younger son as a young man. It may be so. But the narrative does not say so. He may have been in middle life; and it may well have seemed to all concerned that a desire on his part to begin to build up his own house was altogether right and fitting. The separation of his goods from his father's at all events appears in the parable only as the precedent condition of his spending them, not as the beginning of his downfall.

We need not go further, however, into detail. Enough that the story has a single point. And that point is the joy of the father at the return of the son, a joy which is the expression, not of the natural love of the father for a son, but of the overwhelming emotion of mingled relief and thankfulness and overmastering rapture which fills the heart of a father on the recovery of a lost son. The point of the narrative is not, then, that this prodigal is a son, though that underlies and gives its verisimilitude to the picture. The point is that this son is a prodigal. It is because he has been lost and is now found that the joy of the father is so great. The elder

son is a son too; and the father loves him also. Let him who
doubts it read again the exquisite narrative of the father's
tender and patient dealings with him. There is not in all
literature a more beautiful picture of parental affection
pleading with unfilial passion. This father knew perfectly
how to fulfil the injunction later laid down by the apostle
Paul: "And ye fathers, provoke not your children to wrath;
but nurture them in the chastening and admonition of the
Lord." From this point of view that soothing admonition,
"Child, *thou*" (the emphasis on the "thou" must not be
neglected) "art always with me; and all that is mine is thine;
but it was meet to make merry and be glad, because this thy
brother was dead and is alive, and was lost and is found"—is
simply perfect. So clear is it that the lesson of the parable
does not turn on the prodigal's being a son, but on this son
being a prodigal.

In other words, its lesson is not that God loves His
children, but that God loves sinners. And thus this parable is
seen ranging with the preceding ones. The lost sheep, the lost
coin, the lost son, have only this one thing in common, that
they are lost; and the three parables unite in commending the
one common lesson to us, that as men rejoice in the recovery
of what is lost, so God rejoices in the recovery of sinners—
since sinners are the things that to Him are lost. We must not,
then, use this parable to prove that God is a father, or draw
inferences from it as if that were its fundamental teaching. It
does not teach that. What it teaches is that God will receive
the returning sinner with the same joy that the father in the
parable received the returning prodigal; because as this son
was to that father's heart above all other things that he had
lost, his lost one, and his return was therefore above all other
things that might have been returned to him his recovery; so
sinners are above all else that God has lost in the world His
lost ones, and their return to Him above all other restorations
that may be made to Him His recovery. The vivid picture of

the father not staying to receive the returning son, but, moved with compassion as he spied him yet a great way off, running out to meet him and falling on his neck and kissing him in his ecstasy again and again; cutting short his words of confession with the command that the best robe be brought to clothe him, and shoes for his blistered feet, and a ring for his finger, and the order that the fatted calf be killed and the feast be spread, and the music and the dance be prepared— because, as he says, "This my son was dead and is alive, was lost and is found"—all this in the picture is meant to quicken our hearts to some apprehension of the joy that fills God's heart at the return of sinners to Him.

O brethren, our minds are dulled with much repetition, and refuse to take the impression our Lord would make on them. But even we—can we fail to be moved with wonder today at this great message, that God in heaven rejoices— exults in joy like this human father receiving back his son— when sinners repent and turn to Him? On less assurance than that of Jesus Christ Himself the thing were perhaps incredible. But on that assurance shall we not take its comfort to our hearts? We are sinners. And our only hope is in one who loves sinners; and has come into the world to die for sinners. Marvel, marvel beyond our conception; but, blessed be God, as true as marvellous. And when we know Him better, perhaps it may more and more cease to be a marvel. At least, one of those who have known Him best and served Him most richly in our generation, has taught us to sing thus of His wondrous death for us:

> That He should leave His place on high,
> And come for sinful man to die,
> You count it strange?—so do not I,
>   Since I have known my Saviour.

Nay, had there been in all this wide
Wide world no other soul beside
But only mine, then He had died
     That He might be its Saviour;

Then had He left His Father's throne,
The joy untold, the love unknown,
And for that soul had given His own,
     That He might be its Saviour!

Is that too high a flight for us—that passion of appropriation
by which the love of Jesus for me—my own personal soul—is
appreciated so fully that it seems natural to us that He,
moved by that great love that was in Him for me—even
me—should leave His throne that He might die for me,—just
me,—even were there none else beside? At least we may
assent to the dispassionate recognition that in the depths of
our parable is hidden the revelation of that fundamental
characteristic of Jesus Christ by virtue of which He did
become the Saviour at least of sinners. And seeing this and
knowing ourselves to be sinners, we may acknowledge Him
afresh today as our Saviour, and at least gratefully join in our
passionate sinner's prayer:

And oh! that He fulfilled may see
The travail of His soul in me,
And with His work contented be,
     As I am with my Saviour!

Yea, living, dying, let me bring
My strength, my solace from this spring,
That He who lives to be my King,
     Once died to be my Saviour!

ACTS iv. 12:—And in none other is there salvation: for neither is there any other name under heaven, that is given among men, wherein we must be saved.

JESUS ONLY

A notable miracle had been wrought. As Peter and John were entering the temple at the hour of afternoon prayer, they had encountered a poor cripple who was in the habit of having himself laid at the gateway to beg alms of the passing worshippers. Him they had healed, attracting his attention and faith by the great word, "In the name of Jesus Christ the Nazarene, walk!" To the confounded crowd that ran together Peter had improved the opportunity to preach Jesus, whose mighty name, on faith having been awakened in it, had wrought this wonderful cure. The Sadducean leaders of the people had been, as the narrative puts it, greatly "worked up" by the occurrence; and, apprehending Peter and John, they had cast them into prison overnight and brought them on the morrow before the Sanhedrin. The question put to the apostles in their examination before this body was studiedly insulting in its every phrase, and runs up into an explosion of angry contempt: "What sort of power is it, and what sort of a name is it that you have done this thing by—you?" There is here an open relegation of the apostles to that herd of "vagabond Jews" who infested every city, working strange things by the power of some great name which they pronounced in their incantations.

"Then Peter," says the narrative, "filled with the Holy Spirit, said to them: 'Rulers of the people, and elders, if it can possibly be we' "—note the emphasis of personal protest in this "we,"—" 'who are today called to account, for a good deed' "—note this emphatic "good deed;" not the misdeed for which it is customary to call men to account—" 'to an infirm man, by what it is that he has been saved,—be it

23

known to all of you and to the whole people of Israel' "–
here Peter it will be seen is rising to his climax,–" 'that it is
by the name of Jesus Christ the Nazarene, whom ye' "–an
emphatic "ye" locating the persons with clear and strong
assertion–" 'whom *ye* crucified, whom God raised from the
dead,' "–oh, the tremendous poignancy of that contrast!–
" 'by this name it is that he stands before you whole. This is
the stone that was despised by you the builders, that is
become the head of the corner.' "

Assuredly, we will say, pungency of rejoinder, boldness
of proclamation, could go no further. And there stood the
healed man in their midst, the living witness of the truth of
the declaration. But Peter does go further than even this. Not
content with so ringing an assertion of the reversal in the
court of heaven of their earthly verdict on Jesus the despised
Nazarene, and of the living presence among them of Him
whom they had foully slain, doing wonders, Peter now suddenly rises to the height of his great argument and sets His
Master on the pinnacle of His glory as the sole Prince and
Saviour of all the earth. "This," he says, "is the stone that
was set at nought by you the builders, that has been made
the head of the corner, and in none other," he adds,–"in
none other is there salvation; for neither is there any other
name under heaven given among men, by which we must be
saved!"

It is too late now to speak of the fine note of defiance,
of holy and chastened challenge, that rings in this trumpet-
like speech of Peter's. In these last words it has passed
beyond defiance and even beyond challenge, and taken on
the note of summons and high proclamation. In them Peter
steps forth unabashed before the world, as the herald of the
Prince of Life, and asserts His crown prerogatives. Into the
face of the sneering Sanhedrin before whom he stands ar-
raigned he, an unlearned and ignorant man, flings this great
and sweeping declaration: that Jesus Christ of Nazareth–

whom they had crucified—was not only God's Holy Servant, by way of eminence the Holy and Righteous One, against whom they had therefore grievously sinned when they laid their wicked hands upon Him; but is actually (though they have slain Him) the very Lord and Source of Life, into whose sole hands are gathered all the issues of Being, whether in this world or in the world to come.

We must not pause to seek to picture the effect with which this daring predication to Jesus of the unique empire over salvation must have struck upon those Jewish ears that day. Him they had slain, but truly He had risen from the dead to trouble them, and was showing forth His might in signs and wonders done in His name. Here was this crippled man, saved from his infirmity; and who could gainsay that the cure had been wrought by the name of Jesus? Nay, here are these unlearned and ignorant men themselves, saved from their special infirmities also; Peter, for example, who had denied his Lord at the mere glance of a serving-woman, now stands before the Sanhedrin itself, careless of their frowns and his own chains, and boldly proclaims his Lord's risen glory and dominion over the whole realm of life. Who could gainsay that this cure too had been wrought by the name of Jesus? It is easy to imagine what searchings of heart there were in the Sanhedrin that day; what marvellings; what anxious inquiries as to what could be done to stop the spread of such a gospel. The two thousand years that have passed have taught us how vain all their efforts were; and, having rejected the stone that the Lord had made the head of the corner, how completely was fulfilled in them the further prediction of this same Jesus, that "he that falleth on this stone shall be broken to pieces, while on whomsoever it shall fall it will scatter him to dust."

It is of more importance for us today, however, to inquire what we today—after these two thousand years of enlightenment during which the gospel of Jesus has had free course and been glorified—should learn from this great declaration of Peter, spoken, we are told explicitly, when he was filled with the Holy Spirit. It assures us too, after so long a time, that there is salvation in none other than Jesus, and that there is no other name under heaven given among men whereby we must be saved. What are we to understand by this tremendous assertion?

We shall be counselled, of course, at the outset, to remember that we have before us here an announcement that belongs to the beginnings of the Gospel; that we are listening to words of Peter, not, say, of Paul or John; and to words of Peter even, which were spoken before he had been enlightened by the great vision that visited him on the house-top of Joppa. We shall even be counselled to remember that a miracle of physical healing lay at the root of this announcement, and that in its primary meaning, at least, it must be held to bear its natural reference to it. It would be a pity assuredly to forget such things as these. It is only by bearing them fully in mind that the large and rich comprehensiveness of Peter's great declaration can be apprehended. It is true that the whole situation turns on a miracle of healing; that Peter is addressing himself in his entire speech to a demand for an explanation of the power by which this physical cure had been wrought; that he had just spoken of the healing as a "salvation," making use of the same word that he employs in this great declaration itself. He certainly means to declare, and he certainly does declare, that in none other than Jesus is such physical salvation to be had; and that there is no other name under heaven given among men whereby they must even thus be saved. Exorcists there were and healers enough, who pronounced other names over the afflicted children of men. None of them had power to save. If ever the evils of this life are to be relieved, the forces of disease and decay, of injury and death, to be broken, it will be only by Jesus that it will be done; only His name, by faith in His name, can give that perfect soundness for which we long. It is doubtlessly equally true that Peter had not yet wholly sloughed off the hard casing of Jewish exclusiveness that enclosed and straitened his heart. We know not what elements of crude Messianic hopes may not have still clung to his thought and conditioned his conception of salvation. The Jesus whom he proclaimed was undoubtedly in his view a king, the fruit of David's loins, and seated upon David's throne; a prophet aforepromised by Moses and all who came after Moses, now come primarily to Israel that he might bless them first of all, and others, only in and through Israel. He means to proclaim, and he does proclaim, that there is no national Saviour but Jesus, that there is no other name under heaven, given among men, whereby men must be saved from the. oppressions of society and the organized life of states. Many other national Saviours had offered themselves and were still offering themselves to his hearers. There was, for example, one Theudas, whom they all remembered, who gave himself out to be a somebody; and there was Judas of Galilee who only the other day had presented himself to their acceptance. What had become of those that followed after them? No; if the yoke of the oppressor is ever to be broken, if society is ever to become that promised kingdom of righteousness for which all long, it will only be by Jesus that it will be accomplished; only His name, by faith in His name, can bring in the long-expected reign of God.

But it is beyond all possibility of doubt equally true that salvation in Peter's apprehension of it stretched far beyond these conceptions and found its real significance in the things of the spirit. "Remission of sins," and the gift of the Holy Ghost as an inward power making for holiness,— these are the ideas which, at least from Pentecost onward, dominated his thoughts; the "blotting out of sin" that seasons of refreshing from the presence of the Lord might come—here is expressed the very core of all his longing. No doubt, as regards this spiritual salvation too, he had yet much to learn. No doubt the wideness of God's mercy had not yet been fully revealed in his thought, and no doubt he still expected the Gentiles to become participants in this salvation, not as Gentiles, but only as the result of a spiritual conquest of them by Judaism. But assuredly not the less, but much the more rather, was it therefore inconceivable to Peter that Gentiles could be saved apart from that one Saviour in whom alone was there salvation for even the Jews. That channels of salvation could be open to the "sinners of the Gentiles" which are closed to Jews could not enter his imagination. Any remnants of Jewish exclusivism which may be imagined to have still clung to his thought, cannot be supposed, then, to render it doubtful whether or no the Gentiles too are to be understood to be shut up to this one announced means of salvation, but quite the contrary. "Sinners of the Gentiles," in the very nature of the case, rested in his view under a condemnation indefinitely deeper than the chosen people; and could hope for salvation only by participation in the blessing which came first to them. So that it must remain beyond all question that Peter's declaration was intended to assert and does assert in the most unqualified and the most exceptionless way possible that in none other than Jesus is this spiritual salvation to be had, and that there is no other name under heaven given among men, whereby men in this sphere, above all, must be saved.

    It would seem quite clear, therefore, that to catch Peter's meaning in this great declaration, we must take the conception of salvation in the most comprehensive sense possible for it to bear, and that we must give to his restriction of this salvation to Jesus and His mighty name, the strictest and most stringent interpretation. Doing so, we shall not be subjecting Peter's words to undue pressure, forcing them out of their natural and simple meaning. Rather it is only thus that we can protect them from wresting and preserve to them

their natural and simple meaning. Nor can we affect surprise
that such is the case. In both matters Peter is here only
reflecting in his own way and consonantly with his own
personal stage of growth and the circumstances which were
determining his language, the common Biblical doctrine.

We certainly shall never do justice indeed to the Biblical
conception of salvation taken as a whole, save by giving to
that term its widest conceivable connotation. It may be that
we are prone to narrow and limit it on this side and that, and
then to feel some surprise, perhaps some perplexity, when we
open the pages of Scripture and light upon passage after
passage which will not square with our poor starveling ideas.
In the Biblical conception of it,—we shall not be able to say it
too emphatically—salvation broadens its beneficent reach to
cover every evil that afflicts the afflicted race of man. And
that with the best of reason. For in the centre of its centre, in
the heart of its heart, salvation is deliverance from sin, and
accordingly it is deliverance from all the evils that find their
roots in sin: and every evil of every kind that has ever entered
the sphere of human life is consequent on sin and but the
manifestation of sin's presence and power in humanity. We
open a recent book and find written: "God Himself cannot
prevent the consequences of sin, the sorrow, disgrace and
suffering which are the direct effect of evil doing." We bless
the God and Father of our Lord and Saviour Jesus Christ, the
Lord of heaven and earth, that such is not the teaching of
this blessed Bible. "They shall hunger no more," we read,
"neither thirst any more; neither shall the sun strike upon
them, nor any heat, . . . and God shall wipe away every tear
from their eyes . . . and death shall be no more, neither shall
there be mourning, nor crying, neither shall there be any
more pain." Symbolical this language no doubt is, but it is
such, nevertheless, because it expresses much more, not less,
than it directly says: and so far as faithfulness to Biblical
teaching goes it could be read with the literalness of a legal

document. The favourite expression for salvation in the Biblical record is that great word Life; which is set over against
the equally great word Death, as the best comprehensive term
to gather up all the evils from which we shall be saved.
Whatever Death is, and all that Death is, and all that leads up
to, accompanies and follows Death, in any one of its possible
applications, physical and temporal, spiritual and eternal—
that is what we shall be saved from in this salvation. And
whatever Life is, and all that Life is, and all that leads up to,
accompanies and expresses, and grows out of and crowns
Life—in every possible application of that great conception—
that is what we shall be saved to in this salvation: or rather
that, in Biblical language, *is* salvation. "In the day that thou
eatest thereof, thou shalt surely die"—in these terms was
couched the great prohibition of "the fruit of that forbidden
tree whose mortal taste," as Milton, not a whit too compre-
hensively, puts it, "brought death into the world and *all* our
woe." Everything that vexes and troubles human life in every
sphere of its manifestation is but the issue of this first
disobedience. Conceive man as a physical organism held together by the subtle forces which govern material life; all that
brings him pain, disease and death, emerges as the unavoida-
ble result of sin and therefore the necessary object of salvation. Conceive him as a social being bound in fellowship with
his companions by those mutual ties which hold together the
fabric of society; all that brings him discontent, strife, injustice, oppression, want or neglect, equally truly is the fruitage
of sin and equally truly is therefore the object of salvation.
Or conceive him at the height of his nature, as a spiritual
being standing in relation to that spiritual world above him
which stretches upwards to the throne of God itself; all that
breaks the free play of this high communion and rouses in
him the sense of incompatibility with his higher environment;
all that rises within him as a bar to that favour of God which
is life, whether in the form of guilt or corruption,—this above

all is the bitter fruit of sin and therefore above all the immediate object of salvation. We must conceive salvation as reaching out with its healing hand to the utmost confines of the effects of sin, or else fail to recognize with the poet the Restorer as a "greater man" than him through whom we suffered this grievous loss. The Scriptures certainly will not permit us to entertain fancies so derogatory to the glory of the Redeemer. They do not content themselves indeed even with an equation of the spheres in which the forces of destruction and restoration work as if it were enough to say that the gift of life shall supplant the curse of death—following it into all the ramifications of its baneful effects that it may work their reversal. Nay, no sooner have they drawn the parallel than they at once correct it with a fervid, "but *not* as the trespass, so also is the free gift. For if by the trespass of the one the many died, *much more* did the grace of God and the gift by the grace of the one man Jesus Christ *abound* unto the many." There is a superabundance of grace, and an extension of it immeasurably beyond the ravages wrought even by sin.

Would we do justice to the Scriptural representations, then, we must conceive nobly of salvation. We must enlarge its borders if we would give to it all the land which the Lord has promised it. It belongs to the glory of Christ that His salvation enters into every region of human need and proclaims in all alike complete deliverance. Even the lower creation, by virtue of the relation in which it stands to man, partakes in his redemption. If the very ground was cursed for man's sake that the place of his abode might sympathetically partake in his punishment, no less shall it share in his restoration. Man's sighs are not the only expression of the evil that curses human life in its sinful development. The whole creation groans and travails together with him. But it shares also in the hope of the coming deliverance. For there shall be a new heaven, we are told, and a new earth. Under these new heavens, in this new earth, shall gather redeemed humanity, in the perfection of its idea, and in perfect harmony with its perfected environment. In the perfection of physical vigour: for what is sown in corruption shall have been raised in incorruption, what is sown in dishonour shall have been raised in glory, what is sown in weakness shall have been raised in power, what is sown in selfishness shall have been raised in spirituality. In the perfection of social organization and intercourse: for there shall be none to hurt or destroy in all God's holy mountain, and all the people of the Lord shall have learned righteousness. In the perfection of spiritual communion with God: for then it is that the Lord shall make Himself known to His people and shall dwell with them, and they shall need no Temple to which men should require to repair in order to meet the Lord, for the Lord God the Almighty and the Lamb are the Temple thereof, and the grace of the Lord shall flow down the streets in a river of the water of Life washing into every nook and corner. Such is the picture the Scriptures draw for us of the salvation of our God. And let us not fail to note that it is a picture of a saved world. As no sphere of human life is left untouched by it; as on its touch, every sphere of human life is transformed; so the completeness and the profundity of its renovation of man is matched by the wideness of its extension over man. It is the renewed heavens and the renewed earth that we are bidden to contemplate; and dwelling in them in endless bliss renewed humanity. Renewed *humanity;* not a meagre company withdrawn from the sin-festering race, but the race itself, cleansed and purified and gathered home to the Father's arms; not without loss suffered by the way, it is true, for there are some who shall not enter into this holy city; but with all losses made good, all breaks in the ranks filled up, and all lacks and wants supplied by Him who has redeemed it to Himself and led it to its new estate of perfection in itself and eternal communion with Him. Such is the salvation that has been wrought out for us by Christ.

Now the point to which the words of Peter, which are particularly engaging our thought today, energetically direct our attention is that neither this salvation as a whole, nor any least part of or element in it, can possibly be attained save in Jesus Christ. "And in none other," he declares with tremendous emphasis, "in none other is there *this* salvation," this well-known salvation which fills all our hopes and longings:— "in none other is there this salvation: for neither is there any other name, under heaven, given among men, wherein we must be saved." Peter's interest, we will observe, is absorbed, not in the greatness of the salvation, but in the greatness of Jesus Christ the Nazarene, who is the Lord and sole disposer of this great salvation. He assumes that the idea of this salvation and its indescribable greatness, and an insistent craving for it, are all present, persistent, controlling in the minds and hearts of his auditors. What he is concerned with is to carry home to their minds and hearts the autocracy of Jesus Christ the Nazarene over it. Hence the negative form given to his declaration. He does not say, you observe, "You ask by what power or by what name this cure has been wrought. I reply by the power and name of Jesus Christ of Nazareth, in whose mighty hands rests power to heal all the ills of men." No, he gives quite a different tone to his declaration when he turns forward its negative edge and declares with enormous energy of expression: "You ask by what sort of power or by what sort of name we have done this thing. I reply it is by the name of Jesus Christ the Nazarene, and there is not in any other this salvation; for neither is there another name, under heaven, given among men by which we must be saved." Observe the accumulation of emphatic phrases to enhance the stress laid on the exclusiveness of Jesus' power to save. First of all, there is the redoubled assertion: "in none other is there salvation," and then again that none might miss it, "there is no other name

under heaven, given among men, whereby we must be saved."
Then there is the heaping up of clauses, in almost superfluous
reiteration of the absoluteness of the exclusion of all but
Jesus from the power of saving: there is "none other," there
is "no other name," "under heaven," "given among men"—as
if it should be said, "Seek you wherever men can be found,
search to the utmost limits of the encanopying sky,—nowhere
among men, nowhere under the stretch of heaven's roof, will
you find a whisper of another name in which salvation can be
found." And then, at last, there is the curious turn given to
the phrase: "in which we *must* be saved." We weaken it
vastly in our careless current reproductions of it, saying,
"neither is there any other name under heaven given among
men wherein we *may* be saved,—wherein we *can* be saved."
Peter does not so phrase it. He says, "wherein we *must* be
saved." The accent of necessity is in it. It is not merely that
we may be saved by Jesus, or that we can be saved by Jesus;
but, if we be saved at all, it *must* be in Him that we are saved.
There is no possibility otherwise or elsewhere. And with the
emergence of this vigorous *must* at the end of the sentence
the last hammer falls, the last rivet is clinched, and the last
band of steel is fixed around this tremendous assertion of the
exclusiveness of salvation in Jesus Christ alone.

The note of Peter's declaration here, you will observe,
is, "Jesus only!" "Jesus only!" There is a note of severity in
the mode in which he declares it, for the occasion of its
declaration was such as to call for assertion,—assertion in the
face of hard unbelief, of persistent denial of the crown-rights
of the King. But through all the severity there sounds also a
note of exuberance. This is the account to be given indeed of
the almost unexampled piling up of phrases to which we have
adverted, adding little to one another as they do except an
ever-growing emphasis for the main declaration; expressive in
a word only of the overflowing emotion that was flooding
the speaker's heart. The name of Jesus was inexpressibly

precious to him because it was the saving name, nay, we will
not express it adequately until we say it outright—because it
was the *only* saving name in all the universe. It was much to
him, no doubt, that he had come to perceive that there had
been given to that broken and suffering man whom he had
seen but yesterday hanging on the cruel cross, the Name that
is above every name, that in the name of Jesus every knee
should bow, of things in heaven and things on earth and
things under the earth, and that every tongue should confess
that Jesus Christ is Lord, to the glory of God the Father. This
supreme exaltation of his Master alone must have filled his
soul with swelling delight. But there was something beyond
this supreme exaltation itself that was suffusing his whole
being with unutterable joy. It was the exuberant sense of the
uniqueness of Jesus' office of Saviour that pressed for utter-
ance and found it haltingly in an accumulation of phrases
that must appear extravagant to all who do not with him rise
to the height of the great vision. Jesus exalted to the throne
of the universe,—that is a great vision; but Jesus the sole Lord
of salvation, holding in His hands the keys of life, and
dividing to each as He will,—Jesus the only Name under
heaven given among men whereby man must be saved—to
sin-stricken and despairing men, surely this is a much greater
vision. It was this greater vision that had caught Peter's
uplifted eyes.

Not, of course, as if it were to his eyes alone that it was
given to see it. There is nothing that Peter tells us here that is
not told us over and over again by every writer of this New
Testament. It belongs indeed to the very heart of the Gospel
that these writers preached, which centred not precisely in
the proclamation of salvation, but in the preaching of Jesus
as Saviour. To them indeed Jesus *is* the Gospel; and where
Jesus is not, there there is no gospel at all. It is of the very
essence of the Gospel, therefore, that salvation can be obtained through Jesus alone. And so it was preached from the

beginning. "I am the way, the truth, and the life," said Jesus
Himself as plainly as majestically: "no man cometh unto the
Father, but by Me." And equally plainly again, in that
equally majestic assertion reported to us by Matthew and
Luke on which He founds one of the most touching of His
invitations: "All things have been delivered unto Me by My
Father; and no one knoweth the Son, save the Father; neither
doth any know the Father, save the Son, and *he to whom the
Son willeth to reveal Him.*" That as there is one God, so there
is only "one mediator between God and men, the man Christ
Jesus," after whose once offering of Himself "there remain-
eth no more sacrifice for sins," became accordingly the
centre of the Gospel proclamation by His accredited messengers. And therefore they did not hesitate to proclaim boldly
that only they who believe in Jesus Christ shall be saved: and
that those who are without Christ have no hope and are
without God in the world. The life that God has given us,
explains John in his searching way, is deposited for us "in the
Son," and therefore, "he that hath the Son hath the life; he
that hath not the Son of God hath not the life."

It was, in fact, this arrogant exclusiveness of the Gospel
in which its offence in large part consisted. Even the Jew
might have been persuaded to accept Jesus as a Rabbi,
teaching a way to God; and the Gentiles in that syncretistic
age would have welcomed with acclamation such a teacher
among the multitude of their other masters. But neither Jesus
nor His followers would accept such an assignment. He and
they alike claimed for Him the sole empire over salvation and
would brook no fellow by his side. When we contemplate the
wide liberality of the Roman world, and consider the ease
with which the most varied cults found room for themselves
side by side in that spacious toleration, we are sometimes
tempted to wonder why, among all this crowd of religions,
Christianity alone was singled out for violent and indeed
relentless persecution. The solution is of course that Chris-

tianity was not, and would not consent to be considered, one
of these multiform religions. It was and it proclaimed itself to
be the one only valid religion; and, thus pitting itself against
them all, it drew the hatred and the assault of all against
itself. A recent writer, seeking to draw for us a picture of the
exclusive attitude of Christianity in those old days of the
beginning of the Gospel, commences with a string of quota-
tions from the great representative writers of the time,—
Irenaeus and Tatian and Commodian and Tertullian and
Cyprian himself, that man of moderate, one might say even
politic, spirit, from whom more smooth speech might have
been expected: but wearying of his task he breaks off suddenly with the remark that to present the whole case it
would be necessary to cite the whole body of Christian
authors, and well-nigh the whole list of Acts of Martyrs with
them—since there is, he says, no one of them who does not
assert the exclusiveness of Christianity. It brought them ridicule; it brings us ridicule yet. It brought them persecution of
unexampled ferocity, as it brings us the scorn of man yet.
But in that sign they conquered. Heathenism, throwing itself
upon them with fury, did not break them: it broke itself
upon them. And they have handed on the banner to us still
bearing the unsullied legend of "Jesus only,"—Jesus the sole
author of salvation.

   Now, it is not a popular thing today any more than it
was two thousand years ago to assert the exclusiveness of
Christianity. Men no longer cast us to the lions when we
proclaim Jesus the only Saviour the world can know; His
name the only name under heaven given among men wherein
they must be saved. But the world of today endures with no
more real patience than that older world two thousand years
ago the arrogance of such lofty claims. This is above all
others that have preceded it the day of eager and appreciative
study of other faiths; and equally with the others that have
preceded it, the day of indifference, if not hostility, to the

high claims of Jesus. You will be pressed on every side to give some recognition to the large element of truth and good that is found in the historical religions of the earth; to the high conceptions of God that are enshrined in some of them, the noble ethical teaching that is the essence of others, the poignant pity for suffering humanity that throbs through others. You will be pressed on every side to accord an appreciative hearing to the voice of the religious spirit speaking in the hearts of men, who, nevertheless, have not learned to express their religious emotions in the formulas with which you have been made familiar. What, you will be asked, will you refuse your welcome to the aspirations of the soul that is naturally Christian; will you not give hearty recognition to the service that is rendered to the "essential Christ" by thousands who have never heard His earthly name, or who, having heard it, have failed rightly to estimate His unique character? Will you forget that the man Christ Jesus was the Word of God before He became flesh, and remains through all the ages that Light that lights every man that comes into the world? Will you dare to deny to His sovereign grace the right to quicken whom He will, under whatever sky and calling on God by whatever human name; or refuse to recognize the movings of His inspiration in the hearts of men—because, forsooth, they speak not your words and swear not in your symbols? It will be hard for you to resist the specious pleas with which you will be plied and to preserve in your heart—I will not say now on your lips—the echoes of Peter's great declaration that in none other than Jesus is there salvation, that there is none other name under heaven, given among men, whereby we must be saved.

I beg you, when the temptation to admit other saviours to a place by His side, to acknowledge other names as equally potent with this unique name of Jesus, is strong upon you to remember three things. Remember the great commission: remember the peril of your own souls: remember the honour of Jesus Christ your Saviour.

Remember the great commission! "All authority is given unto me in heaven and earth," declared our Saviour when He was about to ascend to His throne. "Go ye, therefore," He commanded His disciples, "and make disciples of all the nations." Was this great commission the great mistake of history? It has required all the heroism the Church could command to make even the tentative efforts she has been able to make to fulfil it; and every step of the way has been watered by floods of her best blood. Have we now come at last to see it in a clearer light and to understand the error of judgment, or rather the profoundly deflected point of view, on which it was all founded? From our higher standpoint, shall we say that all the nations are already in the right path, and need no instruction from us to find the way: that the essential truth is already in their grasp and they may be trusted to its guidance: that having thus the leading of the Logos they cannot fail of the life? Such clearly was not our Saviour's view, whom we recognize as the Logos, to the guidance of whom we would trust the world, and who proclaimed Himself the Truth indeed, or He would never have sent His Church upon this—in that case—useless if not noxious mission. And if such be our view, we will never go upon this great mission in which consists, nevertheless, the very reason for the existence of the Church on earth. Only if we catch the apostles' view-point, and can say to our souls with the clearness of conviction which they felt, that there is salvation in Jesus alone, will we be inspired with the zeal that filled them, to evangelize the world. The nerve of the missionary spirit after all is embalmed for ever in Paul's great sorites. Only they that call upon the name of the Lord shall be saved. "How then shall they call on him in whom they have not believed? and how shall they believe in him whom they have not heard? and how shall they hear without a preacher? and how shall they preach except they be sent?"

The salvation of the world hangs, thus, in our human mode of speaking, on the clearness and the strength of our conviction that there is salvation in none other than Jesus, that there is none other name under heaven, given among men, wherein they must be saved. O the cruelty of that indifferentism, miscalled broadness of mind, that would withhold from a perishing world the only healing draught, on the pretence, forsooth, that it is not needed. O remember that the whole world lies in iniquity—ill to death with the dreadful disease of sin,—and that you have in your hands the one curative potion, the only water of life which can purge away sin and restore to spiritual health and beauty. Remember the great commission!

And remember the peril of your own souls! Jesus Christ has come into the world to save sinners. And He calls you to Him, you who are weary and heavy laden with the burden of your sins. He points you to His wounded hands and feet and to His riven side. He points you to His outpoured blood. He points you to His finished sacrifice and to the Father's great, It is enough! In Him he proclaims to you there has been opened up at last access to the Father, and to the Father's forgiveness, and to the Father's love. He is able to save unto the uttermost all that come unto God through Him. He pleads with you to come. He presses upon you the greatness of the opportunity, the greatness of the peril. He urges you with the great promise: He that believeth shall be saved. He importunes you with the sharp warning: He that believeth not shall be lost. Will you neglect so great salvation, which has at the first been spoken by the Lord, and has been confirmed unto us by those that heard Him, God also bearing witness by the wonders of His grace without us and within? And all because, forsooth, we cannot believe there is no other way? Other masters enough will demand your attention; other teachers essay your guidance. The wisdom of the world will laugh at your narrowness and point you to other ways of approach to God. I charge you, by the welfare of your own souls—and what should a man give in exchange for his soul? —to bear steadily in mind that the world by its wisdom has never yet attained to the knowledge of God. Where is the wise? Where is the scribe? Where is the disputer of this world? Has not God made foolish the wisdom of this world? Let those who are set on perishing despise the word of the cross as foolishness. You who are set on salvation—bear it well in mind that it is the power of God unto salvation, apart from which there is no salvation. On the peril of your souls, I charge you to remember that Jesus Christ is the only way, the only truth, the only life; that no man comes or can come to the Father except by Him, that all the life that is in the world is in Him, and he only that hath Him hath the life, while he that hath not Him hath not the life. Listen to the solemn words of the apostle of love: "Whosoever denieth the Son, the same hath not the Father: he that confesseth the Son," he, and he only, "hath the Father also." Let us note it clearly and note it whole: there is no access to God for sinners save in the blood of Jesus Christ.

Ah, I know what is rising upon your lips to say! You are of these who have believed in Jesus; your hearts are full of joy because you find yourselves in Him, and, being in Him, in the enjoyment of His salvation. I charge you, then, brethren, companions of the blessed life, remember the crown rights of your Lord and Saviour! Let His honour be precious in your sight! I have charged you in the words of Paul to let no man rob you of your crown: I charge you now in yet more insistent tones, to let no man rob your Saviour of His crown. In Him and in Him alone is redemption. In His hands He holds, as sovereign Lord of salvation, all the issues of life. Being at the right hand of God exalted, and having received of the Father the promised Holy Spirit, it is He and He alone that sheds down on earth all the currents of influence that make for salvation. Say in your heart and shout abroad with your lips, that all men may know it assuredly, that God has made this Jesus both Lord and Christ, and beside Him there is no other. See to it that you ever honour Him in your hearts and ceaselessly proclaim Him with your voice as the one only Saviour the world can ever have; since in none other is there any salvation; and there is no other name under heaven given among men, wherein we must be saved. Only so will you render to Him the glory that is His due. For when there was no one in the heavens or on the earth or under the earth who was able to open the book of salvation or to break the seals thereof, this man was counted worthy; worthy to endure the pangs of death for the offences of men, worthy to rise from the dead for their justification, worthy to be exalted to the throne of God and to receive the power, and riches, and wisdom, and might, and honour, and glory, and blessing. He by whose hand has been wrought salvation, He is and remains the only Lord of Salvation, and beside Him is no fellow. Let this good confession, I beg you, echo throughout all the corridors of your life and fill with its voice all the recesses of your souls. Above even the great commission, above even the peril of your own souls, remember—remember as those should remember who owe their all to Him, remember the honour due to Jesus Christ, the Saviour, the sole Saviour, of this lost world.

)

JOHN i. 29:—Behold the Lamb of God, which taketh away the sin of the world.

THE LAMB OF GOD

John the Apostle was the pupil of John the Baptist. Alone of the evangelists, he had not merely heard the preaching of this last and greatest of the prophets, but had formed one of the inner circle of his disciples, closely attached to his person and intimately acquainted with his entire thought. And he had brought to this teaching the same receptive and brooding heart, attuned to the higher truth, which he afterwards brought to the teaching of Christ. The result was very much the same. There are scattered here and there through the sayings of Jesus recorded by the other evangelists, deep sayings enough to assure us that, even as they would set it forth, there was this element in the teaching of the Master; but John's record of our Lord's discourses is compacted of these deep sayings. So there are hints enough in the record of the Baptist's preaching given by the other evangelists, to make it clear that there was such a side to it as John records; but it is John alone who throws this aspect of it into the foreground. In both alike, the Baptist is purely the forerunner of the Lord, whose whole work consisted in making ready for the Lord's coming. But the attention of the other evangelists is directed to the pathway prepared for the feet of the Lord; John's is focused upon the figure advancing over the road. They tell us, therefore, of the trumpet-call to repentance which the Baptist sent ringing through the land, of his searching inquisition into the hearts of men, of his unsparing rebuke of evil whether in high places or in low, of

his flaming proclamation of judgment; John tells us rather of
the testimony of the Baptist to Christ. From them we learn
accordingly what the Baptist thought of man; from John,
what he thought of Jesus.

And when we learn from John what the Baptist thought
of Jesus, we are startled by the clearness and fulness of his
prophetic vision. We have already reminded ourselves that
John was a pupil of the Baptist. Let us now give its full
validity to this fact. At least this much he obviously would
himself have us say,—that all he ever came to know of Jesus
he saw, when he looked back upon the teaching of his first
master, to have been already contained in germ in his prophetic instruction. It is therefore that he lays such stress on
the testimony of the Baptist to Jesus. Even from the reports
of the Baptist's teaching given in the other evangelists, we
may perceive that he saw in Jesus a person, and expected of
Him a work, which marked Him out as the divine Saviour of
the world. What is thus implicit in their report, however, is
made explicit in John's. We need not suppose that John fully
understood from the beginning all he heard from the Baptist's lips. But, like Mary, he belonged to that class of profound religious natures who are accustomed to hide the deep
declarations of the prophets in their hearts, that they may
ripen under the influences which the experiences of later life
bring. And thus, after John had lain on Jesus' bosom as he
had sat at the Baptist's feet, and had drunk from that fuller
and richer fountain, he was in a position to tell us that there
was included in the Baptist's declaration a true knowledge of
Jesus, a knowledge of who and what He was and what He
came into the world to do, a knowledge of Him, in the
fulness of the meaning of that great designation, as the "Son
of God," and, in the fulness of the meaning of that great
declaration, as "the Lamb of God, that takes away the sin of
the world."

It is easy to say that such fulness of apprehension is

incredible in the Baptist. That, standing as he did, in the grey dawn of the new dispensation, it is incongruous to bathe him in the full light of noonday, a noonday which did not shine upon Christ's own disciples until long afterwards—which, indeed, never shone upon them until their Master's work had been accomplished and was bearing its own witness to itself, until He had not only died for our sins, but risen again for our justification and had sent His Spirit to teach their laggard understandings things which earlier they had been unable to bear. Nay, are we not attributing to the Baptist, it is asked, a knowledge to which even Jesus Himself attained only slowly, as He learned by the things which He suffered; for did not He Himself begin His ministry animated by the hope of establishing the Kingdom He came to erect through the mere force of His winning proclamation, and only gradually learn, as the cross threw more and more deeply its baleful shadow over His pathway, that it was only through suffering that He could attain His glory? How shall we believe that to the Baptist there lay open from the beginning all that the Lord Himself and all His disciples learned only at the end; and even, that the Baptist taught it all, on his prophetic authority, both to Jesus and to Jesus' disciples, who were his pupils,—although certainly with so little effect that they forthwith forgot it and required painfully to recover it in the hard school of experience? If indeed we must not even say that the Baptist forgot it himself; for how else can we suppose that he could send to Jesus that perplexed inquiry, "Art Thou He that should come, or do we look for another?"

Plausible, however, as such doubts and hesitations may be made to appear, the answer to them is easy and decisive. They are utterly without historical foundation. They are purely the fruit of an attempt to reconstruct the historical sequences of the evangelical narrative in the interests of an *a priori* theory,—of an *a priori* theory, moreover, the principle of which is rejection of the supernatural factor in the history, though this supernatural factor is no less the nerve of the whole historical development than the very heart of the Christian religion. If we are to credit the evangelical narrative (and what other source of information have we?) it is not true that our Lord began His ministry with the expectation of accomplishing His mission through the instrumentality of successful preaching alone. Every one of the evangelists represents Him as undertaking His work with a clear perception of precisely what lay before Him; as coming into the world, in a word, not that He might live and build up a Kingdom, but that He might die and through His death purchase a people to Himself; as entering from the beginning, that is to say, upon the conscious fulfilment of the programme which the Baptist marked out for Him when He called Him the Lamb of God that takes away the sin of the world. It is true the disciples are represented as, in their preoccupation with another Messianic ideal, slow of heart to believe that it should be thus and not otherwise with their Master, that it should be through the sufferings and death of the cross that He should accomplish His work and enter into His glory. But the significance for this of the Baptist's preannouncement falls into the background in view of the repeated declarations of the Lord Himself, running up at last into careful and precise instruction, which only their dullness of spirit was able to resist; and, indeed, in view of the broad preadumbrations of the Old Testament itself, which the evangelists would have us understand laid down beforehand the entire plan of our Lord's life. When the risen Christ turned to His despondent disciples with the sorrowful rebuke, "O foolish men and slow of heart to believe all that the prophets have spoken, ought not the Christ to suffer these things and to enter into His glory?" He but put into direct words once again before He was taken up the teaching of His whole life, which has become the teaching of all His biographers as well.

From the point of sight of our Lord Himself and of these narratives which embalm His memory for us, there was really nothing new in the Baptist's proclamation and nothing exceptional in it, beyond its designation of the man Jesus as the expected Messiah. It was but the summary presentation of the essential teaching of the Old Testament, and particularly of that great prophet of whom as truly as of Elijah the Baptist was a revival, and in whose prophecies his testimony, as recorded by John, is steeped. Little marvel that those who could forget Isaiah, could forget also the Baptist's crisp summary of Isaiah's teaching. Little marvel that, in the hour of his own trial, even he himself should sink into a certain measure of despondency and need to reassure himself that He on whose head he had seen the Spirit descend and rest, was really He that should come, and he need not look for another. In the progress alike of the individual and of the Kingdom of God upwards towards those heights of knowledge and privilege which at the start, perchance, stand out clearly in view touched with the glow of sunrise, it often happens that they are temporarily lost from sight as the lower valleys and shaded paths are traversed, by which they are approached. The very process of attaining the fuller possession of them involves the hiding of them for a time from view. There is nothing psychologically unnatural, therefore, either in the clear perception of the Baptist, from the vantage-ground of the opening of the new dispensation, of the true character of the Messiah and the real nature of His work; or in the evangelist's recalling the fulness of this prophetic teaching after the event had justified it and he had himself through his inspiration attained a firm grasp of its elements. What John, in effect, invites us to do, is to come back with him to the dawn of the Christian proclamation, and to observe with him how this lonely peak was "fired by the red glow of the rushing morn." "Listen," says he to us, "listen, to these marvellous words which fell from the great prophet's lips in the rich flow of his inspiration. When I heard them, then, they kindled a flame in my heart which has not yet died down; in their impulse I turned and followed Jesus. When I recall them now I see in them nothing less than a direct witness from God to what Jesus was and did. Hearken to them as a voice from heaven, declaring what in truth is the central fact of the Gospel."

So we seem to hear the evangelist speaking to us out of the records of his Gospel this morning, and we would not be disobedient to the heavenly message. Let us, then, ask what it is that the Baptist, thus reported to us, bids us behold in Him whom he declares to be the Lamb of God that takes away the sin of the world.

We remark, then, in the first place, that he bids us see in Jesus the suffering servant of God.

In the preparation for the coming of redemption which forms the main burden of the Old Testament revelation the promised redeemer is presented in a great variety of aspects, corresponding to the multifarious functions which he was to perform as the Saviour of His people. Among these, none fell in so completely with the popular temper, or appealed with such force to the popular imagination, as that which foretold Him as the Son of David, the great warrior-king who should subdue the world to the God of Israel and for ever rule over the whole race of man. Fired with hopes kindled by this great prediction, the prevailing conception of the Messiah very naturally came to be that of a monarch, whose dominion was inevitably transmuted into a more or less carnal kingdom of power over the enemies of Israel. Meanwhile the other lines of prophetic description were neglected; and among them most of all that culminating in the fifty-third chapter of Isaiah, in which the Messiah is depicted as the righteous servant of Jehovah, preserving his integrity amid the contradictions of sinners, and by his patient endurance of the sufferings inflicted upon Him not merely earning the favour of God, but purchasing blessings for the people. What it concerns us to observe now is that the Baptist, in designating Jesus the Lamb of God that takes away the sin of the world, recalls his hearers from the one Messianic ideal to the other. His prophetic announcement is the authoritative designation of Jesus as the long-expected Messiah, the Hope of Israel; but along with that, the authoritative definition of the Messianic ideal to be fulfilled in Jesus, as very especially that set forth in the figure of the servant of Jehovah. It is the prophetic proclamation of the great doctrine of the suffering Messiah, in terms and tones which imperatively claimed a hearing and admitted no misunderstanding.

In this, indeed, consists the offence of the Baptist's announcement. It was its offence at the time. Had the Baptist come proclaiming the advent of a warrior-king, who should, with the rod of His anger, break in pieces the oppressors of Israel, Herod might still have slain him, but the Pharisees would have believed in Him, and no Jew would ever have questioned whether his mission were from heaven. It remains his offence to the present day. This doctrine of a suffering Messiah, we are asked,—what unheard-of doctrine is this? No Jew ever dreamed of it, we are told, until he had been taught it by the Christians; and the Christians invented it only to reconcile the catastrophe which had befallen their Christ with their hope that it would have been He who should redeem Israel. It concerns us little when the Jews, in their engrossment with the expectation of a Messianic King of the earth rather than of heaven, first began to lend tardy ear to the Isaian proclamation of a suffering Messiah; it is a historical question of some obscurity whose solution has little bearing on our practical life. But it is obvious that the contention that the doctrine of a suffering Messiah was first introduced by the Christians to save the situation when their Messiah succumbed to the machinations of His foes and poured out His blood at Calvary, involves the complete rewriting of the

New Testament in the interests of an *a priori* theory. Here stands written in the forefront of the Gospel narrative, a crisp proclamation of the doctrine of the suffering Messiah from the mouth of John the Baptist; and over and over again from the very outset of the narrative of His life it is represented as underlying the announcements of Jesus Himself, as it is later made the prime topic of His instruction to His disciples and the staple of the preaching of all His followers. In very truth, if we conceive the great religious movement inaugurated by John the Baptist, and carried through by Jesus and His followers, from the point of view of the development of the Messianic conception, its significance is precisely that of a sustained effort to revolutionize the dominant Messianic ideal,—to substitute for the conception of Messiah the king of Israel, that of Messiah the suffering servant of Jehovah. This is written large over the whole face of the New Testament. Every one of the evangelists as he seeks to present a vital picture of how Jesus comported Himself on earth, makes his appeal to the fifty-third chapter of Isaiah, as laying down the programme on which His life was ordered (Matthew viii. 17, Mark xv. 28, Luke xxii. 37, John xii. 35; also Matthew xi. 5, xii. 18, xxi. 5, Luke iv. 18, etc.). In the didactic portions of the New Testament this conception is simply carried forward and developed into its doctrinal implications (Rom. x. 16, I Peter ii. 22, Acts viii. 28, Rev. v. 6, xiii. 8). The doctrine of the suffering Messiah may thus be truly said to be the nerve of the whole New Testament presentation. There is nothing peculiar, therefore, in the Baptist's proclamation except its initial position at the head of a development which has revolutionized, not the Messianic ideal merely, but the world itself. Historically speaking its entire significance is that it announces in a clear, sharp, startlingly worded proclamation at the very outset of the new dispensation, its whole programme. Precisely what characterizes the New Testament most profoundly as the documentation of a movement issuing from the bosom of Judaism is its ideal of the Messiah as the suffering servant of Jehovah. Precisely what differentiates Christianity most sharply from the Judaism from which it issued is its proclamation of this Messianic ideal. Precisely the distinction of the Baptist is his initial announcement of this altered hope.

"Behold," cries the Baptist, pointing to Jesus,—"behold the Lamb of God, which taketh away the sin of the world." In that meek and lowly figure passing yonder, in bearing so simple and unassuming amid His fellow-men, see the Hope of Israel, the Chosen of God. Lay aside your national passions, your fierce chafing under the foreign yoke; man suffers from something worse than political bondage or alien oppression; there is a higher deliverance than that from the dominion of the stranger. It is not a king you need so much as a redeemer; and the God of our fathers knows it. Behold, there is the Lamb of God which takes away the sin of the world. To his first hearers, that is substantially what the proclamation of the Baptist meant. To us, today, it means, that if we would know Jesus, we must dismiss from our minds all preconceived notions of what it behoved the Lord of all the earth to be, and how it behoved Him to bear Himself in the world, and, under the Baptist's direction, go to the fifty-third chapter of Isaiah and read in that prophetic picture what Jehovah's righteous servant was and how He lived in the earth. And certainly it is no attractive portrait, as men count attractiveness, that the prophet draws of Him. "His visage," he writes, "was so marred, more than any man, and his form more than the sons of man." "He hath no form nor comeliness; and when we see Him, there is no beauty that we should desire Him." "He was despised and rejected of men," we are told, "a man of sorrows and acquainted with grief; and as one from whom men hide their face He was despised and we esteemed Him not." "He was stricken, smitten of men, and afflicted"—wounded, bruised, chastised, oppressed, led like a

lamb to the slaughter, put to grief. Epithet is piled upon
epithet almost beyond measure, to convey to us a sense of
the depth of His humiliation. This, says the prophet to
us,—this is our Redeemer. If we would see Jesus as He was,
looking beneath the appearance to the actual reality and
faultless truth, the Baptist tells us to look at Him in this
portrait,—subjected, to put it shortly and sharply, to the
most fathomless humiliation that ever befell or will ever again
befall a sentient, feeling, palpitating being in all God's universe. There never has been, there never will be, another to
stoop as He stooped. You know how Paul put it, seeking to
suggest the depth of the humiliation by the interval between
that which He was by nature and that which He became by
His condescension. God on His throne—a broken slave on the
cross; these are the end terms. As God, He was the Lord of all
the earth; when He became man, He became servant to the
whole world; and not content with that, being found in
fashion as a man, He humbled Himself still further even unto
death itself, and that the death of the cross. Enough: words
cannot paint this humiliation. We read the prophetic portrayal in the fifty-third chapter of Isaiah; we read the historical
portraiture in the pages of the Gospels, culminating in the
agony of Gethsemane and the anguish of the Passion; we read
the dogmatic representation in the arguments of the Epistles.
They fill our minds with wonder; they wring our hearts with
compassion; but we remain conscious through all that even
the bloody sweat of Gethsemane and the forsaken cry on the
cross are an insufficient index of the soul-anguish which was
endured by this greatest of earth's sufferers, this most humili-
ated of all those who from the primal curse have trodden
with bloody feet the thorny surface of this sin-smitten world
of ours. Surely the Baptist was right when he bade us see in
this Jesus, the type of all righteous sufferers, the suffering
servant of Jehovah.

But a great deal more is to be said of this sufferer than

merely that He stands before us as the type of all sufferers. His sufferings were not endured for their own sake; nor did the Baptist suppose that they were. We need to remark, in the second place, therefore, that the Baptist bids us see in Jesus the substitutive sacrifice for sin.

"Behold the Lamb of God," cries the Baptist, "which taketh away the sin of the world." Not, Behold the Prophet like unto Moses, whom ye shall hear; nor yet, Behold the Israelite without guile, in whom meet perfect purity, wisdom and truth; nor even, Behold the Lion of the tribe of Judah, who shall scatter your foes and deliver you from all your enemies. He might have said any one or all of these things. They are all true of Jesus. Christ is our teacher, and our example, and our king. But there is something more fundamental than any of these things; something which underlies them all and from which they acquire their value. And it is this that the Baptist saw in Christ and sends us to Christ to find. "Behold," says he, "the Lamb of God, which taketh away the sin of the world." That image could mean but one thing to an humble, sin-conscious Old Testament saint. He would think first of the righteous sufferer of the fifty-third chapter of Isaiah: and that righteous sufferer is not merely described there, we will remember, as a lamb that is led to the slaughter, and as a sheep that before her shearers is dumb, the very embodiment of meekness and patience in enduring the violence of the despoiler; but, in well-remembered words which throw a glory over these sufferings to which even meek patience and uncomplaining endurance can lend nothing, we read: "Surely he hath borne our griefs and carried our sorrows; he was wounded for our transgressions, he was bruised for our iniquities; the chastisement of our peace was upon him, and with his stripes we were healed." "All we like sheep have gone astray; we have turned, every one, to his own way; and the Lord hath laid on him the iniquity of us all." "For the transgression of my people was he stricken . . . yet it pleased the Lord to bruise him. He hath put him to grief: when thou shalt make his soul an offering for sin, he shall see his seed, he shall prolong his days, and the pleasure of the Lord shall prosper in his hand. . . . By his knowledge shall my righteous servant justify many, and he shall bear their iniquities. . . . He bare the sin of many and made intercession for the transgressors." And along with the fifty-third chapter of Isaiah, the Old Testament saint, when directed to the Lamb of God which takes away sin, would inevitably think also of the paschal lamb, the fundamental national symbol of deliverance; along with it, beyond question, also of the lamb of the daily sacrifice and of the underlying significance of the whole sacrificial system, with its typical finger pointing forward to something better,—to God's own Lamb, who should really take away sin, a lamb of God's providing, able and willing to bear on his own head the sin of the world.

It is through the eyes of such an Old Testament saint that we of these later days may hope to catch for ourselves the Baptist's meaning. Men have no doubt wearied themselves with efforts to derive from his declaration some less explicit reference to sacrifice. Jesus might well be compared to a lamb, it has been said, merely because of His mild and inoffensive disposition, the gentleness of His bearing, the patience of His demeanour under the injuries of His foes; and He might well be said to take sin away from the world with reference merely to His zeal for purity of conduct and heart, the loftiness of His ethical character, the winning example of the holiness of His life. It may certainly be doubted whether those who take this line of remark, have fully understood Jesus—whether they remember the sternness of His demeanour in the presence of sin, the excoriation of His rebuke, that scourge of cords with which He drove the traders from the Temple, that bearing which, when He set his face to go up to Jerusalem, caused even His followers to draw back from Him afraid, leaving Him to rush on alone in the van. We must beware, because Jesus is described as bearing with patience the sufferings He came to endure, of picturing Him therefore to ourselves as without the power of indignation or without the will to use it. And it may equally be doubted whether those who suppose that the sin of the world may be taken away by any power of persuasion or example, rightly understand man, or his love of sinning, or the power of sin in him. But let all this pass. The artificiality of such attempts to explain away the plain significance of the Baptist's declaration is too glaring to require formal refutation. Jesus is not merely compared with a lamb in it; He is identified with a specific and particular lamb,—the well-known "Lamb of God." And whether this be taken as Isaiah's lamb of the fifty-third chapter of Isaiah, or the passover lamb, or the lamb of the common sacrifices, it is in each and every case a sacrificial lamb which is indicated. Nor is Jesus said here in some broad and general way to take away sin. He is said to be the sin-bearer as the Lamb of God: and there is but one way in which from the beginning of the world, or in any nation, a lamb has ever been known to bear sin, and that is, as a piacular sacrifice, expiating guilt in the sight of a propitiated God. The Lamb of God which takes away sin, is and can be nothing other than the lamb of God's providing upon whose head sin is laid, and by whose blood expiation is wrought.

When, then, the Baptist pointed out Jesus as the Lamb of God who takes away the sin of the world, he pointed Him out as the divinely provided sacrifice for sin: he pointed Him out as the substitute for sinners, by whose stripes they are healed. Thus he preached beforehand the Gospel of the blood of Jesus—that blood of Jesus by which alone can our sins be washed away. Following his direction, we shall see in Jesus not merely and not primarily our king—our prophet and our king though we adoringly recognize Him as being, by whom alone we are effectively instructed in the truth, or protected from the most intimate enemies of our peace and safely directed in our way. Nay, we shall recognize in Him not merely our priest who represents us before God and makes satisfaction for our sins; but before all and above all, as our sacrifice,—the victim itself upon whose head our sin is laid, and by whose outpoured blood our guilt is cleansed. It is, in a word, the Gospel of the cross—of the cross of Christ—which the Baptist commends to us here; that Gospel, not only of Christ *simpliciter*, but of Christ as crucified, which has ever remained to the Jews a stumbling-block and to Gentiles foolishness, but which has also ever remained, and will ever remain, to the called themselves, Christ the power of God and the wisdom of God. The blood of Jesus,—O, the blood of Jesus!—when we have reached it, we have attained not merely the heart, but the heart of the heart of the Gospel. It is as a lamb as it had been slain, that He draws to Himself most mightily the hearts, as He attracts to Himself most fully the praises of His saints.

But not even in this high testimony is the witness of the Baptist exhausted. We reach its height only when we remark, in the third place, that he calls upon us to see in Jesus the Saviour of the world.

"Behold," he cries, "the Lamb of God, which taketh away the sin of the world,"—not "our sin" merely, though we praise God that may be gloriously true; nor "the sin of His people" merely, though that too, when properly understood, expresses the entire fact; but, with clear vision of the ultimate issue, "the sin of the world." The propitiatory sacrifice which the Baptist sees in Jesus, is a sacrifice of world-wide efficacy: the salvation which he perceives to issue from it stretches onward in its working until it embraces the whole world. The sin of the world, as a whole, he gathers, as it were, into one mass; and, laying it upon the head of Jesus, cries, "Behold the Lamb of God, which taketh away the sin of the world." It is in this universalism, we say, that we reach the height of the Baptist's declaration.

And it is in this universalism that it has become common to discover the element in the Baptist's proclamation which is specifically new. The suffering Messiah, it is often said, is no doubt an Old Testament doctrine; Messiah the sin-bearer, yes, even that may be found in the fifty-third chapter of Isaiah: but Messiah the bearer of the sin of the world,—was it not reserved to the opening of the new dispensation, characterized by spiritual breadth, and to John the Baptist, harbinger of Christ, to give explicit expression to this great truth? It will be well, however, to walk warily even here. The narrowness of the ordinary Jewish outlook cannot, perhaps, be easily overstated,—the pride of the Jews as the special favourites of heaven, and their ingrained determination to confine the grace of God to the limits of their own nation. But they certainly were never encouraged in this restricted view of the reach of God's mercy by the revelation of His purposes which Jehovah had made to them. From the moment when He promised to the mother of all living a seed by whose bruised heel the serpent's head—the source of all evil in the world—should be crushed, the extension of His grace was never confined within narrower limits than the race itself. The normative promise to the father of the faithful,— typical of all the other promises of redemption that fill the Old Testament,—was that in his great Seed (for He saith not seeds, as of many, but Seed, as of one) should all the nations of the earth be blessed. Least of all in this wonderful chapter of Isaiah to which the Baptist's words carry us most immediately is the sacrifice of the righteous sufferer circumscribed in its efficacy by the cleansing of the sins of Israel. "When He shall have made His soul an offering for sin," we read, "He shall justify many;" and, bearing the sins of many, "so shall He sprinkle many nations." No doubt the Baptist's declaration, in the springing growth of prophetic annunciation, goes beyond even this, and asserts not a relative but an absolute universalism. Not many nations, but the whole world, is what he bids us see redeemed in Christ: the Jesus he proclaims as the God-provided sacrifice bears upon His broad and mighty shoulders nothing less than the world's sin.

It is the note, then, of pure universalism, we perceive, that is sounded in the Baptist's great proclamation. He does not think, of course, of denying that salvation is of the Jews. This Lamb of God was a Jew of the Jews, and came as the Hope of Israel: and only as the Hope of Israel does He become also the Hope of the world. No more does He think of doubting that only as it should work its way out from Israel, perhaps by slow and even tentative stages, could this redemption of Israel extend into and throughout the world. We cannot credit him, to be sure, with detailed foresight of the actual process by which the salvation in Jesus has been conveyed to the world: through the scattering of the disciples from Jerusalem, the preaching of Paul and his companions, the slow missionary advance of the Church and slower leavening of the ingathered mass, through all these two thousand lagging years—and no one knows how many more thousands of years the secular process must continue before the great goal is attained and the great promise fulfilled that the whole shall be leavened. But the Baptist certainly expected the redemption he saw in its potency in Jesus to take effect only through the process of discipling; and accordingly he directs his own disciples to Jesus that they might attach themselves to Him whose very nature it was to "increase," and he himself remains through life an interested observer of the work and career of Him whose pathway it was his own highest ambition to smooth. Least of all does the Baptist ever think of obscuring that dark, that terrible fact, that as the redemption in Jesus thus makes its way surely to its ultimate goal of the salvation of the world, there are multitudes of sinners left to this side and that, out of the direct line of its advance; there are many who fail to hear the call; there are many who hearing refuse to hearken to it; there are whole masses of men that are extruded in the progress of the perfecting whole to its consummate end. Though the progress be continuous, therefore, and the goal sure, yet so long as it is progress to a goal as yet unreached, there must ever remain among the saved, unsaved—dross amid the gold, chaff to be winnowed out from the wheat. This Saviour, accordingly, whom the Baptist proclaims as the Lamb of God who takes away the sin of the world, he presents also as the husbandman who prunes and weeds His garden, and cuts down the unfruitful trees to cast them into the flames; as the Lord of the harvest who has His fan in His hand and thoroughly purges His threshing-floor, burning up the chaff with unquenchable fire. The Baptist neither denies nor glozes such things as these. But neither does he focus his eye upon them as if they were the end which Jesus had in view in coming into the world. Rather, looking through and beyond them, he fixes his gaze upon the ultimate goal which, after the process attended by these effects is over, shall at length be attained, and in this great declaration points to Jesus as bearing in His own body on the tree nothing less than the sin of the world.

You will observe, that what I am endeavouring to do, is to make as plain as I can that the Baptist's gaze, when he declares that Jesus takes away the sin of the world, is directed to the end of a process—a process of long continuance and of varied appearance through the several stadia of its course. He sees in Jesus the Saviour of the world and perceives in Him a saved world. Through the turmoil and the labour which accompany the accomplishment of this great task; through the long years of progress towards the goal, the centuries and millenniums of but partial success and oft-times even of apparent failure, which we know as the history of the Church and which even we (let us praise God for it) can recognize as the history of the expansion of Christianity; he looks out upon the end, that end to which all has been steadily advancing, when the knowledge of the glory of the

Lord shall cover the earth even as the waters cover the
sea,—with the same breadth and expansion, leaving no nook
or cranny unfilled, and with the same depth of fulness,
overwhelming all. It is the spectacle of a saved world thus
which fills his vision. And with this spectacle full in his eye,
he may well afford to neglect all that intervenes, and to
proclaim Jesus simply as the Lamb of God that takes away
the world's sin. He is unquestionably the husbandman who
prunes His garden well, and casts the improfitable plants and
branches to the flames: but on that very account He is not a
Husbandman who gives over His garden—the garden of the
Lord—to thorns and weeds and unfruitful trees, but rather
one who cleanses it and makes it in effect—this very garden in
its entirety—what it has in principle been from the beginning,
is now, and ever shall be, the Garden of the Lord in which
shall grow at last, luxuriantly filling it in its whole extent,
only plants of worth and trees of delight. He is beyond doubt
the winnower of men, whose fan is in His hand, to beat out
the chaff and cast it in the fire: but on this very account He
does not give over His threshing-floor to the worthless and
cumbering chaff, but thoroughly purges it that, after the
chaff is burned, it may remain the garner of the Lord heaped
with the precious grain. Accordingly the Baptist does not
teach us that in Jesus the sin of the world is so taken away in
the mass, that there has not been and shall not yet be in the
process by which the world has been and is being saved by
Him, unfruitful trees cut down and chaff cast into the fire;
but rather that in the end, when the process is over, no
unfruitful trees will be found growing in God's garden, the
world, no chaff be found cumbering God's threshing-floor,
the world. The vision he brings before us, let us repeat it, is
the vision of the ultimate salvation of the world, its complete
conquest to Christ when at last Jesus' last enemy shall have
been conquered and the whole world shall bow before Him as
its Lord and its Redeemer. On the basis of this great consum-

mation seen hanging on the margin of the future by his
prophetic eye, he declares of Jesus that He bears in His body
on the tree the whole world's sin, and in very truth is to be
acclaimed as the Saviour of the World.

Such, then, is the Jesus to whom the Baptist would
direct our eyes, when he bids us behold in Him the Lamb of
God that takes away the sin of the world. Let us not fail to
derive at least two great lessons from his exhortation.

The first of them is this: we must never despair of the
world. This is certainly a much-needed lesson. For are we not
very prone to despair of the world? And is there not very
good apparent reason why we should despair of it? For who
can deny that the world is very evil? Only, we must not add
in the words of the old hymnist, that therefore "the times are
waxing late." This world is not to rot down into destruction,
but to become, however slowly and by whatever tentative
processes, the very garden of the Lord. That the world is very
evil is no proof, then, that the times are waxing late; but, if
any inference can be drawn from it, the contrary rather. The
world has always been very evil, ever since there entered it,
through that forbidden fruit, the sin of man and all our
human woes. Throughout all the ages, its sin has gone up
reeking before God to heaven. Viewed in itself we could not
but despair of it. But the great fact—the great fact, greater
even than the fact of the world's sin—is that Christ has
redeemed this sinful world. In Him we behold the Lamb of
God which takes away the sin of the world. Not, who strives
to take it away and fails; not, who takes it away in some
measure, but is unable to take it away entirely; not, who
suspends its taking away upon a gigantic *IF*—as though His
taking it away were dependent on some aid given Him by the
world itself—that world which loves its sin and will never give
it up of itself and which will, of course, always act when left
to itself in accordance with its nature as the sinful world. No,
but who actually, completely, finally, takes away its sin.

This,—I beg you to bind the great truth on your heart,—this, despite all appearances that smite the astounded eye and the slowness of its realization of its great destiny—is a redeemed world, in which we live. It has been purchased unto God by the most precious blood of His Son. Its salvation, in God's own good time and way, can no more fail than the purpose of God can fail, than the blood of Jesus Christ can be of none effect. God's ways, to be sure, are not as our ways: there is none of us fitted to be His counsellor; we cannot review His plans nor bid Him stay and justify to us His methods of working. It must ever remain a mystery to us why He works in this world by process; why He created the world by process, why He has peopled it by process, why He has redeemed it by process, why He is saving it by process—by process so slow and to our human eye so uncertain, cast so much to the mercy of the currents that flow up and down through the earth, that we are tempted at times to doubt whether it is directed to a goal at all. We know only that it is by process that God chooses to work in the world,—except this further: that, though He works by process, He ever gloriously attains His ends. This wicked world in which we live is, then, God's world, Christ's world; it belongs to Christ by right of purchase and nothing can snatch it out of His hands. The day will surely come when the kingdoms of the world shall become the kingdom of our God and His Christ; and we—you and I—are co-workers with God in bringing about the great consummation. O lift up your eyes from the dust and noise of the strife and its apparently fitful fortunes, and, shall I not even say? doubtful issue; and under the direction of the Baptist, fix them upon the end: lift them from the world's sin and its just doom for its sin, to the world's Saviour and its abounding life in Him. See the redeemed world in its redeeming Lord, clothed in righteousness; and let your hearts beat high with the vision and gather courage for your daily tasks as messengers of God to a world lost indeed in its sin, but found again in its Saviour.

The second lesson is: we must not despair of ourselves. Living in this sinful world, as constituent members of it, we are partakers of its sin; or, as it may be more fair to put it, its sinfulness is but the expression of our sin. How can we, sinners, cherish hope of life? In ourselves, surely, we can find no ground for such a hope: and that we know right well. Our hearts condemn us and God is greater than our hearts. If we look at ourselves, how can we not despair? Let us look, therefore, not at ourselves but at Jesus; for Jesus, the Baptist tells us, is the Lamb of God which takes away sin. And, note it well, troubled heart, the Baptist did not make this declaration to those who had no sin, or even to those who, having it, knew not that they had it. What appeal, in fact, could such a declaration make to such men as that? He made it to those whom he had called with flaming speech to repentance; and who, with burning hearts, had come to his baptism of remission of sin. The message is, then, to you too whose hearts are sore with the sense of sin. To you and me also he cries today: "Behold the Lamb of God, which taketh away sin." Is it not a joyful message to sin-stricken souls? Let others think of Jesus as they may. Let them hail him as a king: let them sit at His feet as a prophet: let them eagerly seek to follow in His steps. For you and me, sinners, He is most glorious and most precious, as a Saviour. Let others make elaborate inquisition into the possible reasons which led Him to come into this sinful world of ours. He Himself tells us that there were but two reasons which could have brought Him into the world— to judge the world, or to save the world. And, blessed be His name, He has further told us that it was actually to save the world that He came. This is the only reason that can satisfy our hearts, or even our reason,—that Jesus Christ came into the world to save sinners. It is only as the Lamb of God that has been slain, to purchase unto God by His blood of every tribe and tongue and people and nation, and to make them unto God a kingdom and priests who shall reign on the earth,—that the heavenly hosts in the apocalyptic vision hymn Him; and it is only as we catch a glimpse of this His true glory that we can worthily add our voices to His praise. It is only when we see in Him a slaughtered lamb, lying on a smoking altar, from which ascends the sweet savour of an acceptable sacrifice to God for sin, that we can rise to anything like a true sense of the glory of Jesus Christ, or in any degree give a sufficing account to our souls of His presence in the world.

> *"The Lord has come into His world!"*
>   Nay, nay, that cannot be;
> The world is full of noisomeness
>   And all iniquity:
> He is the Lord of all the earth—
> How could He stoop to human birth?
>
> *"The Lord has come into His world!"*
>   A slaughtered Lamb I see,
> A smoking altar on which burns
>   A sacrifice for me!
> O blessed Lord! O blessed day!
> He comes to take my sin away!

GOD'S IMMEASURABLE LOVE

To whom we owe this great declaration of the love of God, it is somewhat difficult to determine; whether to our Lord Himself, or to that disciple who had lain upon His bosom and had imbibed so much of His spirit that he thenceforth spoke with his Master's voice and in his Master's words. Happily it is a matter of no substantial importance. For what difference does it make to you and me whether the Lord speaks to us through His own lips, or through those of His servant, the Apostle, to whom He had promised, and to whom He had given, His Holy Spirit to teach him all the truth? What concerns us is not the instrumentality through which the message comes, but the message itself. And what a great message it is,—the message of the greatness of the love of God! Let us see to it that, as the words sound in our ears, it is this great revelation that fills our hearts, fills them so full as to flood all their being and wash into all their recesses. The greatness of the love of God, the immeasurable greatness of the love of God!

This exhortation is not altogether superfluous. Strange as it may sound, it is true, that many—perhaps the majority—of those who feed their souls on this great declaration, seem to have trained themselves to think, when it falls upon their ears, in the first instance at least, not so much of how great, how immeasurably great, God's love is, as rather of how great the world is. It is the world that God loves, they say,—the world: and forthwith they fall to thinking how great the world is, and how, nevertheless, God loves it all. Think, they cry, of the multitudes of men that swarm over the face of the earth; and have swarmed over it through all the countless generations from the beginning; and will swarm over it in ever-increasing numbers through perhaps even more countless generations yet to come, until the end: and God loves them all, each and every one of them, from the least to the greatest; so loves them that He has given His only begotten Son to die for them, for each and every one of them—and for each and every one of them with the same intent,—the intent, namely, that he may be saved. O how great the love of God must be to embrace in its compass these uncounted multitudes of men; and so to embrace them that every individual that enters as a constituent unit into the mass of mankind receives his full share of it, or rather is inundated by its undivided and undiminished flood!

Certainly this is a great conception. But it is just as certainly not a great enough conception to meet the requirements of our text. For, look you, will you measure the immeasurable greatness of God's love by the measure of man? All these multitudes of men that have lived, do live, or shall live, from the beginning to the end of the world's entire span,—what is their finite sum to the infinitude of God? Lo, the world, and all that is in the world,—and all that has ever been in the world or can ever be in the world,—lies as nothing in the sight of the Infinite One, floats as an evanescent particle in His eternal vision. How can we exalt our conception of the greatness of the divine love by thinking of it as great enough to embrace all this? Can we praise the blacksmith's brawn by declaring it capable of supporting a mustard-seed on an outstretched palm? This standard is too small: we cannot compute such masses in terms of it. Conceive the world as vastly as you may, it remains ever incommeasurable with the immeasurable love of God.

And what warrant does the text offer for conceiving so greatly of the world, or indeed for thinking of it at all under the category of extension, as if it were its size that was oppressing the imagination of the speaker, and its parts—down to the last analysis—that were engaging his wondering attention? Evidently the text envisages the world, of which it speaks in the concrete, as a whole. This world is made up of parts, no doubt, and the differing destinies that await the individuals which compose it are adverted to. But the emphasis does not fall upon its component elements, as if their number, for example, could form the ground of the divine love, or explain the wonder of its greatness. Distribution of it into its elements and engagement with the individuals which compose it, is merely the result of the false start made when the mind falls away from contemplating the immensity of the love of God with which the text is freighted, to absorb itself rather in wonder over the greatness of the world which is loved.

And having begun with this false step it is not surprising if the wandering mind finds itself shortly lost in admiration not even of the greatness of the world, but rather of the greatness of the individual soul. These souls of men, each and every one of which God loves so deeply that He has given His Son to die for it,—what great, what noble, what glorious things they must be! O what value each of us should place upon this precious soul of ours that God so highly esteemed as to give His Son to die for it! A great and inspiring thought, again, beyond all doubt: but, again, obviously not great enough to be the thought of the text. Clearly, what the text invites us to think of is the greatness of the love of God, not the greatness of the human soul.

And how can we fancy that we can measure the love of God by what He has done for each and every human soul? Persist in reading the text thus distributively, making "the world" mean each and every man that lives on the earth, and what, after all, does it declare that the love of God has done for them? Just open a way of salvation before men, give them an opportunity to save themselves. For, what, in that contingency, does the text assert? Just this: that "God so loved the world"—that is, each and every man that has lived, does live, or shall live in this world,—"that He gave His only begotten Son, that *whosoever believeth on Him* should not perish, but have eternal life." "Whosoever believeth on Him,"—those only. Is this, then, the measure of the immeasurable love of God—that He barely opens a pathway to salvation before sinful men, and stops right there; does nothing further for them—leaving it to their own unassisted initiation whether they will walk in it or not? Surely this cannot be the teaching of the text; and that, for many reasons,—primary among which is this: that we all know that the love of God has done much more than this for multitudes of the children of men, namely, has not merely opened a way of salvation before them, but has actually saved them. Nor is our text silent on this point. It is not in this mere opening of a way of salvation before each and every man that the love of God for the world is declared by it to issue, but in the actual saving of the world. We read the next verse and we discover it asserting that God sent His Son into the world for this specific end, that the world should be "saved by Him." God did not then only so love the world as to give it a bare chance of salvation: He so loved the world that He saved the world. And surely this is something far better: and provides a much higher standard by which to estimate the greatness of God's love.

We discover, then, that the distribution of the term "world" in our text into "each and every man" in the world not only begins with the obvious misstep of directing our attention at once rather to the greatness of the world than to the greatness of God's love and only infers the latter from the former; but ends by positively belittling the love of God, as if it could content itself with half-measures,—nay, in numerous instances, with what is practically no measure at all. For if it is satisfied with merely opening a way of salvation and leaving men to walk in this way or not as they list, the hard

facts of life force us to add that it is satisfied with merely
opening a way of salvation for multitudes to whom it should
never be made known that a way of salvation lay open before
them, although their sole hope lies in their walking in it. And
why dwell on special cases? Shall we not recognize frankly
that so meagre a provision would be operative in no case? For
even when it is made known to men that a way of salvation is
opened before them—can they, being sinners, walk in it? Let
our passage itself tell us. Does it not explicitly declare that
every one that doeth ill hateth the light and cometh not to
the light? And who of us does not know that he, at least,—if
not every man,—doeth ill? Does the love of God expend itself
then in inoperative manifestations? Surely not so can be
measured the love of God, of which the Scriptures tell us that
its height and depth, and length and breadth pass knowledge:
of which Paul declares that nothing can separate us from it,
not death, nor life, nor angels, nor principalities, nor things
present, nor things to come, nor powers, nor height, nor
depth, nor any other creature: of which he openly asserts,
that if it avails to reconcile us with God, through the death of
His Son, much more shall it avail to bring us into the fruition
of salvation by His life.

Obviously, then, the distribution of the notion "world"
in our text into "each and every man" in the world, does less
than justice to the infinitude of the love of God which it is
plainly the object of the text to exalt in our thought. React-
ing from the ineptitudes of this interpretation, and determined at all costs to take the conception of the love of God
at the height of its idea, men of deeper insight have therefore
suggested that it is not the world at large that is in question
in the text, but God's people, the chosen of God in the
world. Surely, it is God's seeking, nay, God's finding love
that is celebrated here, they argue; the love which goes out to
its object with a vigour which no obstacle can withstand, and,
despite every difficulty, brings it safely into the shelter of its

arms. The "world" that God so loved that He gave His Son for it,—surely that is not the "world" that He loved so little as to leave it to take or leave the Son so given, as its own wayward heart might dictate; but the "world" that He loved enough, after giving His Son for it, prevalently to move upon with His quickening Spirit and graciously to lead into the offered salvation. The "world" of believers, in a word, as they are called in the following clause; or, as they are called elsewhere in Scripture, the "world" of God's elect. It was these whom God loved before the foundations of the world with a love beyond all expression great and strong, constant and prevailing, a love which was not and could not be defeated, just because it was *love*, the very characteristic of which, Paul tells us, is that it suffereth long, is not provoked, taketh no account of evil, beareth all things, endureth all things, yea, never faileth: and therefore was not and could not be satisfied until it had brought its objects home.

It is very clear that this interpretation has the inestimable advantage over the one formerly suggested, that it penetrates into the heart of the matter and refuses to evacuate the text of its manifest purport. The text is given to enhance in our hearts the conception of the love of God to sinners: to make us to know somewhat of the height and depth and length and breadth of it, though truly it passes knowledge. It will not do, then, as we read it to throw limitations around this love, as if it could not accomplish that whereto it is set. Beyond all question the love which is celebrated is the saving love of God; and the "world" which is declared to be the object of this love is a "world" that is—not merely given an opportunity of salvation—but actually saved. As none but believers—or if you choose to look at them *sub specie æternitatis,* none but the elect—attain salvation, so it seems but an identical proposition to say that it is just the world of believers, or the world of the elect, that is embraced in the love of God here celebrated. When the text declares, therefore, that God so loved the world that He gave His only begotten Son for it, is not what is meant, and what must be meant, just the elect scattered throughout the world? It may seem strange to us, indeed, to speak of the elect as "the world." But is not that largely because, in the changed times in which we live, we do not sufficiently poignantly appreciate or deal seriously enough with the universalism of Christianity, in contrast with the nationalism of the old dispensation? In this universalistic and anti-Jewish Gospel of John, especially, what more natural than to find the "world" brought into contrast with Jewish exclusivism? In fine, is not the meaning of our text just this: that Jesus Christ came to make propitiation for the sins not of Jews only, but of the whole world, that is to say, not of course for each and every man that lives in the world, but in any event for men living throughout the world, heirs of the world's life and partakers in the world's fortunes? Certainly it is difficult for us to appreciate the greatness of the revolution wrought in the religious consciousness of men like John, bred in the exclusivism of Judaism and accustomed to think of the Messiah as the peculiar property of Israel, when the world-wide mission of Christianity was brought home to their minds and hearts. To John and men like John its universalism was no doubt well-nigh the most astonishing fact about Christianity. And the declaration that God so loved the world—not Israel merely, but the world—that He gave His only begotten Son, that whosoever—from every nation, not from the Jews merely— should believe on Him should have eternal life: this great declaration must have struck upon their hearts with a revelation of the wideness of God's mercy and the unfathomable profundities of His love, such as we can scarcely appreciate in our days of age-long familiarity with the great fact. Is not this, then, the real meaning of the immense declaration of the text: that Jesus Christ is the world-wide Saviour, that now the middle-wall of partition has been broken down and God has called to Himself a people out of all the nations of the earth, and has so loved this His people gathered thus from the whole world, that He has given His only begotten Son to die for them? And is not this a truth big with consequences, worthy of such a record as is given it in our text, and capable of awakening in our hearts a most profound response?

Assuredly no one will doubt the value and inspiration of such suggestions. The truth that lies in them, who can gainsay? But it is difficult to feel that they quite exhaust the meaning of the great words of the text. In their effort to do justice to the conception of the love of God, do they not do something less than justice to the conception embodied in the term "the world"? In identifying "the world" with believers, do they not neglect, if we may not quite say the contrast of the two things, yet at least the distinction between the two notions which the text seems to institute? "God so loved the world," we read, "that He gave His only begotten Son, that whosoever believeth on Him should not perish, but have eternal life." Certainly here "the world" and "believers" do not seem to be quite equipollent terms: there seems, surely, something conveyed by the one which is not wholly taken up in the other. How, then, shall we say that "the world" means just "the world of believers," just those scattered through the world, who, being the elect of God, shall believe in His Son and so have eternal life? There is obviously much truth in this idea: and the main difficulty which it faces may, no doubt, be avoided by saying that what is taught is that God's love of the world is shown by His saving so great a multitude as He does save out of the world. The wicked world deserved at His hands only total destruction. But He saves out of it a multitude which no man can number, out of every nation, and of all tribes and peoples and tongues. How much must, then, God love the world! This interpretation, beyond question, reproduces the fundamental meaning of the text. But does it completely satisfy all

its suggestions? Does there not lie in the text some more
subtle sequence of thought than is explicated by it? Is there
not implied in it some profounder and yet more glorious
truth than even the world-wide reach of God's love, manifested in the Great Commission, and issuing in the multitude
of the saved, the voice of whose praise ascends to heaven as
the voice of many waters and as the voice of mighty thun-
ders?

Neither of the more common interpretations of the
text, therefore, appears to bring out quite fully its real
significance. The one fails to rise to the height of the conception of the love of God embodied in it; the other appears to
do something less than full justice to the conception of the
world which God is said by it to love. The difficulty in both
cases, seems to arise from a certain unwillingness to go deeply
enough: a surface meaning, possible to impose upon the text,
seems to be seized upon, while its profundities are left
unexplored. If we would make our own the great revelation
of the love of God here given us, we must be more patient.
Renouncing the easy imposition upon it of meanings of our
own devising, we must just permit the text to speak its own
language to our hearts. Its prime intention is to convey some
conception of the immeasurable greatness of the love of God.
The method it employs to do this is to declare the love of
God for the world so great that He gave His Son to save it.
The central affirmation obviously, then, is this,—and it is a
sufficiently great one to absorb our entire attention—that
God loved the world. "God," "loved," "the world"—we must
deal seriously with this great assertion, and with every element of it. We must first of all, then, thoroughly enter into
the meaning of the three great terms here brought together:
"God," "loved," "the world."

We shall not make the slightest step forward in understanding our text, for instance, so long as we permit ourselves
to treat the great term "God" merely as the subject of a

sentence. We must endeavour rather to rise as nearly as may be to its fullest significance. When we pronounce the word we must see to it that our minds are flooded with some wondering sense of God's infinitude, of His majesty, of His ineffable exaltation; of His holiness, of His righteousness, of His flaming purity and stainless perfection. This is the Lord God Almighty whom the heaven of heavens cannot contain, to whom the earth is less than the small dust on the balance. He has no need of aught, nor can His unsullied blessedness be in any way affected—whether by way of increase or decrease—by any act of the creatures of His hands. What we call infinite space is but a speck on the horizon of His contemplation: what we call infinite time is in His sight but as yesterday when it is past. Serene in His unapproachable glory, His will is the resistless law of all existences to which their every motion conforms. Apparelled in majesty and girded with strength, righteousness and judgment are the foundations of His throne. He sits in the heavens and does whatsoever He pleases. It is this God, a God of whom to say that He is the Lord of all the earth is to say so little that it is to say nothing at all, of whom our text speaks. And if we are ever to catch its meaning we must bear this fully in mind.

Now the text tells us of this God—of *this* God, remember,—that He loves. In itself, before we proceed a step further, this is a marvellous declaration. The metaphysicians have not yet plumbed it and still protest inability to construe the Absolute in terms of love. We shall not stop to dwell upon this somewhat abstract discussion. Enough for us that a God without emotional life would be a God without all that lends its highest dignity to personal spirit whose very being is movement; and that is as much as to say no God at all. And more than enough for us that our text assures us that God loves, nay, that He is Love. What it concerns us now to note, however, is not the mere fact that He loves, but what it is that He is declared to love. For therein lies the climax of the great proclamation. This is nothing other than "the world." For this is the unimaginable declaration of the text: "God so loved the world." It is just in this that lies the mystery of the greatness of His love.

For what is this "world" which we are so strangely told that God loves? We must not throw the reins on the neck of our fancy and seek a response that will suit our ideas of the right or the fitting. We must just let the Scriptures themselves tell us, and primarily that Apostle to whom we owe this great declaration. Nor does he fail to tell us; and that without the slightest ambiguity. The "world," he tells us, is just the synonym of all that is evil and noisome and disgusting. There is nothing in it that can attract God's love,—nay, that can justify the love of any good man. It is a thing not to be dallied with, or acquiesced in: they that are of it, are by that very fact not of God; and what the Christian has to do with it is just to overcome it; for everything that is begotten of God manifests that great fact precisely by this—that he overcomes the world. "Love not the world, neither the things that are in the world," is John's insistent exhortation. And the reason for it he states very pungently: because "if any man love the world, the love of the Father is not in him." God and the world, then, are precise contradictions. "Nothing that is in the world is of the Father," we are told; or, as it is put elsewhere in direct positive form: "The whole world lieth in the evil one." "The world, the flesh and the devil"—this is the pregnant combination in which we have learned from Scripture to express the baleful forces that war against the soul: and the three terms are thus cast together because they are essentially synonyms. See, then, whither we are brought. When we are told that God loves the world, it is much as if we were told that He loves the flesh and the devil. And we may, indeed, take courage from our text and say it boldly: God does love the world and the flesh and the devil. Therein indeed is the ground of all our comfort and all our hope: for

we—you and I—are of the world and of the flesh and of the
devil. Only,—we must punctually note it,—the love wherewith
God loves the world, the flesh and the devil—therefore, us—is
not a love of complacency, as if He the Holy One and the
Good could take pleasure in what is worldly, fleshly, devilish:
but that love of benevolence which would fain save us from
our worldliness, fleshliness and devilishness.

That indeed is precisely what the text goes on at once to
say: "For God so loved the world, that He gave His only
begotten Son, that whosoever believeth on Him should not
perish, but have eternal life." The world then was perishing:
and it was to save it that God gave His Son. The text is, then,
you see, in principle an account of the coming of the Son of
God into the world. There were but two things for which He,
being what He was as the Son of God, could come into the
world, being what it was: to judge the world or to save the
world. It was for the latter that He came. "For," the next
verse runs on, "God sent not His Son into the world to judge
the world, but that the world through Him should be saved."
Not wrath, then, though wrath were due, but love was the
impelling cause of the coming of the Son of God into this
wicked world of ours. "For God so loved the world, that He
gave His only begotten Son." The intensity of the love is
what is emphasized: it was so intense that it was not deterred
even by the sinfulness of its objects. You will perceive that
what we have here then is, in effect, but the Johannean way
of saying what Paul says when he tells us that "God commendeth His own love towards us, in that while we were yet
sinners, Christ died for us." The marvel, in other words,
which the text brings before us is just that marvel above all
other marvels in this marvellous world of ours—the marvel of
God's love for sinners. And this is the measure by which we
are invited to measure the greatness of the love of God. It is
not that it is so great that it is able to extend over the whole
of a big world: it is so great that it is able to prevail over the

Holy God's hatred and abhorrence of sin. For herein is love, that *God* could love the *world*—the world that lies in the evil one: that God who is all-holy and just and good, could so love this world that He gave His only begotten Son for it,—that He might not judge it, but that it might be saved.

The key to the passage lies, therefore, you see, in the significance of the term "world." It is not here a term of extension so much as a term of intensity. Its primary connotation is ethical, and the point of its employment is not to suggest that the world is so big that it takes a great deal of love to embrace it all, but that the world is so bad that it takes a great kind of love to love it at all, and much more to love it as God has loved it when He gave His Son for it. The whole debate as to whether the love here celebrated distributes itself to each and every man that enters into the composition of the world, or terminates on the elect alone chosen out of the world, lies thus outside the immediate scope of the passage and does not supply any key to its interpretation. The passage was not intended to teach, and certainly does not teach, that God loves all men alike and visits each and every one alike with the same manifestations of His love: and as little was it intended to teach or does it teach that His love is confined to a few especially chosen individuals selected out of the world. What it is intended to do is to arouse in our hearts a wondering sense of the marvel and the mystery of the love of God for the sinful world—conceived, here, not quantitatively but qualitatively as, in its very distinguishing characteristic, sinful. And search the universe through and through—in all its recesses and through all its historical development—and you will find no marvel so great, no mystery so unfathomable, as this, that the great and good God, whose perfect righteousness flames in indignation at the sight of every iniquity and whose absolute holiness recoils in abhorrence in the presence of every impurity, yet loves this sinful world,—yes, has so loved it that He has given His only

begotten Son to die for it. It is this marvel and this mystery
that our text would fain carry home to our hearts, and we
would be wise if we would permit them to be absorbed in its
contemplation.

At the same time, however, although we cannot permit
the passage to be interpreted in the terms of the debate in
question, it would not be quite true to say it has no bearing
upon that debate.

One thing, for instance, which the passage tells us, and
tells us with great emphasis, is that the love which it celebrates is a saving love; not a love which merely tends towards
salvation, and may—perhaps easily—be defeated in its aim by,
say, the unwillingness of its objects. The very point of the
passage lies, on the one side, in the mightiness of the love of
God; and on the other in the unwillingness not of some but
of all its objects. The love here celebrated is, we must
remember, the love of *God*—of the Lord God Almighty: and
it is love to the *world*—which altogether "lies in the evil one."
It is a love which is great, and powerful, and all-conquering;
which attains its end, and will not stand helpless before any
obstacle. It is the precise purpose of the passage to teach us
this, to raise our hearts to some apprehension of the inconceivable greatness of the love of God, set as it is upon saving
the wicked world. It would be possible to believe that such a
love as this terminates equally and with the same intent upon
each and every man who is in "the world," only if we may at
the same time believe that it works out its end completely
and with full effect on each and every man. But this the
passage explicitly forbids us to believe, proceeding at once to
divide the "world" into two classes, those that perish and
those that have eternal life. The almighty, all-conquering love
of God, therefore, certainly does not pour itself equally and
with the same intent upon each and every man in the world.
In the sovereignty that belongs of necessity to His love as to
all love, He rather visits with it whom He will.

But neither will the text allow us to suppose that God grants this His immeasurable love only to a few, abstracted from the world, while the world itself He permits to fall away to its destruction. The declaration is, not that God has loved some out of the world, but that He has loved the world. And we must rise to the height of this divine universalism. It is the world that God has loved with His deathless love, this sinful world of ours: and it is the world, this sinful world of ours, that He has given His Son to die for: and it is the world that through the sacrifice of His dear Son, He has saved, this very sinful world of ours. "God sent not His Son into the world," we read, "to judge the world, but that the world should be saved by Him:" that is to say, God did not send His Son into the world for the purpose of judging the world, but for the purpose of saving the world: a declaration which could not be true if, despite His coming, the world were lost and only a select few saved out of it. The purposes of God do not fail.

You must not fancy, then, that God sits helplessly by while the world, which He has created for Himself, hurtles hopelessly to destruction, and He is able only to snatch with difficulty here and there a brand from the universal burning. The world does not govern Him in a single one of His acts: He governs it and leads it steadily onward to the end which, from the beginning, or ever a beam of it had been laid, He had determined for it. As it was created for His glory, so shall it show forth His praise: and this human race on which He has impressed His image shall reflect that image in the beauty of the holiness which is its supreme trait. The elect—they are not the residuum of the great conflagration, the ashes, so to speak, of the burnt-up world, gathered sadly together by the Creator, after the catastrophe is over, that He may make a new and perhaps better beginning with them and build from them, perchance, a new structure, to replace that which has been lost. Nay, they are themselves "the world;" not the world as it is in its sin, lying in the evil one; but the world in

its promise and potency of renewed life. Through all the
years one increasing purpose runs, one *increasing* purpose:
the kingdoms of the earth become ever more and more the
kingdoms of our God and His Christ. The process may be
slow; the progress may appear to our impatient eyes to lag.
But it is God who is building: and under His hands the
structure rises as steadily as it does slowly, and in due time
the capstone shall be set into its place, and to our astonished
eyes shall be revealed nothing less than a saved world.

Meanwhile, we who live in the midst of the process see
not yet the end. These are days of incompleteness, and it is
only by faith that we can perceive the issue. The kingdom of
God is as yet only in the making; and the "world" is not yet
saved. So, there appear about us two classes: there are those
that perish as well as those that have eternal life. With the
absoluteness which characterizes the writer of this Gospel,
these two classes are set before us in the text and in the
paragraph of which it forms a part, in their intrinsic antagonism. They are believers and unbelievers in the Son of God:
and they are believers and unbelievers in the Son of God,
because they are in their essential natures good or bad, lovers
of light or lovers of darkness. "For every one that doeth evil
hateth the light and cometh not to the light; but he that
doeth the truth cometh to the light." Throughout the whole
process of the world's development, therefore, the Light that
has come into the world draws to Itself those that are of the
light: He, that is, who through love of the world came into
the world to save the world,—yea, and who shall save the
world—in the meantime attaches to Himself in every generation those who in their essential nature belong to Him. How
they came to be His, and therefore to be attracted to Him,
and therefore to enter into the life that is life indeed—to
become portions no longer of the world that lies in the evil
one, but of the reconstructed world that abides in Him—the
paragraph in which our text is set leaves us much unin-

formed. Accordingly some rash expositors wish to insist that to it the division of men into the essentially good and the essentially bad is an ultimate fact. They speak therefore much of the ineradicable dualism of Jesus' conception, not staying to consider the confusion thus wrought in the whole paragraph. For in that case how could there be talk of the Son of God coming into the world to *save* the world? Obviously, to the text, those that belong to the Son themselves require saving; that is to say, no less than the lost themselves, they belong by nature to the "evil one," in whom the whole world—not a part of it only—we are told explicitly "lieth."

And if we will but attend to the context in which our paragraph is set, we will perceive that we are not left without guidance to its proper understanding. For we must remember that this paragraph is not an isolated document standing off to itself and complete in itself, but is a comment upon the discourse of our Lord to Nicodemus. It necessarily receives its colour and explanation, therefore, from that discourse of which it is either a substantive part or upon which it is at least a reflection. And what does that discourse teach us except this: that all that is born of flesh is flesh, and only what is reborn of Spirit is Spirit; that no man can enter the Kingdom of God, therefore, except he be born again of God; and that this birth is not at the command of men, but is the gift of a Spirit which is like the wind that bloweth where it listeth, the sound whereof we hear though we know not whence it cometh and whither it goeth—but can say of it only, Lo, it is here! Here then is the explanation of the essential difference in men revealed in the varying reception they give to the Son of God. It is not due to accident of birth or to diversity of experience in the world, least of all to inherent qualities of goodness or badness belonging to each by nature. It is due solely to this,—whether or not they have been born again by the Spirit and so are of the light and come spontaneously to the light when it dawns upon their waiting eyes. The sequence in this great process of salvation, then, according to our passage, when taken in its context, is this: the gift of the Son of God to save the world; the preparation of the hearts of men to receive the Son of God in vital faith: the attraction of these "children of the light" to the Light of the world; and the gradual rebuilding of the fabric of the world along the lines of God's choosing into that kingdom of light which is thus progressively prepared for its perfect revelation at the last day.

Thus, thus, then, it is that God is saving the world—the world, mind you, and not merely some individuals out of the world: by a process which involves not supplanting but reformation, recreation. We look for new heavens and a new earth, it is true; but these new heavens and new earth are not another heaven and another earth, but the old heaven and old earth renewed; or as the Scriptures phrase it "regenerated." For not the individual merely but the world-fabric itself is to be regenerated in that "regeneration when the Son of Man is to sit on the throne of His glory." During the process there may be much that is discarded: but when the process is completed, then also shall be completed the task which the Son of Man has taken upon Himself, and the "world" shall be saved—this wicked world of sinful men transformed into a world of righteousness.

Surely, we shall not wish to measure the saving work of God by what has been already accomplished in these unripe days in which our lot is cast. The sands of time have not yet run out. And before us stretch, not merely the reaches of the ages, but the infinitely resourceful reaches of the promise of God. Are not the saints to inherit the earth? Is not the recreated earth theirs? Are not the kingdoms of the world to become the Kingdom of God? Is not the knowledge of the glory of God to cover the earth as the waters cover the sea? Shall not the day dawn when no man need say to his neighbor, "Know the Lord," for all shall know Him from the least unto the greatest? O raise your eyes, raise your eyes, I beseech you, to the far horizon: let them rest nowhere short of the extreme limit of the divine purpose of grace. And tell me what you see there. Is it not the supreme, the glorious, issue of that love of God which loved, not one here and there only in the world, but the world in its organic completeness; and gave His Son, not to judge the world, but that the world through Him should be saved? And He said unto me, "Come hither, I will shew thee the bride, the wife of the Lamb. And he . . . shewed me the holy city Jerusalem, coming down out of heaven from God, having the glory of God. . . . And the city hath no need of the sun, neither of the moon, to shine upon it: for the glory of God did lighten it, and the Lamb, the lamp thereof. And the nations shall walk amidst the light thereof; and the kings of the earth do bring their glory into it. And the gates thereof shall in no wise be shut by day (for there shall be no night there): and they shall bring the glory and the honour of the nations into it: and there shall in no wise enter into it anything unclean, or he that maketh an abomination and a lie; but only they which are written in the Lamb's book of life." Only those written in the Lamb's book of life, and yet all the nations! It is the vision of the saved world. "For God so loved the world, that He gave His only begotten Son, that whosoever believeth in Him should not perish, but have eternal life." It is the vision of the consummated purpose of the immeasurable love of God.

2 CORINTHIANS v. 14-15, 18-19, 21:—For the love of Christ constraineth us; because we thus judge, that one died for all, therefore all died; and He died for all, that they which live should no longer live unto themselves, but unto Him who for their sakes died and rose again. . . . But all things are of God, who reconciled us to Himself through Christ, and gave unto us the ministry of reconciliation; to wit, that God was in Christ reconciling the world unto Himself, not reckoning unto them their trespasses. . . . Him who knew no sin He made to be sin on our behalf; that we might become the righteousness of God in Him.

THE GOSPEL OF PAUL

I have chosen for my text three sentences which do not form a consecutive passage. They stand, however, in very close contiguity within the limits of a single short paragraph, within the narrow compass, indeed, of eight verses. More than that, they stand out upon the face of this short paragraph as marked features, from which it receives its character and chief significance. Glancing over this paragraph, the eye can no more fail to fix itself upon these three sentences than gazing over a rich plain from some high point of sight it could fail to be attracted by a series of bold promontories throwing themselves athwart it; or glancing on the fretted lid of some highly wrought casket it could fail to be drawn and dazzled by the jewels which blaze upon it. We cannot say, indeed, that the paragraph exists for these three sentences: they, rather, are here for the purposes of the paragraph and fulfil these purposes with perfection. But in prosecuting the end he has here in view the apostle is led to make his appeal to considerations of so high an order that the sentences in which they are adduced stand out above the general drift of the discussion like mountain-peaks in a plain, glow on its surface like jewels in their setting.

What Paul is engaged upon in this section of his Epistle is the vindication of his integrity as a minister of grace, and of the purity of the Gospel he preached. It is in full view of the judgment-seat of Christ, he asserts, that he prosecutes the mission that has been committed to him; and he has permitted nothing to deflect him by a hair's-breadth from the message which has been placed on his lips. In giving force to this contention he is led to enunciate the contents of the message of which he has been made the bearer: and it is this enunciation which is thrown up to our view in these sentences I have chosen for my text.

In these sentences is contained therefore the announcement of Paul's Gospel; and it is this fact which gives them their distinction. Search throughout the whole compass of Paul's Epistles and it is doubtful if you will find another such succinct, complete and pungent statement of the Gospel which Paul preached; of what he deemed the very touchstone and heart of the message he brought to men. Certainly you will find none more formally set forth as the apostle's own declaration of the essence of his Gospel. If we wish to know precisely what Paul preached and precisely in what he conceived all that he preached to centre and to be summed up, we cannot do better than attend to these crisp sentences.

I have called them crisp sentences, and I might almost have spoken of them as detached sentences. For part and parcel as they are of Paul's argument, fitting into it and bearing their part in it with the perfection of sentences born of the discussion of the moment, they yet have an odd air of detachment about them, which seems to assure us they were not struck out in the heat of this debate, but have been brought into it from without. One of them is introduced by what we may almost call a formula of citation: "because we thus judge"—"seeing that our judgment is this,"—viz. what follows. All of them are phrased with that sharply cut frugality of language which belongs to proverbial speech, and is the result, no doubt, of the attrition which sentences suffer from much repetition, by which all the rough edges, like superfluous particles, are worn off. "One died for all: therefore all died: and He died for all that, living, they might no longer live to themselves, but to Him who died and rose for them." "All is of God; who reconciled us with Himself through Christ and gave us the ministry of reconciliation, since it was

God who in Christ was reconciling the world with Himself."
"Him that knew no sin He made sin for us, that we might
become the righteousness of God in Him." There is not a
redundant word in any of these sentences; there is even a
notable parsimony of words; even what might have been
deemed the necessary connecting particles are omitted. I
think we may be quite sure that these sentences were not
first framed as Paul set them down on the sheets of this
letter; that they had often been on his lips before; and that
they went down on the sheets he was writing here in the
form they had taken on his lips after numerous repetitions.
In a word, we have here the phrases in which Paul was
accustomed to give expression to the heart of his Gospel.

It is tempting to turn aside to remark upon the analogy
supplied by this discovery to a phenomenon characteristic of
the so-called Pastoral Epistles, in which we repeatedly meet
with gnome-like announcements of the great truths of the
Gospel, encysted, as it were, in the tissues of the Epistle. It
would seem that from the beginning Paul was accustomed to
imbed in his Epistles the "faithful sayings" in which he was
wont to find adequate expression given to the mighty truths
it was his life-work to make effective among men. It is
important, however, that we should not permit our attention
to be distracted from the main point which now claims it.
This is that we have in the sentences now before us not only
an announcement of the essence of Paul's Gospel, perhaps
the most clear and formal announcement of its essence to be
found in his Epistles, but also this announcement in the form
which he habitually gave it. It was in these precise words that
Paul was accustomed to express himself when he desired to
carry the essence of his Gospel home to the minds of men
and fix it there with precision and in unmistakable and
unalterable distinctness. We may approach the study of these
sentences, then, with the utmost confidence that we have in
them not some chance, perhaps one-sided, deliverance valid

only for the immediate purpose of a particular controversy, but the well-weighed and carefully compacted expression of the very core of his Gospel, that Gospel which had been committed to him by the Lord Himself, by which he won the world, upon which he nourished his own spirit, and which he offers to us as the very word of life.

What, then, is this Gospel of Paul, brought before us here with such directness and energy of expression?

Casting our eye over the sentences in which it is embodied, we are struck at once with the fact that it is a universalistic Gospel. We should have expected this of Paul. The hinge upon which his whole life-work turned was the universalizing of the Gospel of Christ. It was therefore that he was the Apostle of the Gentiles. And it was out of this that all his conflicts, trials, sufferings arose. The bitter strife in which he was engaged in this very Church of Corinth, one campaign of which is fought out in this letter, was itself rooted in the universalism of his Gospel. It could not be that the note of this universalism should be unheard in anything that can put in the slightest claim to be the embodiment of Paul's Gospel.

It is so little unheard here that it would be truer to say that it forms the ground-tone of the whole enunciation. "One died for all: therefore all died"—that is the key-note which is struck at the beginning. "God was in Christ reconciling the world with Himself"—that is the great announcement in which it culminates. We may be perfectly sure that neither statement was here made by Paul for the first time. Rather, these were the things on which he had fed his courage in those days of afflictions, necessities, distresses, stripes, imprisonments, tumults, labours, watchings, fastings, in which his life had been spent. We may fancy him in the midst of the deaths which he died daily repeating to himself over and over again these great words: "One died for all: therefore all died:" "God was in Christ reconciling the world with Himself"—and deriving from them the force by virtue of which, though he died yet behold he lived again, though he was chastened yet he was not destroyed, though he was brought to grief yet he always rejoiced, though he was himself poor he yet enriched many, though he had nothing he yet possessed all things. They constitute indeed the battlecry of Paul's whole immense conflict and give its character to his entire life-history. Eliminate this note of universalism from Paul's Gospel and you do away with his significance in history; you cut up the Gospel to which he freely gave his life by the roots.

You cannot exaggerate, therefore, the significance to his Gospel of Paul's universalism. In important respects this universalism was his Gospel. But unfortunately it is very possible to misconceive and to misrepresent this universalism: and unhappily it is commonly very gravely misconceived and misrepresented. After all, Paul's universalism was *Paul's* universalism; and *Paul's* universalism stood in opposition, not to the particularism of divine grace, but to the exclusiveness of Jewish nationalism. What he gave his life to, what he directed all his teaching toward, was not a passionate assertion of absolute indiscrimination on God's part in His dealings with sinners of the human race, but the vindication to the Gospel of God's grace in Christ Jesus of a world-wide reference. If he argues at one time that "there is no difference" between men, he makes it plain that he means this in point of claim upon God for His mercy; and so soon as he comes to speak of the distribution of the divine gifts, he makes it equally plain that there is a great difference and that this difference depends on the will of the Divine Giver. When Paul therefore nailed to his mast-head the great declaration: "One died for all; therefore all died," he was as far as possible from intimating that Jesus' death was equally and without distinction in behalf of every individual of the human race, and that therefore every individual of the human race, past, present and to come, died with Christ on the cross. This crass distributive universalism of redemption apparently never once entered his mind. And equally, when he inscribed upon his banner, "God was in Christ reconciling the world with Himself," he thought of nothing so little as teaching that this reconciliation concerned itself equally with each and every individual who has ever lived in the world, lives in it now, or ever shall live in it. Such a conception is quite alien to his entire thought. What he means is just that God, who is the God not of the Jews only but also of the Gentiles, has given His Son to die not for the Jews only but for the world. His eye has caught this great vision; and, his mouth being open and his heart enlarged, he cries, Not one people only, but the world for Christ! It is the great missionary cry which Paul gives us here. "The world for Christ!" That is the cry that sounds in our ears today and fills us with enthusiasm in our service of the cross. It is the cry which Paul heard in his heart two thousand years ago, and under the impulse of which he inaugurated that great mission work which still occupies our hearts and hands. "The world for Christ"—not one nation, not one class, not one race or condition of men, but the world and nothing less than the world for Christ!

It would certainly be exceedingly unfortunate in any event to eviscerate Paul's whole Gospel for the sake of gratuitously imposing on his language an inoperative universalism of redemption which does not actually save. That men could perish for whom Christ died, Paul never imagined that human minds could conceive. The very nerve of his great declaration that "Christ died for all; therefore all died," is that participation in the death of Christ is salvation. Therefore he goes on to declare that those who thus died with Christ live, live with the Christ who not only died for them but also rose again for them. So little was it possible for him to admit a distinction between dying with Christ, which is the unconscious lot of all, and living with Christ, which is the conscious attainment of only some, that he even founds elsewhere an *a fortiori* argument on participation in Christ's death as removing all doubt of participation in His life. "But God commendeth His own Son towards us," he reasons, "in that while we were yet sinners Christ died for us. Much more then, being now justified by His blood, shall we be saved from wrath through Him. For if while we were sinners, we were reconciled with God through the death of His Son, much more, being reconciled, shall we be saved by His life." "But if we died with Christ," he reasons again, "we believe that we shall also live with Him;" and again, "For if we have become united with Him by the likeness of His death, we shall be also by the likeness of His resurrection." Paul therefore will have nothing to do with a distinction between men who have only died with Christ and those who also live with Him. With Paul, to die with Christ means to live together with Him; to be reconciled with God through the death of Christ means to enter into the full inheritance of life. When he passionately declares that when Christ died He died not for Jews only but for all, that in Him God was reconciling nothing less than the world with Himself, he is thinking of no half-measures. He is proclaiming the world-wide reach, the world-wide destiny of God's salvation.

How impossible it is to read Paul as teaching here a purely potential universalism in the death of Christ, to be made effective in each instance by the individual's own act of appropriation, is rendered clear by another prime characteristic of his Gospel as here enunciated. This is what we may perhaps call, for lack of a better phrase, its high supernaturalism. By this we mean to refer to the emphasis and persistence with which he ascribes the whole saving process—in its initiation and outworking alike—to God. This too we should have expected of Paul. There is no more marked feature of his total thought than the vision of God which informs it: and no matter from what point of departure his argument takes its start, it can find its point of rest only when it arrives at "the good pleasure of His will, to the praise of the glory of His grace, which He freely bestowed on us in the Beloved." It can cause us no surprise therefore when we find him in our present passage insisting, of the new life which he discovers in those—in all those—who have died with Christ, that it is all of God; and representing the whole tremendous transaction by which we sinners are transformed into the likeness of Christ as inaugurated and carried through by God alone. All those for whom Christ died He tells us died with Him and rose again with Him, and are consequently a new creation, the old things having passed away and become new. And then he adds with what might almost seem superfluous emphasis—for how could these things be, except by the power of God?— "But all these things are of God, who it is that has reconciled us with Himself through Christ and has given to us the ministry of reconciliation, seeing that it was God" (observe the emphasis again) "who in Christ was reconciling the world with Himself." Accordingly, when a few verses later he alludes to the redemptive process again, he tells us quite naturally, not that "He who knew no sin was made sin for us," but that "Him who knew no sin God made sin for us, that we might become the righteousness of God in Him." So eager is the apostle that his readers shall take off from his page at least this assurance, that what they are in Christ Jesus and all that they shall become they owe to God and to God alone. It was He, he tells us, who made Christ, the sinless one, to be sin for us; it was He who reconciled us with Himself through Christ; it is of Him that we are new creatures in Christ. In the whole saving process we supply nothing but the sinners to be saved, and the consequent activities induced in us by the saving process, as, in accordance with our nature, we move as we are moved upon.

It surely belongs to the most astonishing curiosities of exposition, then, that in the face of this abounding emphasis upon the sole efficiency of God in salvation, there should be found those who insist that, according to Paul's teaching, the decisive act in salvation is supplied by an action of the human will. See, we are told, the apostle in this very context beseeches his readers not to permit the grace of God to come to them in vain, but to be reconciled with God. Does not this imply that all that God has done lies without us, and it belongs to us, in our sovereign freedom, to give it validity each for his own person? We need not pause to point out that the inference thus so confidently drawn is explicitly contradicted a score of times elsewhere by the apostle, who consistently represents it as "of God" that men differ in their spiritual endowments; and declares that no one has the least advantage over another which he has not received from above, and therefore cannot glory in it as if it were of his own production,—that, in a word, in the matter of spiritual standing, it is not of him that willeth nor of him that runneth but of God that showeth mercy. Nor need we pause to point out that there is a great difference, which we dare not neglect in a matter like the present, between an exhortation to action in accordance with the really moving force, and exhortation to action designed to set this force in motion. When this same apostle exhorts us to work out our own salvation with fear and trembling, "for it is God who is working in you both the willing and the doing for His good pleasure," we certainly cannot infer that our salvation so hangs upon our own will that God's energizing waits upon our act: the contrary is openly asserted—that our act rests rather on His energizing; it is He that works our very willing as well as our doing. Similarly it can scarcely be inferred from Paul's exhortation to us "to be reconciled with God," that reconciliation with God so depends on the unmoved action of our own free-will that all of God's action looking to our salvation must wait upon it. Apart from all this, it would seem to be enough to observe that no inference of this kind can set aside Paul's explicit and emphatic ascription here of this very reconcilia-

tion to God. For it is precisely our reconciliation which Paul
ascribes to God with what seems almost an excessive energy
of emphasis: "All these things are of God, who it was that
reconciled us with Himself through Jesus Christ:" "It was
God who, in Christ, was reconciling the world with Himself."
When, immediately after this strong assertion of the divine
production of reconciliation, he entreats his readers to be
reconciled with God, the one most certain thing of all is that
he does not mean to imply that their reconciliation is so in
their own hands that the act of God waits upon their act.
And this becomes the more evident when we observe that
even in this exhortation itself the verb is thrown into the
passive voice, and points therefore not to something which
we are to do, but to something which we are to suffer. The
exhortation, in other words, is not that we should "reconcile
ourselves" to God, but that we should assume an attitude
consonant with the reconciliation which God has wrought
with respect to us. That is to say, we have a conception here
which ranges perfectly with that other exhortation which we
have already illustratively adduced: that we should work out
our own salvation, knowing it is God who is working in us
both the willing and the doing. It is an exhortation to
consonant, not to determining activity.

We are led thus, however, to advert to a further prime
characteristic of the Gospel of Paul, as set forth in our
passage. That is that it finds its key-note in a doctrine of
reconciliation. The core of Paul's Gospel is indeed expressed
in this one word, Reconciliation; and it behoves us to consider carefully what he means by it. There are several things that
are told us about it in our present passage. In the first place
we are very emphatically told, as we have just seen, that the
author of it is God: it is God Himself, not man, who works
this reconciliation. "All these things," says the apostle, "are
of God, who it is that has reconciled us with Himself through
Christ." "For it was God who in Christ was reconciling the

world with Himself." Next we are told that the effects by
which this reconciliation manifests itself among men are
relief from the burden of their sin, and the proclamation of
free pardon. "It was surely God who in Christ was reconciling
the world with Himself, since He does not impute to them
their trespasses and has placed in us the word of reconciliation." Then we are told that it finds its ground in the
sin-bearing of Christ. "We beseech you in the behalf of
Christ, Be ye reconciled with God: Him who knew no sin He
made sin for us, that we may be the righteousness of God in
Him." From such suggestions as these it is perfectly easy to
see what Paul means by this reconciliation, the ministry of
which he declares to be his only function, the proclamation
of which his one duty—or rather privilege—in the world. It is,
shortly, not the reconciliation of man to God, as the short-
comings of our English version might mislead us into supposing: but the reconciliation of God to man—a reconciliation which God has Himself undertaken and which He has
accomplished at the tremendous cost of the death of His Son,
on the ground of which He is able to release men from their
trespasses. Of course men are at enmity with God: they do
not like even to retain God in their knowledge, and they turn
against Him with unconcealed dread and hatred. But this is
not the thing which most disturbs Paul. What most disturbs
him is that God is at enmity with man: that His wrath is
revealed from heaven against their abounding unrighteousness. And what fills his heart with joy—the joy that made him
the zealous missionary he was,—is the assurance that this
enmity has been removed, that this wrath has been appeased
and that by God Himself, who has reconciled us with Himself
through Christ, by making Him who knew no sin to be sin for
us,—and so enabling Himself not to impute our trespasses to
us. The proclamation of this great transaction seemed to Paul
so glorious that he joyfully made the ministry of reconciliation his life-work; the word of reconciliation his Gospel. In it

lies, in a word, the very heart of Paul's Gospel.

Now the presupposition of this Gospel, you will perceive, is a deep and keen sense of human sin and that in the
aspect of guilt. The reason why Paul's heart was filled with
such joy at the thought of a reconciled God was that his
heart was oppressed with a sense of guilt in the presence of a
just God. A holy and righteous God, he knew, could not
possibly look upon him, or his partners in guilt, without
abhorrence and indignation. In his conscience the wrath of
God was revealed against the abounding iniquity of men. O
wretched men that we are, his soul of souls cried out, who
shall deliver us from this mass of sin? It was because he felt
so deeply and keenly the guilt of sin, and knew so clearly the
depth and heinousness of his own and of the world's guilt,
that he broke out with such rejoicing at the sight of a
reconciled God, and made the proclamation of His reconciliation his Gospel—the substance of the glad tidings which he
bore to a sin-stricken and hopeless race. The underlying
conception of sin,—of sin oppressing, of sin removed—thus
dominates the passages which are now engaging our attention. Why should Christ,--the "One"—need to die for men:
and why is it glad tidings that all for whom He died, died
with Him? Why should the Gospel of reconciliation be announced as manifesting itself precisely in the non-imputation
of men's trespasses to them? Why above all should the
exhortation to be reconciled with God be supported by the
great declaration that He who knew no sin has been made sin
for us? Is it not clear that underneath all Paul's Gospel lies
the most profound and poignant sense of sin, and that his
Gospel consists precisely in a proclamation of relief from the
intolerable burden of guilt? This then was the word of
reconciliation, the ministry of which was committed to him:
that the righteous wrath of God against sin has been appeased
and the face of God has been turned to us again clothed in a
smile of favour.

It has seemed worth while to dwell upon this, partly because of the apparent dying out of a deep sense of sin in wide circles of present-day life, but more because this sense of sin though it may be temporarily obscured cannot really die out, but will sooner or later assert itself in every human breast and bring despair when it does not find its antidote in a sense of a reconciled God. No doubt our age is marked by a "vanishing sense of sin," and there are multitudes about us who seem never to have awakened to any adequate realization of their moral condition, or of the significance of their moral condition with respect to their relations to God and to that future over which the righteous award of God rules. It would not be strange if there were some sitting here today to whom Paul's strong agony under the consciousness of sin seems wholly alien to normal human experience, something at any rate into which they find it impossible sympathetically to enter. I do not say that this condition of apathy in face of the most tremendous fact of human life is scarcely creditable to you: I do not even say that it ought to be viewed by you as a signal of extreme danger, because it is the index of an indurated heart, a heart callous to its own wickedness, and therefore should cause you the deepest concern and call out your best endeavours to see things more truly even if less comfortably. What I wish to say now to you is, that it is a condition that cannot last. We are all sinners: and, being sinners, we are under the condemnation of the just God, who does righteousness in heaven and on earth. We cannot always conceal from ourselves this state of things. Sooner or later our troubled eyes will open with fright upon it: and all our smug contentment with ourselves will be gone. Now, life may run on upon oiled axles. Then, Time will seem to us "a maniac scattering dust, and Life a Fury slinging flame." And then, having discovered what sin is and what we are as sinners, we shall discover also the joy which Paul felt at the vision of a reconciled God. It will no longer seem strange to us that our Lord declared that there is joy in heaven over one sinner that repents, more than over ninety and nine just persons who need no repentance. It will no longer be difficult for us to understand that the gladdest of all glad tidings which the apostle knew to bring to the world, was the glad tidings of reconciliation in the blood of Jesus Christ.

I say, reconciliation in the blood of Jesus Christ. For we do not get to the heart of Paul's doctrine of reconciliation, until we bring clearly before us what he teaches us of the way in which it has been accomplished. That way is, briefly, by a great act of substitution: of the substitution of Jesus Christ for us before the judgment-seat of God and the expiating of our guilt by Him on the tree. If Paul's doctrine of reconciliation is the heart of his Gospel, his doctrine of substitution is the heart of the heart of his Gospel. In it all the glad tidings he had to proclaim to man culminate and find their true significance. What does Paul mean by that great declaration which stands in the forefront of our present passage: "One died for all: therefore all died"? And what does he mean by that even greater declaration with which the passage closes: "Him who knew no sin God made sin for us"? Obviously what he means is just substitution. We must not lose ourselves here in possibly learned but certainly meaningless discussions of the precise fundamental significance of the preposition "for." Of course its fundamental meaning is "for the sake of," "for the benefit of." It was for the sake of the all that Christ died; and it was precisely because He died for their sakes that they share in that death of His which was for *their* benefit and not for *His.* It was for our sakes that God made Him who knew no sin to be sin; and it is precisely because this great transaction was done for our benefit that it avails for us. And what else could Paul have meant when he cries out in the joy of his salvation, "Christ died for me," "God made Him sin for me," than just that Christ had died for his sake and it inured to his benefit that He had been made sin? Would you expect a beneficiary of this tremendous transaction, suffused with a sense of the immense benefit received, to employ in describing it language which was wholly denuded of all emotional recognition that it was all for him, for his sake? And this is the real account to give of the prevalence in the allusions of the Biblical writers to the death of Christ of the broad preposition "for," with the primary implication of "for the sake of," rather than of the more precise "for" with the primary implication of "instead of," in relating that death to themselves. They were not putting together a systematic statement of the exact relation of Christ's death to human salvation: they were giving expression to their deepest religious convictions, and they could not but choose language charged with their profound emotions. When they employ the particular preposition they do employ, they derogate nothing from the substitutive nature of the death they are describing, but they couch their description of it in language freighted with their answering gratitude and love. When Paul declares that when Christ died in behalf of all, then all died with Him—that God made Him sin in our behalf though He Himself knew no sin—he asserts substitution just as clearly as if he had said that He died in our stead and had been made sin in our place; and at the same time he uncovers to us his own heart, throbbing with grateful response to such an unheard-of benefit.

The glad tidings which Paul's Gospel brings to men, then, is just, to put it briefly and in familiar language, salvation from sin in the blood of Jesus Christ. What it means is, in the crispest form of statement, just that Jesus has done it all. He has taken our place and borne in His own body on the tree all our iniquities: He has died our death: and He grants us His righteousness that hereafter we may live and live to Him. This, according to Paul, is the very heart of the heart of the Gospel.

And now let us observe finally what according to Paul is

the issue of all this for life. Here we have brought before us
yet another primary characteristic of his Gospel. Shall we
say, Because Jesus has done it all, there remains nothing for
us to do? So says not Paul. We could not save ourselves, or do
the least thing towards, or contributing to, our salvation.
Until Jesus had died for us there was nothing for us to do but
to die. We were dead in sin, and held under death for sin. But
now since He has died for us, we can work our salvation out
into life. And that is what Paul teaches us. We cannot save
ourselves: but having been saved, we can illustrate our salvation in newness of life. "One died for all," he says, "therefore
all died: and He died for all, that, living, they might no longer
live for themselves, but to Him who for them died and rose
again." "He that knew no sin was made sin for us, that we
might become the righteousness of God in Him." "So then, if
anyone is in Christ, he is a new creature: the old things have
passed away, behold, they have become new." There is, it
will be observed, a declaration here and an exhortation. The
declaration is that this newness of life is the result of salvation in Christ. The exhortation is that we shall walk in
accordance with this newness of life. The apostle does not
leave it an open question whether those for whom Christ has
died (and who, therefore,—so he says—have died with Him)
shall possess this new life. He says they *are* "a new creation;"
and a new *creation* is not a self-made thing, which waits upon
our own choice whether it is made or not; but a product of
the almighty power of God. And therefore the apostle at
once adds that it has God for its author: "And all these
things are of God." If Christ died for us, He died for us only
for this end—that we may live and, living, may live not for
ourselves, but to Him. If He was made sin for us, He was
made sin for us only for this end—that we may be the
righteousness of God in Him. The end can no more fail than
the means. He who is in Christ Jesus is a "new creation." To
him the old things have passed away; all has become wholly

new. Paul had found it so: and he makes his finding it so the substance of his defence to the Corinthians. He could not but be true to his mission and office as an apostle of Christ: for it was the love of Christ—not *his* love *to Christ*, but *Christ's* love *to him*—which constrained him—held him in—that he should not give himself to aught but that to which he was sent. Being in Christ, he was a new creation, and everything that was of the flesh had fallen away from him.

And every one who, like Paul, has been made the object of Christ's love, for whom Christ has died, and who has been made partaker of Christ's death, will like Paul find the love of Christ constraining him, will find the life of Christ flowing into his veins, will discover himself a new creation, looking out as such on a new world, filled with new enthusiasms, directing himself to new ends. You cannot die with Christ and not rise again with Him: it cannot be that He who knew no sin shall have been made sin for you, and you who have known no righteousness shall not be made the righteousness of God in Him. This is Paul's declaration to you: and there could be no declaration of greater joy. Being in Christ Jesus, you have within you the powers of a new life, and they will grow, and grow, and grow. Sinner that you are, Christ who knew no sin has been made sin for you, and you shall become the righteousness of God in Him. Could there be a greater inducement to effort brought to bear upon us than this great declaration? It is God that is working in us: shall we not then work out our own salvation with fear and trembling? This is Paul's exhortation to you. In effect he says: Seeing that you are a new creation, live as becomes those who are a new creation. Desert the old plane of your living; it is not worthy of new creatures. Having died with Christ, live with and for Him. He has been made sin for you. See that you become the righteousness of God in Him. You are released from the bondage of sin and freed for a new life of holiness. Live it. Adorn the Gospel you profess: for God has called you not to sin but to holiness, and if you walk not in this holiness,—are you in Him? have you died with Him? He who dies with Him lives also in and with Him, and living in and with Him lives to Him.

So the apostle mingles declaration and exhortation, warning and encouragement; and the upshot of it all is, as we cannot have failed long ere this to have told ourselves, that the Gospel he preaches is an eminently ethical Gospel. Righteousness in Christ, righteousness through Christ,—justification, sanctification—these things do not stand with the apostle as separable entities over against one another, one of which can be had without the other. They are distinctly correlatives, implying and implicating one the other. It would be inconceivable to him that there could be sanctification which did not rest on justification, or that there could be justification which did not issue in sanctification. To die with Christ is to live with Him; to live with Him means to live to Him. To be reconciled with God by Christ's death means a new creation through His Spirit. Analysis of parts and stages there may be; distinguishings of inceptions from continuations and continuations from consummations: but to the apostle there is but one salvation, and that salvation is an indivisible whole. The holy life ripening into that perfection without which no man shall see the Lord, is not with Him an arbitrary addition to acceptance by God in Christ Jesus, but its natural and necessary outgrowth: and therefore, with all his proclamation of life in Christ, the life of faith, and of an objective salvation in the blood of Jesus, he never looses sight of the essence of salvation in holiness of life. So, in our present passage, the whole movement of which turns as on its hinge upon the substitution of Christ for sinners and His death in their behalf and their consequent righteousness in Him, the issue of all is found nevertheless in holiness of life. Those for whom Christ has died are, in their new creature-hood, to live no longer for themselves but for Him who died and rose again for them. The revolution in standing is marked by a revolution in living. If their trespasses are no longer imputed to them, they are also no longer to have trespasses to be imputed to them. In a word, their salvation is not merely from the penalty but from the power of sin: and the mark of it is the life that is free not only from the condemnation but from the commission of sin. We are saved while yet sinners, but not that we may remain sinners, but that we may glorify God and His saving power by becoming under His guidance saints.

This is what, according to Paul, we are saved to: this is what, in his conception of it, salvation is. It is the promise to us of a perfected life. And surely there is no promise which could come to us with a more penetrating appeal. There is no one of us so degraded that he would not fain be good: the desire that stirs within us may be so faded and so weak that we can scarcely call it a desire, but we secretly admire the good even when we pursue the bad. Paul points the way not to an inoperative admiration, but to an effective accomplishment. He says to us in effect that all which the best of men have longed for and vainly striven after and the worst have dully admired while impatiently spurning is placed within our reach in Christ Jesus. He says that in Him there is the potency of a new life and that this potency shall surely pass into actualization for all those that are in Him. Or if we choose, we can give form to his message to us today rather in the words of his Master and our Master. For what does he say in effect but this: Blessed are they that hunger and thirst after righteousness, for they shall be filled? For they shall be filled! Let these words be our encouragement today. Let them become from today the strength of our life. "They *shall* be *filled!*"

HEBREWS ii. 9:—But we behold Him who hath been made a little lower than the angels, even Jesus, because of the suffering of death crowned with glory and honour, that by the grace of God He should taste death for every man.

THE GLORIFIED CHRIST

The words I have chosen as a text form a part of a great passage, the proximate purpose of which is to set in a clear light the surpassing glory of Jesus Christ. In the first chapter of the Epistle to the Hebrews the unapproachable greatness of our Lord's person is exhibited. No mere "interpreter" of God He, like the prophets; no mere "messenger" of God, like the angels. The Jewish-Christian readers of this Epistle had been prepared by their traditional teaching to expect the coming of a culminating interpreter of God, of a final messenger from God, and they readily greeted Jesus Christ as such. Our author reminds them that, greeting Jesus Christ as such, they had found in Him something much more. No doubt they had found in Him the supreme interpreter of God, who, alone, having seen God, is in a position to "declare" Him,—or, as our author expresses it, who, being the very effulgence of God's glory and the very impress of His substance, can, alone, manifest all that God is. And they had found in Him the final messenger of God who had come to do a service, for the sake of them that shall inherit salvation, which no angel could do, or in His own words, who had come not to be ministered unto but to minister. But our author reminds his readers that they had found in Jesus something more glorious than even these great things, seeing that He had received by inheritance the much more exalted name of Son. The ineffable glory of Jesus Christ lies, he tells us, in this,— that even the great functions of interpreter of God and messenger of God, great as these functions as exercised by Him are, are not the source and not the measure of His greatness. As the Son of God, the effulgence of God's glory, and the impress of God's substance, all the prophets are but His servants, and before His majesty the very angels veil their faces and do Him homage.

The greatness of His work, of course, he now goes on to remind them, corresponds with the greatness of His person. In the second chapter our author advances to exhibit this surpassing greatness of the work of the Son of God. The salvation He wrought is called with pointed directness "so great a salvation," and is contrasted by this epithet with all that even the divinely given law could accomplish. To exhibit its greatness it is set before us in the height of its idea on the positive side. That we are saved by it from sin is taken for granted, and alluded to as a matter well known to all. But the negative side of salvation is not treated as the measure of its greatness. We are asked to attend, not to what we are saved from, but to what we are saved to. And that is presented as nothing less than dominion over the universe. This dominion God has destined for man from the beginning. But man had failed of his destiny. How hopelessly, how dismally, he had failed, none knew better than those the author of this Epistle was addressing,—Jews, who had lost even their Jewish ideals, and were now doubting whether in Christianity they had not lost all. He points them to Jesus as one who had saved them out of this depth to that height. Lordship,—not over "this world," with its troubles and trials, its incompletenesses and make-believes, and after all done, the end of death,—but over the "world to be," was theirs. True, they had not entered as yet into their heritage: the "world to be," by that very token, is not yet. But Jesus had entered upon it; and in Him they held the reversion to it. "But now, not yet do we see all things subjected to man: but Him who has been made a little lower than angels for the suffering of death, Jesus, we behold crowned with glory and honour, in order that by the grace of God His tasting of death should be for every man." He is on

the throne; and He is there not for Himself but for us. It was
for us that He died, nay, that He took upon Himself mortality; and now He is on the throne that this dreadful experience
of death might really avail for us.

Had He only died for us, perhaps salvation might have
consisted solely in relief from this penalty of sin which He
bore for us. That He ascended out of death to the throne,
conquers the throne itself for us. When we behold Jesus on
the throne for us, we may see how great a salvation He has
wrought for us. For on that throne we too shall sit, not
merely in Him but with Him. It has always been the Father's
good pleasure to give us the Kingdom; not apart from the
Son but along with that Son who is not ashamed to call us
brethren. And because this has always been and still is the
Father's will, it behoved Him who orders all things for His
own glory, in leading many sons into glory, to bring the
leader of their salvation through sufferings to the full accomplishment of His great task.

The verse which we have chosen out of this noble
context as our text is so remarkable, even in its form, that we
must pause for a moment to observe some of its characteristics. The first thing that strikes us about it is the way in
which it takes all the great Christian verities for granted, not
formally asserting them, as if it were instructing us as to their
reality, but assuming them as things fully established, which
could be counted upon to be fully understood, if only
suggested. The Incarnation, the Atoning Death, the Session
on the right hand of God, the Kingly rule of the exalted
Christ, all these are in this verse touched upon with clearness, confidence, emphasis. But no one of them is asserted, as
if the purpose were to inform us of it. They are all assumed
as the common conviction of writer and reader, and built
upon as such for the conveyance of the special message of the
passage.

Note the simplicity and effectiveness with which this is

done. What the text wishes to do is, to put it briefly, to turn our eyes from ourselves to Jesus. But it does not speak of Jesus by His bare name, but designates Him by a descriptive phrase taken from the eighth Psalm which had just been quoted. What is this descriptive phrase? "Him that hath been made a little lower than angels:" "But now, we see not yet all things subjected to him," *i.e.* to man: "but Him who hath been made a little lower than angels, we behold, Jesus." Now, how could this phrase be thus employed to describe Jesus as a man? You observe, it is not, properly speaking, a "quotation" from the Psalm. It is not employed here in the sense of the Psalm. As it stands in the Psalm, it is a proclamation of man's amazing greatness and dignity: God, it is declared, "made man but little lower than angels, and crowned him with glory and honour." Here, it is not a proclamation of dignity, but a recognition of humiliation: "Him that hath been made a little lower than angels for the suffering of death, we behold, Jesus." It is merely the application of certain words taken out of the Psalm in a new sense to designate Jesus according to a habitual mode of thinking of Him. The writer is making a quick transition, and he feels that when he says, "Him who has been made a little lower than angels," everybody will be struck at once with a little shock of pleased surprise at seeing the words of the Psalm suddenly given a new meaning and will anticipate him in saying to themselves, Why, it is Jesus he means: He was made a little lower than angels when he became man. In other words, the author counts confidently on the doctrine of the Incarnation as present to the thought of his readers, to which he can therefore allude, even in the most unexpected language, with the assurance that they will take his point.

Similarly, he says nothing directly about the Atoning work of Christ, but simply alludes to it in a word or two which in themselves might bear a less profound significance, but which he knows cannot but be taken in just this meaning by his readers: "Him," he says, "who hath been made a little lower than angels, for the suffering of death." He speaks only of death. Other men besides Jesus have suffered death: every other man, sooner or later, suffers death. In themselves the words, therefore, carry no suggestion of anything unusual in Jesus' case. But the writer knew that every Christian heart would respond, when he spoke of Jesus suffering death, and that with a turn of phrase which called attention to the suffering which He endured in His death, with a thrill of joyful recognition that this suffering of death was not merely the usual payment of the debt of nature, common to man, but was fraught with high significance. This indeed, he subtly suggests, by speaking of Jesus' becoming a little lower than angels for the suffering of death: it was for this purpose that He became man, that He might endure this death. Other men do not become men to die: Jesus did and in this he separated Himself from man. Death to Him is His voluntary act, and must be endured, not of necessity, but for an end. With such a suggestion embedded in it, our author can easily trust his bare mention of the death of Jesus to suggest forcibly to his readers all that a full reference to the atonement could convey.

The same is true of his allusion to the Ascension. Of the Ascension itself he says nothing, nor of the Resurrection which preceded it and forms its presupposition. He merely says, still in words borrowed from the description of man's high destiny in the eighth Psalm, that Jesus has been "crowned with glory and honour." With what sort of glory? With what kind of honour? Perhaps the glory and honour of the grateful memory of men? The inscription of His name on some monument, in some hall of fame? Or, possibly, on the hearts of His grateful followers? Does he mean that all history will ring with His praise, and, like the widow who cast in her mite at the treasury of the Temple, this that He did shall be remembered in His honour through all generations?

Nothing of the kind. He means the actual session of Jesus upon the throne of the universe, that He may reign with a real rule over all principalities and powers and mights and dominions. But the words which he employs do not themselves say this. That he leaves to the natural understanding of his readers, whom he knows he can trust to read into his bare allusion to the crowning of Jesus with glory and honour the whole body of facts concerning His exaltation, including His resurrection and ascension and session at the right hand of God, thence expecting till He shall make His enemies His footstool.

You see how remarkable our text is for its confident dealing with this great circle of Christian doctrines by way of allusion. It is as plain as day that these things were not novelties to the writer or to his readers. They were not things about which he felt that he must instruct his readers; or even which they required to be reminded of in detail. They were things which stood to them and himself, alike, as the basis of their faith and hope. It is, therefore, also clear that these doctrines, thus suggested by way of allusion, do not constitute the specific teaching of our text. We do not deal with our main purpose in writing by way of allusion. The burden of the text is found, therefore, not in these great doctrines of the Incarnation, the Atonement, the Session at the right hand of God, which are brought before us in it, richly, powerfully, movingly, indeed, but, in point of mode of presentation, allusively. It is to be found in the final clause of the text, up to which they lead, and which describes the purpose, for which the incarnated Son of God, having become man and suffered death, has been crowned with glory and honour. This purpose was—I retranslate the words in an effort to bring out their true sense and relations—"in order that this, His bitter experience of death, may by the grace of God redound to the benefit of every man."

As it is in these words that the real message of the text

is delivered to us, they demand our most careful scrutiny. To place them in their proper relation, let us observe in the first place that the clause goes back to the preceding words, "Because of the suffering of death;" and finds its true sense only when read in reference to them. Jesus Christ became man that He might die; and He has been crowned with glory and honour that this, His death, might by God's grace redound to the benefit of man. We are justified in rendering the strong Greek verb—"that He may taste of death"—by the strong English substantive—"that His bitter experience of death," on the general rule, which used to be so fertilely emphasized by Edward Thring, that it is the verb in the one language and the substantive in the other that is the strong word, and that our translations, if they are to be true to the stress of the original, must bear this in mind.

But perhaps it is worth while to pause to point out that the idea intended to be conveyed by the phrase "tasting of death" is a strong and not a weak one. Many, no doubt, when they read of our Lord's "tasting death," take it as implying that He merely "had a taste of death," as we say,—passed through it with the minimum of conscious experience of its terror. Precisely the contrary is what is really meant. What the phrase signifies is that He was not a merely passive subject of death, of whom it is merely to be said that He died, and that is all of it: but that He drained this bitter cup to its dregs. It is the horror and the pains of death that are thrown up boldly for our contemplation by this phrase; and therefore it is used to take up again the preceding phrase,— "the suffering of death," a phrase which by an unexpected turn of expression itself emphasizes the sufferings of death. Jesus became a man not merely that He might suffer death, but that He might endure the sufferings of death. He was not merely the object on which death wrought; He in dying suffered, had strong agonies to endure. And now, our present clause adds that this dreadful cup of death was drunk by

Him, for a high end,—that by God's grace benefits might be secured for men.

Let us not pass on too rapidly to remind ourselves that in these words lies the emphasis not only of our text, but of this entire Epistle. For one of the great objects of this Epistle was to exhibit the glory of the death of Christ. To those old Jewish Christians for whom the Epistle was written, the offence of Jesus was—what the offence of Jesus has been ever since to all who, though not of Jewish blood, are of Jewish hearts—just the cross. Jesus as God's "interpreter," the supreme prophet, revealing by word and deed what God is and what God intends for man: Jesus as God's "messenger," the supernal agent in the divine work of gathering His people to Himself: these were ideas familiar to them, to which they gave immediate and glad hospitality. But Jesus, the bruised and broken sufferer hanging on the accursed tree,—it was hard for them to adjust themselves to that; and this it was which, first of all things, as the cruelties of their lot shook their courage and faith, they were in danger of drifting away from. This it was, therefore, which, first of all things, the author of this Epistle desired to fix in their hearts as too precious to lose hold of; as, indeed, the very centre and core of their Christianity, first spoken by the Lord Himself, and confirmed to them by those who heard Him, God bearing witness with them with signs and wonders and divers miracles and gifts of the Holy Ghost, distributed according to His will. And therefore he gives his strength in the paragraph of which our text forms a part to carrying home to them these two great truths: that it became God—seeing that He it is to whom all things tend as their end and through whom all things come to pass as their director and governor,—without whom, therefore, as end and means, nothing takes place—to lead many sons to glory; and that it became Him equally to make the Leader in their salvation perfect—that is, to bring His saving work to the completion which is its accomplishment—through suffering. These are the two ideas, you will perceive at once, which, though they are announced in the form in which I have just stated them only in the next verse, yet already dominate our text. For precisely what our text seeks to emphasize is that Jesus passed through sufferings to glory; and that the reason why these sufferings were crowned with glory was in order that they might be made to inure to the benefit of every one.

There still remain two or three points which require elucidation before the precise message of the text may be grasped with clearness. Perhaps the first of these that will strike us is that the text does not directly announce the reason why Jesus suffered. As I have already pointed out, it does not say explicitly that Jesus suffered that many might enter into glory; but rather only that He has been crowned with honour and glory that His sufferings might inure to the good of every one. For all that is openly asserted in this verse by itself, it might be plausibly argued that the saving power of Jesus resided in His session at the right hand of God, rather than in His death; though no doubt we should be given pause in pushing this notion by observing that after all His kingly power is not represented as itself the saving force, but only as needed to secure its proper efficacy to His death: "That the bitterness of His death should inure to the good of every one." And the context speedily supplies all that may be thought wanting in the text itself. We are immediately told that it was becoming in our Lord as the Leader in our salvation to partake in all that belongs to those whom He would lead to glory, since only so could he open the way for them to this glory: He must through death bring to naught Him that had the power of death, that is the devil, and deliver all them who through fear of death were all their lifetime subject to bondage. Obviously it is sin that blocks the way to their ascent to glory, and soon we find it express-ly declared that the reason why our Lord was made in all

things like unto His brethren was that as a merciful and
faithful high priest He might make propitiation for the sins of
the people. We must not, therefore, infer from the absence of
express mention of it in our text that the author of our
Epistle did not look upon the sufferings and death of Christ
as primarily and above all the expiation of sin: or imagine
that this idea does not underlie and colour the language of
the text and need not be held in mind by us as part of its
presupposition. On the contrary, this is one of the main
foundations, as of the whole argument of the Epistle, so of
our text as well.

Meanwhile it is not thrown forward in our text, and the
reason is, as has already been intimated, that the aspect of
salvation which is for the moment engrossing the mind of the
author is not that of deliverance from the curse of sin. He is
looking at salvation at this point of his argument not on its
negative, but on its positive side. His mind is not full at the
moment of what man is saved from, but with what man is
saved to. He cannot help speaking of the sufferings of Christ,
and throwing these sufferings out in the highest relief: for it
was in and through these sufferings that Christ saved us. But
His eye is set, not on the depths out of which this salvation
has raised us, but on the heights to which it promises to
elevate us. This is what is swelling in his heart when he calls it
"so great salvation." And the specific aspect of its greatness
which is occupying his attention is the universal dominion
which it brings to saved mankind. O the greatness of this
salvation, which Jesus Christ has wrought for us, he seems to
cry; by it we are elevated well-nigh to the throne of God
itself, and all creation is placed beneath our feet!

It is especially important to note the completeness of
the writer's preoccupation at this point with the positive side
of salvation, and, indeed, with the particular aspect of the
positive side of salvation which consists in the establishing of
mankind in its destined dominion over the creation, in order

that we may understand another peculiarity of his exposition. This is the apparent inclusion of Christ Himself among those who share in the salvation adverted to. Nothing could be further from our author's mind than that theory of the atonement, sometimes vividly called the theory of "salvation by sample," which conceives our Lord in His incarnation to have taken sinful flesh, and to have participated in His own work of saving humanity from sin. Our author is express in his assertion that our Lord was "without sin," although He was offered specifically to bear the sins of many; and He makes it a part of our Lord's superiority to the priest of the shadow-dispensation that He did not require as the priest did to offer sacrifice for Himself as well as for the people. Our author no more than the other writers of the New Testament imagined Jesus to participate in His own propitiation for sin. Yet, in this context, he speaks of Him as "the Leader in salvation," making use of a term variously rendered, "Author," "Captain," "Prince," of salvation, which may seem to imply that He leads in salvation because He is the first to take part in it, as well as the principal cause of it; as we may speak of a bad man as the leader in all the evil in which a coterie under his influence indulges; or, more appropriately in this connection, of a good man as the leader in all the good works his example inspires; or, even better still, of a great popular saviour like Washington as the leader of his people into freedom and power. And, indeed, our whole passage is cast in some such mould as this. For what does it do but bid us see in the exaltation of Jesus to the throne of the universe, the fulfilment in principle of the promise in the Psalm of universal dominion to man, which is here identified with the great salvation earned by Christ? The explanation of this apparent inclusion of Jesus Himself in His own saving work, is found in the engrossment of the writer with the positive aspect of salvation, and that as manifested in dominion over the creation, to the exclusion for the moment of contemplation of its whole negative side.

The negative aspect of salvation, no doubt, enters too deeply into the very essence of salvation ever to be wholly out of mind when the work of Christ is spoken of. And therefore, though the immediate interest of the writer, in our text, rests not so much on the relation of Christ's death to the guilt which it expiates, as on its relation to the glory which it purchases, yet he not only alludes to His death, but throws it into prominence as the basis of all that Jesus has obtained for men. And certainly there is no forgetfulness apparent that it was for others, not for Himself, that all our Lord's work was done. The very purpose for which the whole passage was written is to emphasize the fact that it was not for Himself but for others that our Lord wrought: and that purpose is nowhere more emphatically asserted than in this very culminating clause of our text, the assertion of which is precisely that our Lord's bitter experience of death was on behalf of others: "In order that, thus, His tasting of death might by God's grace inure to the benefit of every man." The energy of this expression is so great, in fact, that we may possibly be misled by it into attaching a meaning to it which was certainly not intended by its author. By his use here of the term "every man"—"in order that He might taste of death for every man"—the author has no intention of asserting a universal salvation. As we are reminded by a recent commentator, he "nowhere expresses hope or expectation of universal redemption." His interest is not in asserting that each and every man who lives in the world, or has lived or will live in it, shall attain to the universal dominion promised through the Psalmist. He knows very well that this will not be the case; no one could be more earnest than he is in warning his readers against neglecting this great salvation and incurring the fate of thorns and thistles whose end is to be burned. And the refinement of a universal redemption which does not take universal effect, but hangs for its realization upon a condition to be fulfilled by the redeemed themselves, is foreign to his whole thought. He is speaking in our text moreover not of the intention with which Christ died, but of the realization of that intention through the power of the ascended Christ. His interest is absorbed in the contrast between Jesus' earning the promised dominion for Himself alone, and His earning it for others. What he asserts, and that with the highest energy, is that Jesus did not act for Himself in the great transaction which he speaks of as this "so great salvation," but for others: and that the result of it is not that by it He Himself attained to honour and glory, but that He by it led a multitude of sons of God into glory. And therefore the "every one" of this verse is immediately translated into the "many sons" of the next: "For it became Him, for whom are all things, and through whom are all things, to bring many sons into glory."

Certainly there is a sense in which this "every one" is the human race. Jesus' endurance of death for every one is set forth as the ground on which the fulfilment of the Psalmist's promise is based. And that promise was that to man should be given dominion over creation. The nerve of the assertion our author makes is that Christ's ascension to His glory is in order that His death, suffered on earth, should bring about this great consummation: "In order that by God's grace His endurance of death may be for every one,"— that is, may redound to the glorification, the establishment on its destined throne, not of Himself, but of the human race. The promise is to the human race; Christ is but the instrument of securing its fulfilment to the race. He enters His glory not for Himself, any more than He died for Himself; but that He might bring about the glorification of the race. "Every one" means here, thus, simply the race at large, and its peculiar form is not intended to distribute the race into its units, and to declare that the consummation shall fail for no one of these units; but with the greatest possible energy to assert the racial effect of our Lord's work. Not for Himself, but for man it was that He died; not for Himself, but for man it was that He has ascended into heaven and has seated Himself on the right hand of God; not for Himself, but for man is it that He has been crowned with glory and honour, that His death may not be of no effect, but by God's grace His endurance of death may inure to the benefit of mankind.

And now, perhaps, we are prepared tardily to throw into its proper relief the especial message of the text for us. What is it but this: The necessity of the exaltation of Christ for the completion of His saving work? We are accustomed to think of Christ dying for us. Let us remember that He not only died for us, but rose again for us: Paul says that He who was delivered up for our trespasses was raised for our justification. And let us remember that He was not only raised for us, but ascended into heaven for us and sits at the right hand of God for us. It was therefore that our Lord declared that it was expedient for us that He should go away, and that Paul exhorts us to remember Jesus Christ, risen from the dead, of the seed of David. What our author does when he declares that we behold Jesus, made a little lower than angels for the suffering of death, crowned with glory and honour, that His bitter experience of death may be for the benefit of every one, is to fix our eyes on the saving work of the exalted Jesus. If He died to expiate our sins, He reigns in heaven that He may apply the benefits accruing from that expiation to His people, and may thus bring them into the glory He has purchased for them. If, says Paul, while we were enemies, we were reconciled with God through the death of His Son, much more, being reconciled, shall we be saved by His life. Christ no more died for us two thousand years ago at Calvary, than He now lives for us in heaven.

An exhortation to fix our eyes on the exalted Saviour was eminently timely when this Epistle was written; and it is

no less timely today after the passage of these two thousand
years. Then, the Hebrew Christians, puzzled and distressed by
the spectacle of a suffering Christ, needed to have their hearts
cheered and their faith steadied by the great vision of the
exalted Christ: they needed to be continually reminded that
Jesus died, not for Himself but for man, and that His death
cannot fail of its high purpose, seeing that He Himself, sitting
on the throne of the universe, will see to it that the seed that
was sown in sorrow shall produce a harvest which shall be
reaped in joy: He shall see of the travail of His soul and be
satisfied. And we today, in the special trials to faith which an
age of critical doubt has brought to us, need to keep in
constant remembrance that our trust is put not in a dead, but
in a living Christ,—in a Christ who died, indeed, but whom
the tomb could not retain, but lo! He is alive for evermore.
The fashionable, I do not say unbelief, I say the fashionable
belief, about us today, forgets or neglects, or openly turns its
back upon the living Christ, and bids us seek inspiration for
our lives and hope for our future, in a Jesus who lived and
died in Palestine two thousand years ago,—and that was all.
Dimly seen through the ever-increasing obscurity of the gathering years, that great figure has still the power to attract the
gaze and to quicken the pulses—yes, to dominate the lives—of
men. This is, no doubt, much; but so little is it all, that it is
the least of what we are to seek and to find in Jesus Christ.
He is our inspiration; and, knowing Him better than these,
our would-be guides, know Him, He is also our example. But
He is so much more than our inspiration or even our example, that we need scarcely think of these things when we
think of Him: He is our life. And He is our life not only
because He has washed out in His blood the death-warrant
that had been issued against us—giving, as He Himself phrased
it, His life as a ransom for many—but also because, after He
had purchased us to Himself by His precious blood, He has
become to us the living fountain and ever-flowing source of

life and blessedness. Jesus on the cross is our Saviour; and it is our privilege to behold Him on His cross, an all-sufficient sacrifice for our sins. But Jesus on His throne is our Saviour too; and it is our privilege today, as we read the lofty words of this great declaration of the Epistle to the Hebrews, to behold Him on His throne, crowned with glory and honour, that His tasting of death may by God's grace be the actual salvation of our souls.

Let us fix our eyes and set our hearts today, then, on our exalted Saviour. Let us see Him on His throne made head over all things to His Church, with all the reins of government in His hands,—ruling over the world, and all the changes and chances of time, that all things may work together for good to those that love Him. Let us see Him through His spirit ruling over our hearts, governing all our thoughts, guiding all our feelings, directing all our wills, that, being his, saved by His blood, we may under His unceasing control steadily work out our salvation, as He works in us both the willing and the doing, in accordance with His good pleasure. As, in our unrighteousness, we know we have an Advocate with the Father, Jesus Christ the righteous,—or, as our own Epistle puts it, a great High Priest who has entered within the veil and ever liveth to make intercession there for us: so let us know that in our weakness we have the protecting arm of the King of kings and Lord of lords about us, and He will not let us slip, but will lose none that the Father has given Him, but will raise them up at the last day. Having been tempted like as we are (though without sin), He is able to sympathize with us in our infirmities; having suffered as we do, He knows how to support us in our trials; and having opened a way in His own blood leading to life, He knows how to conduct our faltering steps that we may walk in it. Christ our Saviour is on the throne. The hands that were pierced with the nails of the cross wield the sceptre. How can our salvation fail?

Art thou afraid His power shall fail
    When comes thine evil day?
Or can an all-creating arm
    Grow weary, or decay?

Supreme in wisdom as in power,
    The Rock of Ages stands;
Though Him thou canst not see, nor trace
    The workings of His hands.

What matters it if we cannot see? There is a firmer foundation for confidence here than sight. "Who shall separate us from the love of Christ? shall tribulation, or anguish, or persecution, or famine, or nakedness, or peril, or sword? . . . Nay, in all these things we are more than conquerors through Him that loved us. For I am persuaded that neither death, nor life, nor angels, nor principalities, nor things present, nor things to come, nor powers, nor height, nor depth, nor any other creature, shall be able to separate us from the love of God, which is in Christ Jesus our Lord." Let us bless God today that we can behold Jesus, not only made a little lower than the angels for the suffering of death, but, having suffered death for us, crowned with glory and honour, that by God's grace the bitter pains He suffered in our behalf may be efficacious for the saving of our souls.

Just one word, in closing, especially to you who have given yourselves to the service of Christ in the ministry of His grace. Remember that you serve a living, not a dead Christ. You are to trust in His blood. In it alone have you life. But you are to remember that He was not broken by death, but broke death; and having purchased you to Himself by His blood, now rules over your souls from His heavenly throne. He is your master whom you are to obey. He has given you commandment to bring all peoples to the knowledge of Him.

And He has promised to be with you, even to the end of the world. Live with Him. Keep fast hold upon Him; be in complete touch with Him. Let your hearts dwell with Him in the heavenly places, that the arm of His strength may be with you in your earthly toil. Let this be that by which all men know you: that in good report and in bad, in life and in death, in the great and in the small affairs of life—in everything you do down to the minutest acts of your everyday affairs—you are the servants of the Lord Christ. So will you be truly His disciples, and so will He be your Saviour—unto the uttermost.

2 TIMOTHY ii. 8:—Remember Jesus Christ, risen from the dead.

THE RISEN JESUS

The opening verses of the second chapter of the Second Epistle to Timothy are in essence a comprehensive exhortation to faithfulness. The apostle Paul was lying imprisoned at Rome, with expectation of no other issue than death. The infant Church had fallen upon perilous times. False teachers were assailing the very essence of the Gospel. Defection had invaded the innermost circle of the apostle's companions. Treachery had attacked his own person. Over against all these dreadful manifestations of impending destruction, he strenuously exhorts his own son in faith, Timothy, to steadfast faithfulness. Faithfulness to himself, faithfulness to the cause he had at heart, faithfulness to the truth as he preached it, faithfulness to Jesus Christ, their common Redeemer and Lord.

The temptations to unfaithfulness by which Timothy was assailed were very numerous and very specious. Many good men had fallen and were falling victims to them. The perverted teachings of the errorists of the day were urged with a great show of learning and with eminent plausibility. And they were announced with a fine scorn which openly declared that only dull wits could rest in the crude ideas with which Paul had faced the world—and lost. The sword of persecution had been ruthlessly unsheathed, and sufferings and a cruel death watched in the way of those who would fain walk in the path Paul had broken out. It seemed as if the whole fabric which the apostle had built up at such cost of labour and pain was about to fall about his ears.

Paul does not for a moment, however, lose courage,

either for himself, or for his faithful followers. But neither does he seek to involve Timothy unwittingly in the difficulties and dangers in which he found himself. He rather bids him first of all to count the whole cost. And then he points him to a source of strength which will supply all his needs. We called the passage an exhortation. We might better call it, more specifically, an encouragement. And the encouragement culminates in a very remarkable sentence. This sentence is pregnant enough to reveal at once the central thought of Paul's Gospel and the citadel of his own strength. Amid all the surrounding temptations, all the encompassing dangers, Paul bids Timothy to bear in mind, as the sufficing source of abounding strength, the great central doctrine,—or rather, let us say, the great central fact—of his preaching, of his faith, of his life. And he enunciates this great fact, in these words: Jesus Christ raised from the dead, of the seed of David.

It is, of course, to the glorified Jesus that Paul directs his own and Timothy's gaze. Or, to be more specific, it is to the regal lordship of the resurrected Jesus that he points as the Christian's strength and support. The language is compressed to the extremity of conciseness. It is difficult to convey its full force except in diluted paraphrase. Paul bids Timothy in the midst of all the besetting perplexities and dangers which encompassed him to strengthen his heart by bearing constantly in remembrance, not Jesus Christ *simpliciter*, but Jesus Christ conceived specifically as the Lord of the Universe, who has been dead, but now lives again and abides for ever in the power of an endless life; as the royal seed of David ascended in triumph to His eternal throne. It is not from the exaltation of Jesus alone, let us observe, that Paul draws and would have Timothy draw strength to endure in the crisis which had fallen upon their lives. It is to the contrast between the past humiliation and the present glory of the exalted Lord that he directs his eyes. He does not say simply, "Bear in mind that Jesus Christ sits on the throne of the universe and all things are under His feet," although, of course, it is the universal dominion of Jesus which gives its force to the exhortation. He says, "Bear in mind that Jesus Christ has been raised from the dead, of the seed of David—that it is He that died who, raised from the dead, sits as eternal king in the heavens." No doubt a part of the apostle's object in his allusion to the past humiliation of the exalted Lord is to constitute a connection between Jesus Christ and his faithful followers, that they may become imitators of Him. They, the *viatores*, may see in Him, the *consummator*, one who like them had Himself been *viator*, and may be excited to follow after Him that they too may in due time become *consummatores*. But the nerve of the exhortation, obviously, does not lie in this, as the very language in which it is couched sufficiently avouches. How could Timothy imitate our Lord in being of the seed of David? How could he imitate Him by ascending the throne of the universe? Fundamentally the apostle is pointing to Christ not as our example, but as our almighty Saviour. He means to adduce the great things about Him. And the central one of the great things he adduces about Him is that He has been raised from the dead.

It is not to be overlooked, of course, that Paul adverts to the resurrection of Christ here with his mind absorbed not so much in the act of His rising as in its issues. "Bear in mind," he says, "Jesus Christ, as one who has been raised from the dead:" that is to say, as one who could not be holden of the grave, but has burst the bonds of death, and lo! He lives for evermore. But neither can it be overlooked that it is specifically to the resurrection, which is an act, that he adverts; and that he adverts to it in such a manner as to make it manifest that the fact of the resurrection of Christ held a place in his Gospel which deserves to be called nothing less than central. The exalted Christ is conceived by him distinctly as the resurrected Jesus; and it is clear that, had there been no resurrection of Jesus, Paul would not have known how to point Timothy to the exalted Christ as the source of his strength to face with courage the hardships and defeats of life. From this great fact, he derives, therefore, the very phraseology with which he exhorts Timothy, with rich reference to all that is involved in Christ our Forerunner, to die with his Lord that he might also live with Him, to endure with Him that he might also reign with Him. To Paul, it is clear, the resurrection of Christ was the hinge on which turned all his hopes and all his confidence, in life and also in death.

Now, there is a sense in which it is of no special importance to lay stress on the place which the resurrection of Christ held in Paul's thought and preaching. In this sense, to wit: that nobody doubts that it was central to Paul's Gospel. It would seem impossible, in fact, to read the New Testament and miss observing that not only to Paul, but to the whole body of the founders of Christianity, the conviction of the reality of Christ's bodily resurrection entered into the very basis of their faith. The fact is broadly spread upon the surface of the New Testament record. Our Lord Himself deliberately staked His whole claim to the credit of men upon His resurrection. When asked for a sign He pointed to this sign as His single and sufficient credential. The earliest preachers of the Gospel conceived witnessing to the resurrection of their Master to be their primary function. The lively hope and steadfast faith which sprang up in them they ascribed to its power. Paul's whole gospel was the gospel of the Risen Saviour: to His call he ascribed his apostleship; and to His working, all the manifestation of the Christian faith and life.

There are in particular two passages in Paul's Epistles, which reveal, in an almost startling way, the supreme place which was ascribed to the resurrection of Christ by the first believers in the Gospel.

In a context of very special vigour he declares roundly

that "if Christ hath not been raised" the apostolic preaching and the Christian faith are alike vanity, and those who have believed in Christ lie yet unrelieved of their sins. His meaning is that the resurrection of Christ occupied the centre of the Gospel which was preached alike by him and all the apostles, and which had been received by all Christians. If, then, this resurrection should prove to be not a real occurrence, the preachers of the Gospel are convicted of being false witnesses of God, the faith founded on their preaching is proved an empty thing, and the hopes conceived on its basis are rendered void. Here Paul implicates with him the whole Christian community, teachers and taught alike, as suspending the truth of Christianity on the reality of the resurrection of Christ. And so confident is he of universal agreement in the indispensableness of this fact to the integrity of the Christian message, that he uses it for his sole fulcrum for prying back the doctrine of the resurrection of believers into its proper place in the faith of his sceptical readers. "If dead men are not raised, neither hath Christ been raised," is his sole argument. And he plies this argument with the air of a man who knows full well that no one who calls himself a Christian will tolerate that conclusion. The fact that Christ has been raised lay firmly embedded in the depths of the Christian consciousness.

In some respects even more striking are the implications of such phraseology as meets us in another passage. Here the apostle is contrasting all the "gains" of the flesh with the one great "gain" of the spirit—Christ Jesus the Lord. As over against "the excellency of the knowledge of Christ Jesus, his Lord," he declares that he esteems "all things" as but refuse,—the heap of leavings from the feast which is swept from the table for the dogs,—if only he may "gain Christ and be found in Him," if only, he repeats, he may "know Him, and the power of His resurrection, and the fellowship of His sufferings, becoming conformed into His death; if by any means he may attain to the resurrection from the dead." The structure of the sentence requires us to recognize the very essence of the saving efficacy of Christ as resident in "the power of His resurrection." It is through the power exerted by His resurrection that His saving work takes effect on men. That is to say, Paul discovers the centre of gravity of the Christian hope no less than of the Christian faith in the fact of the resurrection of Christ. And of the Christian life as well. From the great fact that Christ has risen from the dead, proceed all the influences by which Christians are made in life and attainments, here and hereafter, like Him.

In the face of such evidence, spread broadcast over the New Testament, no one has been able to question that the founders of Christianity entrenched themselves in the fact of Christ's resurrection as the central stronghold of their hope, faith, and proclamation. We do not need to lay stress, therefore, on this implication in such a passage as that before us, as if we were seeking proof for a doubtful or even for a doubted fact. The importance of our laying stress on its implication here and its open assertion throughout the New Testament, is that we may be able to estimate the real significance of a very wide-spread tendency which has arisen in our own time to question the importance of this event on which the founders of Christianity laid such great emphasis, and to which they attached such palmary consequence. If nobody doubts that the first preachers of the Gospel esteemed the resurrection of Christ the foundation-stone of their proclamation, the chief stay of their faith and hope alike, there are nevertheless many who do not hesitate to declare roundly that the first preachers of the Gospel were grossly deceived in so esteeming it. This is an inevitable sequence, indeed, of the chariness with respect to the supernatural which so strongly characterizes our modern world. The "unmiraculous Christianity" which has, in one or another of its modes of conception, grown so fashionable in our day, as it could scarcely allow that the most stupendous of all miracles really lay at the basis of Christianity in its historical origins, so cannot possibly allow that confidence in the reality of this stupendous miracle lies today at the foundation of the Christian's life and hope. To allow these things would be to confess that Christianity is through and through a supernatural religion—supernatural in its origin, supernatural in its sanctions, supernatural in its operations in the world. And then,—what would become of "unmiraculous Christianity"?

Accordingly, we have now for more than a whole generation, been told over and over again, and with ever-increasing stridency of voice, that it makes no manner of difference whether Jesus rose from the dead or not. The main fact, we are told, is not whether the body that was laid in the tomb was resuscitated. Of what religious value, we are asked, can that purely physical fact be to any man? The main fact is that Jesus—that Jesus who lived in the world a life of such transcendent attractiveness, going about doing good, and by His unshaken and unshakable faith in providence revealed to men the love of a Father-God,—this Jesus, though He underwent the inevitable experience of change which men call death, yet still lives. Lives!—lives in His Church; or at least lives in that heaven to which He pointed us as the home of our Father, and to which we may all follow Him from the evils of this life; or in any event lives in the influence which His beautiful and inspiring life still exerts upon His followers and through them in the world. This, this, we are told, is the fact of real religious value; the only fact upon which the religious emotions can take hold; by which the religious life can be quickened; and through which we may be impelled to religious effort and strengthened in religious endurance.

The beauty of the language in which these assertions are clothed and the fervour of religious feeling with which it is suffused, must not be permitted to blind us to the real issue that is raised by them. This is not whether our faith is grounded in a mere resuscitation of a dead man two thousand years ago; or rather in a living Lord reigning in the heavens. It is not the peculiarity of this new view that it focuses men's eyes on the glorified Jesus and bids them look to Him for their inspiration and strength. That is what the apostles did, and what all, since the apostles, who have followed in their footsteps, have done. Paul did not say to Timothy merely, "Remember that Jesus Christ, when He died, rose again from the dead,"—although to have said that would have been to have said much. Directing Timothy's eyes to the glorified Jesus, reigning in power in the heavens, he said, "Remember Jesus Christ, risen from the dead, of the seed of David." It is not, then, the peculiarity of this new view that it has discovered the living and reigning Christ. The living and reigning Christ has always been the object of the adoring faith of Christians. It is its peculiarity that it neglects or denies the resurrected Christ.

It does not pretend that in neglecting or denying the resurrected Christ it does not break with the entirety of historical Christianity. It freely allows that the apostles firmly believed in a resurrected Christ, and that, following the apostles, Christians up to today have firmly believed in a resurrected Christ. And it freely allows that this firm belief in a resurrected Christ has been the source of much of the enthusiasm of Christian faith and of the Christian propaganda through all the ages. But it hardily affirms that this emphasis on the resurrected Christ nevertheless involves a gross confusion—no less a confusion than that of the kernel with the husk. And it stoutly maintains that the time has come to shell off the husk and keep the kernel only. Religious belief, we are told, cannot possibly rest on or be inseparably connected with a mere occurrence in time and space. What others have seen in a different age from ours—what is that to us? That Jesus rose from the dead two thousand years ago and was seen of men—how can that concern us today? All that can possibly be of any significance to us is that He was "not swallowed up in death, but passed through suffering and death to glory, that is, to life, power, and honour." "Faith has nothing to do with the knowledge of the form in which Jesus lives, but only with the conviction that He is the living Lord."

Here now is a brand-new conception of the matter, standing in express contrast, and in expressly acknowledged contrast, with the conception of the founders, and hitherto of the whole body of the adherents, of Christianity. It is the outgrowth, as we have already hinted, of a distaste for the supernatural. To get rid of the supernatural in the origins of Christianity, its entire historical character is surrendered. The Christianity now to be proclaimed is to be confessedly a "new Christianity"—a different Christianity from any which has ever heretofore existed on the face of the earth. And its novelty consists in this, that it is to have no roots in historical occurrences of any kind whatsoever. Religious belief, we are told, must be independent of all mere facts.

We must not forget that the professed purpose of this new determination of the relation of Christianity to fact is to save Christianity. If Christianity is independent of all historical facts, why, it is clear that it cannot be assailed through the medium of historical criticism. Let criticism reconstruct the historical circumstances which have been connected with its origin as it may; it cannot touch this Christianity which stands out of relation with all historical occurrences whatever. Doubtless it would be a great relief to many minds to be emancipated from all fear of historical criticism. But it is certainly a great price we are asked to pay for this emancipation. The price indeed is no less an one than Christianity itself. For the obvious effect of the detachment of Christianity from all historical fact is to dismiss Christianity out of the realm of fact.

Christianity is a "historical religion," and a "Christianity" wholly unrelated to historical occurrences is just no Christianity at all. Religion,—yes, man may have religion without historical facts to build upon, for man is a religious animal and can no more escape from religion than he can escape from any other of his persistent instincts. He may still by the grace of God know something of God and the soul, moral responsibility and immortality. But do not even the heathen know the same? And what have we more than they? We may still call by the name of "Christianity" the tattered rags of natural religion which may be left us when we have cast away all the facts which constitute Christianity,—the age-long preparation for the coming of the Kingdom of God; the Incarnation of the Son of God; His atoning death on the Cross; His rising again on the third day and His ascension to heaven; the descent of the Spirit on the Pentecostal birthday of the Church. But to do so is to outrage all the proprieties of honest nomenclature. For "Christianity" is not a mere synonym of "religion," but is a specific form of religion determined in its peculiarity by the great series of historical occurrences which constitute the redemptive work of God in this sinful world, among which occurrences the resurrection of Christ holds a substantial and in some respects the key position.

The impossibility of sustaining anything which can be called "Christianity" without embracing in it historical facts, may be illustrated by the difficulty in carrying out their programme which is experienced by men who talk of freeing Christianity from its dependence on facts. For do they not bid us to abstract our minds, indeed, from that imagined resuscitation that occurred in Palestine (if it occurred at all) two thousand years ago, but to focus them nevertheless on the living Jesus, who has survived death and still lives in heaven? Do they forget that when they say "Jesus" they already say "history"? Who is this "Jesus" who still lives in heaven, and the fact of whose still living in heaven, having passed through death, is to be our inspiration? Did He once live on earth? And, living on earth, did He not manifest that unwavering faith in providence which reveals the Father-God to us? Otherwise what is it to us that He "still" lives in heaven? To be free from the entanglements of history; to be immune from the assaults of historical criticism; it is not enough to cease to care for such facts as His resurrection: we must cease to care for the whole fact of Jesus. Jesus is a historical figure. What He was, no less than what He did, is a matter of historical testimony. When we turn our backs on historical facts as of no significance to our "Christianity," we must turn our backs as well on Jesus—any Jesus we choose to rescue for ourselves from the hands of historical criticism. He who would have a really "unhistorical Christianity" must know no Jesus whether on earth or in heaven. And surely a Christianity without Jesus is just no Christianity at all.

Christianity then stands or falls with the historical facts which, we do not say merely accompanied its advent into the world, but have given it its specific form as a religion. These historical facts constitute its substance, and to be indifferent to them is to be indifferent to the substance of Christianity. In these circumstances it is a dangerous proceeding to declare this or that one of them of no significance to the Christian religion. Especially is it a dangerous proceeding to single out for this declaration, one in which the founders of Christianity discovered so much significance as they discovered in the resurrection of Christ. When Paul says to us, not "Remember Jesus Christ enthroned in heaven," but "Remember Jesus Christ, risen from the dead, of the seed of David," we surely must pause before we allow ourselves to say, "It is of no importance whether He rose from the dead or not." And if we pause and think but a moment, we certainly shall not fail to set our seal to Paul's judgment of the significance of His rising from the dead to the Christian religion. For once let us cast our minds over the real place which the resurrection of Christ holds in the Christian system and we shall not easily escape the conviction that this fact is fundamental to its entire message.

Let us recall in rapid survey some of the various ways in which the resurrection of Jesus evinces itself as lying at the basis of all our hope and of all the hope of the world.

It is natural to think, first of all, of the place of this great fact in Christian apologetics. Opinions may conceivably differ whether it would have been possible to believe in Christianity as a supernaturally given religion if Christ had remained holden of the grave. But it is scarcely disputable that the fact that He did rise again, being once established, supplies an irrefragable demonstration of the supernatural origin of Christianity, of the validity of Christ's claim to be the Son of God, and of the trustworthiness of His teaching as a Messenger from God to man. In the light of this stupendous miracle, all hesitation with respect to the supernatural accompaniments of the life that preceded it, or of the succeeding establishment of the religion to which its seal had been set,—nay, of the whole preparation for the coming of the Messenger of God who was to live and die and rise again, and of the whole issue of His life and death and resurrection—becomes at once unreasonable and absurd. The religion of Christ is stamped at once from heaven as divine, and all marks of divinity in its preparation, accompaniments, and sequences become at once congruous and natural. From the empty grave of Jesus the enemies of the cross turn away in unconcealable dismay. Christ has risen from the dead! After two thousand years of the most determined assault upon the evidence which establishes it, that fact stands. And so long as it stands, Christianity too must stand as the one supernatural religion. The resurrection of Christ is the fundamental apologetical fact of Christianity.

But it holds no more fundamental place in Christian

apologetics than in the revelation of life and immortality which Christianity brings to a dying world. By it the veil was lifted and men were permitted to see the reality of that other world to which we are all journeying. The whole relation they bore to life and death, and the life beyond death, was revolutionized to those who saw Him and companied with Him after He had risen from the dead. Death had no longer any terrors for them: they no longer needed to believe, they knew, that there was life on the other side of death, that the grave was but a sojourning place, and, though their earthly tent-dwelling were dissolved, they had a building of God, a house not made with hands, eternal in the heavens. And we who have come later may see with their eyes and handle with their hands the Word of Life. We can no longer speak of a bourne from which no traveller e'er returns. The resurrection of Christ has broken the middle wall of partition down and only a veil now separates earth from heaven. That He who has died has been raised again and ever lives in the completeness of His humanity is the fundamental fact in the revelation of the Christian doctrine of immortality.

Equally fundamental is the place which Christ's resurrection occupies relatively to our confidence in His claims, His teachings, and His promises. The Lord of Life could not succumb to death. Had he not risen, could we have believed Him when He "made Himself equal with God"? By His resurrection He set a seal on all the instructions which He gave and on all the hopes which He awakened. Had the one sign which He chose failed, would not His declarations have all failed with it? Is it nothing to us that He who said, "Come unto Me and I will give you rest;" who has promised to be with those who trust Him "always even unto the end of the world;" who has announced to us the forgiveness of sins; has proved that He has power to lay down His life and to take it again? Whether is it easier to say, "Thy sins be forgiven thee," or "I will arise and walk"? That He could not be holden of death, but arose in the power of a deathless life, gives us to know that the Son of Man has power to forgive sins.

And there is a yet deeper truth: the resurrection of Christ is fundamental to the Christian's assurance that Christ's work is complete and His redemption is accomplished. It is not enough that we should be able to say, "He was delivered up for our trespasses." We must be able to add, "He was raised for our justification." Else what would enable us to say, He was able to pay the penalty He had undertaken? That He died manifests His love and His willingness to save. It is His rising again that manifests His power and His ability to save. We cannot be saved by a dead Christ, who undertook but could not perform, and who still lies under the Syrian sky, another martyr of impotent love. To save, He must pass not merely to but through death. If the penalty was fully paid, it cannot have broken Him, it must needs have been broken upon Him. The resurrection of Christ is thus the indispensable evidence of His completed work, of His accomplished redemption. It is only because He rose from the dead that we know that the ransom He offered was sufficient, the sacrifice was accepted, and that we are His purchased possession. In one word, the resurrection of Christ is fundamental to the Christian hope and the Christian confidence.

It is fundamental, therefore, to our expectation of ourselves rising from the dead. Because Christ has risen, we no more judge that "if one died for all, then all died," "that the body of sin might be done away," than that having died with Him "we shall also live with Him." His resurrection drags ours in its train. In His rising He conquered death and presented to God in His own person the first-fruits of the victory over the grave. In His rising we have the earnest and pledge of our rising: "For if we believe that Jesus died and rose again, even so them also that are fallen asleep in Jesus will He bring with Him." Had Christ not risen could we nourish so great a hope? Could we believe that what is sown in corruption shall be raised in incorruption; what is sown in dishonour shall be raised in glory; what is sown in weakness shall be raised in power; what is sown a body under the dominion of a sinful self shall be raised a body wholly determined by the spirit of God?

Last of all, to revert to the suggestion of the words of Paul with which we began, in the resurrection of Christ we have the assurance that He is the Lord of heaven and earth whose right it is to rule and in whose hands are gathered the reins of the universe. Without it we could believe in His love: He died for us. We could believe in His continued life beyond the tomb: who does not live after death? It might even be possible that we should believe in His victory over evil: for it might be conceived that one should be holy, and yet involved in the working of a universal law. But had he not risen, could we believe Him enthroned in heaven, Lord of all? Himself subject to death; Himself the helpless prisoner of the grave; does He differ in kind from that endless procession of the slaves of death journeying like Him through the world to the one inevitable end? If it is fundamental to Christianity that Jesus should be Lord of *all;* that God should have highly exalted Him and given Him the name which is above *every* name; that in the name of Jesus *every* knee should bow, and *every* tongue confess Him Lord: then it is fundamental to Christianity that death too should be subject to Him and it should not be possible for Him to see corruption. This last enemy too He must needs, as Paul asserts, put under His feet; and it is because He has put this last enemy under His feet that we can say with such energy of conviction that nothing can separate us from the love of God which is in Christ Jesus our Lord,—not even death itself: and that nothing can harm us and nothing take away our peace.

O the comfort, O the joy, O the courage, that dwells in the great fact that Jesus is the Risen One, of the seed of

David; that as the Risen One He has become Head over all things; and that He must reign until He shall have put all things under His feet. Our brother, who has like us been acquainted with death,—He it is who rules over the ages, the ages that are past, and the ages that are passing, and the ages that are yet to come. If our hearts should fail us as we stand over against the hosts of wickedness which surround us, let us encourage ourselves and one another with the great reminder: Remember Jesus Christ, risen from the dead, of the seed of David!

JOHN vi. 38-39:—For I am come down from heaven, not to do Mine own will, but the will of Him that sent Me. And this is the will of Him that sent Me, that of all that which He hath given Me I should lose nothing, but should raise it up at the last day.

THE GOSPEL OF THE COVENANT

In the miracle of the feeding of the five thousand our Lord presented Himself symbolically to man as the food of the soul. For, as Augustine reminds us, though the miracles wrought by our Lord are divine works, intended primarily to raise the mind from visible things to their invisible author, yet their message is not exhausted by this. They are to be interrogated also as to what they tell us about Christ, and they will be found to have a tongue of their own if we have skill to understand it. "For," he adds, "since Christ is Himself the Word of God, even a deed of the Word is a word to us." One of His miracles is accordingly not to be treated as a mere picture, which we may be satisfied to look upon and praise; but rather as a writing, which we are not content to praise though we delight in its beauty, but find no satisfaction until we have read and understood it. We may possibly consider Augustine's detailed decipherment of the signs in which this miracle is written somewhat fanciful. He discovers in it a complete parable of the salvation of man and of men. But we can scarcely refuse, as we read it in the pregnant record of John, to say in Pauline phrase, "These things contain an allegory."

As such, indeed, John presents it. This is the meaning of his care to tell us, as he introduces his recital, that "the passover was at hand;" not a mere chronological note, we may be sure; nor yet merely an explanation of the presence of the multitude, gathered for the pilgrimage to Jerusalem; but a premonition of what is to come,—John's account of the occasion and meaning of the miracle, which itself was the

147

occasion of the great discourse on the bread of life. Christ, the true passover, chose the passover time, when men's minds were upon the type, to present the antitype to them in symbol and open speech. It was therefore also that He tested His disciples with searching questions, designed to bring them to the discovery of whether they yet knew him; and that He taxed the people that "signs" were wasted upon them, and that while they were demanding a sign that they might see and believe, the sign had been given them, and though they had seen, they did not believe. It was therefore above all, that Christ followed up the miracle with the wonderful discourse in which He explains the sign, and declares Himself openly to be "the bread of God that cometh down from heaven and giveth life to the world." This is the tremendous truth which miracle and discourse united to proclaim to the multitudes gathered on the shores of Gennesaret at that passover season; but which, despite type and sign and teaching each a manifest word from God, they could neither receive nor understand. And this is the blessed truth which our text, taken from the centre of the discourse and constituting, indeed, its kernel, presents to our apprehension and belief anew today. May the Spirit of truth, who searches all things, even the deep things of God, illuminate our minds and prepare our hearts, that we may understand and believe.

Let us begin by observing the testimony borne by our Lord and Master here to His heavenly origin and descent: "I am come down from heaven," He says. And the truth here declared is the foundation of the entire discourse. The whole gist of it is to represent Jesus as the "bread out of heaven," "the true bread out of heaven," "the bread of God that cometh down out of heaven," which the Father hath given for the life of the world. I need not remind you how this representation pervades John's Gospel, from the testimony of the Baptist, that He who was to supplant him "cometh from above," and is therefore "above all," to Jesus' own triumphant declaration at the close of His life, that, His work being finished, He is ready to return to the Father who sent Him, and to the glory that He had with Him before the world was. Our present asseveration is but a single instance of the constant self-testimony of the Son of Man to His heavenly origin and descent.

The older Unitarianism was prodigal of miracle. It was not the supernatural, but the mysteries of the Holy Trinity and the God-man that were its scandal. When brought face to face with such passages as these, it was wont, therefore, to explain that Jesus, born miraculously of His virgin mother, but a mere man, was taken up to heaven by the divine power to learn the things of God; whence He again descended to bring divine teaching to men. To the newer Unitarianism, on the other hand, it is precisely the supernatural which is the offence. Its philosophical forms might hospitably receive such mysteries as the Trinity and the God-man, if only they may be permitted to run freely into their moulds. But divine interventions of any kind, and most of all the descent of a personal God from heaven to earth, to be incased in flesh and to herd for a season among men, it cannot allow. It therefore attacks our passages with a theory of ideal, not real, pre-existence, and teaches that Jesus means only that, in the thought and intention of God, His advent into the world had long been provided for, and that, in that sense, He was with God and came forth from God.

How weak, how inconceivably banal, all such expedients are before the majesty of Christ's self-witness: "I am come down from heaven." And when we turn over the pages of this Gospel,—the leading idea of which, it has been said, inadequately indeed, but so far truly, is the divine glory of Christ in the incarnation,—and observe our Lord's constant witness in the discourses recorded in it, not merely to His descent from the Father, but to His essential equality and oneness with God, to His eternal pre-existence with Him, and to His

prospective return to His primal glory with the Father, after
His task on earth is accomplished, how our spirits bow in
worship before that God only-begotten who is in the bosom
of the Father, who became flesh and tabernacled among us
for a season full of grace and truth, and by His very existence
among us "declared" to us that God, not only whom He
came forth from, but who He is.

We should not fail to observe, however, that the incarnation is not spoken of in our text as an end in itself, but rather
as a means to an end. The object of our Lord here is not to
present the bare fact of His having come down from heaven
to the wonder of men, but to expound the purpose of His
coming down from heaven. "I am come down from heaven,"
He declares, *"in order that I may do* the will of Him that sent
Me." You will scarcely need to be reminded that this, too, is
the representation, not of our text only, but of the whole
body of relevant deliverances recorded by John from the
mouth of the Master, and indeed of the entire Gospel itself.
Everywhere and always, it is not the coming down from
heaven itself, but the purpose of the coming, that receives the
emphasis. And this is why it is inadequate to say that the
leading idea of John's Gospel is the glory of Christ in the
incarnation. Its leading idea is, rather, the sufficient end of
the incarnation, or, in other words, its leading purpose is to
present what we may call a satisfactory philosophy of the
incarnation.

And this is the precise amount of truth that lies behind
the assertion so freely made by those who are stumbled by
the heights of John's theology, that his Gospel is not a simple
narrative of fact, but an ideological treatise, which, in their
view, is equivalent to saying that it does not give us fact but
fancy, and is to be looked upon not as a sober history but as
a metaphysical essay. But does history cease to be history
when it passes beyond the mere tabulation of events, and
essays to marshal them according to their relations and under

the categories of cause and effect?—when it ceases to be a mere chronicle, in a word, and becomes what we have learned to call philosophical history? And is it to be made a reproach to a writer of history that he has sought not merely to collect, but also to understand his facts; and to record them in such a way as to bring out their internal nature as well as their external form?

Bishop Alexander, in his delightful little book on *The Leading Ideas of the Gospels,* places the matter relatively to John's Gospel in a very clear light. "A great life," he reminds us, "cannot be rendered by a simple agglomeration of facts." "A great life,—a life whose words and works influence mankind profoundly,—is not sufficiently told by merely relating its facts and dates. What an enigma, for instance, is the life of Napoleon! How many of his biographies are mere masks, concealing those bronze features! We cannot understand any great and complicated life, good or evil, by merely recording the isolated events along which it moved. It is an organic whole, and must be reconstructed as such. . . . This, then, is the great Leading Idea of St. John's Gospel. *Given* the facts of Christ's life, how shall we bind them into unity, and read them as a whole? What theory of His Person and Nature will give us a logical and consistent view? . . . What Christ *did* and *said* becomes explicable only by knowing what Christ *is*. . . . Some who have not lost all reverence for Christianity speak as if St. John's prologue added a difficulty for faith; as if St. Matthew or St. Luke on the incarnation were comparatively easy to receive. Is it so for those who think? Place side by side these statements. On the one side—'When as His Mother Mary was espoused to Joseph, before they came together she was found with child of the Holy Ghost.' On the other side, the four oracular propositions—'In the beginning was the Word, and the Word was with God, and the Word was God. And the Word was made flesh.' Which is easier to receive? . . . In St. John the fact of the Incarnation is lifted up and

flooded with the light of a divine idea. If in the Unity of the
divine Existence there be a Trinity of Persons; if the Second
Person of that Trinity is to assume the reality of flesh and the
likeness of sinful flesh, we can in some measure see why He
needed the tabernacle of a body, framed and moulded by the
Eternal Spirit, to be His fitting habitation. The mystery of a
Virgin Mother is the correlative of the mystery of the Word
made flesh."

Surely this is most admirably said. To be made quite
perfect, it needs only the removal of the emphasis from the
nature of Christ to the work of Christ. "If the Second Person
of that Trinity is to assume the reality of flesh, and the
likeness of sinful flesh." . . . Aye, *if*. . . . Dr. Alexander leaves
this *"if"* hanging in the air. But not so John. To give an
adequate account of it is just the object and chief end of his
Gospel. We need to amend the postulation of the problem,
therefore, so far as not only to insert, but to emphasize this
element. *"Given* the facts of Christ's life, how shall we bind
them together into unity, and read them as a whole? What
theory of His Person and Nature, and *Purpose* and *Work*, will
give us a logical and consistent view?" This is the problem
that John's Gospel answers. And in answering it, it gives us a
philosophy of the incarnation, and thus renders not only the
incarnation itself, but all that Incarnated Life, not only
credible but natural, and not only natural—may we not even
say?—but almost inevitable—impossible to be otherwise. And
thus John fulfils the end of his writing: "These are written,
that ye may believe that Jesus is the Christ, the Son of God;
and that believing ye may have life in His name."

What, then, is the account of the incarnation which this
Gospel thus commends to us as its philosophy? We note at
once that in our text our Lord states it, in the first instance,
relatively not to man, but to God. The reason of the incarnation, rendering it credible, natural, inevitable, is traced back
into the councils of the Godhead. "I am come down from

heaven, not to do My own will, but the will of Him that sent me."

The purpose of the incarnation is therefore primarily to please God the Father, and to perform His will. We cannot avoid the implication that the incarnated one comes, therefore, in a *subordinate* capacity. He came down from heaven not to do His own will, but the will of Him that sent Him. He was sent. He was given a commission, a work, to do. How this conception is repeated over and over again in the discourses recorded by John! Even to John the Baptist He is the "sent of God." When Nicodemus approached Him as a teacher come from God, He explained that He was not come primarily as a teacher, but as one sent by God to do a work. And this is the burden of the great discourses at the pool of Bethesda, at the feast of Tabernacles, on the Light of the World, and as well of the closing discourses at the last passover. In all alike Jesus is the sent of God, come not of Himself to seek His own will, but to do the will of Him that sent Him; and only when He had "accomplished the work given Him to do" to return to the Father who sent Him.

Now this subordinate relation in which Jesus thus pervasively represents Himself as standing to the Father, so as to have been sent by Him, must be a matter either of nature or of arrangement. It must be either essential or economic. It must find its account and origin either in the necessity of nature or else in the provisions of a plan. But side by side with this perfectly pervasive proclamation of His subordination to the Father, in the whole matter of the incarnation itself, and the purpose or "will" that lies behind that incarnation and gives it its justification and its philosophical account, there runs an equally pervasive assertion by Jesus Himself and by His historian as well, of His essential equality and oneness with God. He was not only in the beginning with God: He was God. He is the only-begotten God, who is in the bosom of the Father. To have seen Him is to have seen the

Father also. He draws and receives from Thomas the worship-ping cry, "My Lord and my God." He declares to the Jews, "I and the Father are One." It seems to be clear, therefore, that the subordination in which the Father is recognized as greater than He, prescribing a "will" for Him to come into the world to perform, is economic, not essential; a matter of arrangement, not of necessity of nature.

By such a representation we are, of course, carried at once back into the darkness, or, what is equally blinding, into the blaze of mystery. It may be thought that it is enough to be asked to believe in the mysteries of the God-man and of the Trinity,—that within the unity of the Godhead there exists such a distinction of persons that of each we may assert in turn that from the beginning he has been with God, and has been God. Are we to add this additional mystery of fancying the persons of the Godhead, though numerically one in essence and sharers in all the divine attributes, "act-ing," as Dr. Martineau puts it, "each on the other as outside beings and conducting a divine drama among themselves,"— imposing tasks on one another, requiring conditions of one another, and earning favours from one another? No doubt it is past our comprehension. But do we gain or lose by denying its possibility, its reality? What does the Trinity mean, if it does not mean such a distinction of persons that each may say relatively to the other, "I," and "Thou," and "He"? What can the incarnation of the Second Person mean, if the per-sons may not stand over against one another in a measure far transcending our power to comprehend? And let us remem-ber that John presents this conception to us, not as an added difficulty to faith, but as the philosophy, the explanation of the incarnation. It may well happen here, too, that two mysteries support and render credible each the other,—as two beams of wood, neither of which could stand easily alone, when bowed together not only support each other, but provide a firm foundation upon which you may safely pile

the weight of a slated roof. To adopt Bishop Alexander's
mode of statement,—"If in the Unity of the Divine Existence
there be a Trinity of Persons, and if the Second Person of
that Trinity is to assume the reality of flesh and the likeness
of sinful flesh,"—is it an additional difficulty or an aid to
faith in this supernal mystery to be further told that this
colossal humiliation of the Son of God was not an objectless
display of arbitrary power, nor yet a tentative and unconsid-
ered effort of divine compassion to do somewhat, as yet
undetermined in kind or amount, for sinful mankind, but the
execution in time of an eternal plan,—a plan born of, and
redolent in its every part with the infinite compassion of
God, shaped in all its details from all eternity by brooding
love, and now remaining only to be executed by each person
involved taking and completing his appointed part in its
tremendous work? The mystery of the covenant is the correlative of the mystery of the incarnation. Without its postulation the incarnation would present increased difficulties of
belief. Without the added words, "In order to do the will of
Him that sent Me," the declaration, "I am come down from
heaven," would remain a simple marvel and prove a strain on
faith.

     And now let us not fail to observe that it results from
what we have said, that John's Gospel is the Gospel of the
Covenant. If its leading idea is not merely the glory of the
incarnation, but the philosophy of the incarnation; and if
that philosophy runs back into an economic arrangement or
plan between the Persons of the Trinity, by which the Second Person comes to perform a work committed to Him by
the Father, not to do His own will, but the will of Him that
sent Him: this is but another way of saying that the leading
idea of John's Gospel is the idea of the Covenant. And is it
not so? Search and look, and you will find not only that this
covenant idea recurs again and again throughout the Gospel,
with a frequency and an emphasis which throw it well into

the foreground, but that the book, as a whole, is moulded in
its form and contents upon it. The burden of its first chapters
is Christ's testimony that He has come because sent by the
Father; the burden of the last chapters is His approaching
return to the Father who sent Him; the accomplished work
lies between. And therefore it is that when Nicodemus came
to Him at the opening of His ministry and asked for teaching,
Jesus pointed him rather to His work, and declared the
doctrine of regeneration itself "an earthly thing" compared
with the heavenly mysteries He had to tell,—those mysteries
of His descent from heaven, sent by the Father to save the
world. And therefore it is that in the midst of His ministry
He opens this great discourse from which our text is taken,
by declaring that the Son of Man has been "sealed," appointed and set apart, by the Father for the work of giving
eternal life to men; and when His disciples stumbled at the
height of the great truth involved,—that He had come down
from heaven to give His flesh as the food of the soul,—He
sorrowfully added, "What, then, if you should see the Son of
Man ascending where He was before?" And therefore it is
that at the end of His life He compares His finished work
with the joy a woman has after travail, when at length the
child is born; and declares that, having accomplished the
work which the Father gave Him to do, the covenant condition is fulfilled, and the covenanted reward is at hand, and He
is about to return to His primal glory. John's Gospel,—we
ought not to miss it,—is the Gospel of the Covenant.

How our hearts should burn within us as we approach
the last and most central question of all, and ask what is our
Lord's account of the nature and terms of this mysterious
but most blessed covenant, to fulfil the conditions of which
He came down from heaven. We observe at once,—and with
what emotions of gladness we ought to observe it,—that it
concerns the salvation of men. And equally at once we
observe, with still swelling emotion, that it is complete and

perfect in its provisions,—that it provides for an entire and finished, for a sure and unfailing salvation. And we observe that this involves—as of course it must involve—the consequence that it is definite and precise in its terms,—that it contemplates definite and particularly designated men. "And this is the will of Him that sent Me, that of all that He hath given Me, I should lose nothing, but should raise it up at the last day." The will of the Father which Christ came down from heaven to do, concerned, then, distinctively: "all that He hath given Me." And His will with reference to these, which He sent the Son to perform, was not the making of some indefinite provision looking toward their rescue from sin and shame, but the definite actual, complete, and final saving of them: that "I should lose nothing of it, but should raise it up at the last day."

Let our hearts stand still while we read these great provisions. It is the testimony of the covenanted Son Himself, as to the terms of the covenant which He came to fulfil, that it had a definite and fully-determined end,—not merely the rendering the salvation of men possible; nor merely the removing of the legal obstacles in the way of the salvation of men; nor merely the breaking down of whatever difficulties may stand in the path of the free outflow of God's love to men; much less merely the introduction into the world of a better example of life than had hitherto been before men, or of a new divine force making for righteousness; or the impressing of men with a deeper sense of the love of God for them, or of His hatred of sin; but the actual, complete, and sure salvation of all that the Father had given the Son: "This is the will of Him that sent Me, that all that He hath given Me, I should lose nothing of it, but should raise it up at the last day."

In a word, we have presented to us here, in these pregnant words, not only in outline, but in all its essential details, what has come to be known among us as the Covenant of Redemption. For what element of the doctrine is lacking here? "I am come down from heaven, not to do My own will, but the will of Him that sent Me:" there is the assertion of an economic arrangement as the precondition of the incarnation, and of the prestipulation of the incarnated work. "And this is the will of Him that sent Me, that of all that He hath given Me I should lose nothing, but should raise it up at the last day:" there is the revelation of the contents of the preincarnation arrangement, and the provision through the incarnation for the certain salvation of a chosen body of lost men. "All that the Father giveth Me shall come unto Me;" "No man can come unto Me except the Father which sent Me draw Him:" there is the twin definition of the subjects of the salvation. Or, if we desire further witness than this one passage, it is spread fully on the pages of this Gospel. Let us attend only to those calm and final words which, as His work was accomplishing, our blessed Redeemer addressed, not to us men, but to His Father, in a divinely assured assertion of His righteous claims upon the fruit of His work. "Father, the hour is come: glorify Thy Son, that the Son may glorify Thee: even as Thou gavest Him authority over all flesh, that to all that Thou hast given Him, He should give to them eternal life. . . . I glorified Thee on the earth, having accomplished the work which Thou hast given Me to do. And now, O Father, glorify Thou Me with Thine own self, with the glory which I had with Thee before the world was. I manifested Thy name unto the men whom Thou didst give Me out of the world: Thine they were, and Thou didst give them to Me. . . . I pray for them; I pray not for the world, but for those whom Thou hast given Me." All His work is in fulfilment of an arrangement with the Father; and the whole of it, down to this High-Priestly prayer itself, making intercession for His own, concerns, primarily and in its chief import, those whom the Father gave Him out of the world, and secures beyond failure their complete salvation.

This is the whole doctrine of the Covenant of Redemption: the Reformed theology has grasped it, and teaches it; but it has not added one single thought to it.

And now let us bask a little, before we close, in the comforting assurances of this blessed teaching.

How the love of God is magnified to us by this teaching. It is not from a yesterday only that He has busied Himself with our salvation. In the depths of eternity our foreseen miseries were a cause of care to Him. In that mysterious intercourse between Father and Son, which is as eternal as the essence of Godhead itself, we—our state, our sin, our helplessness, and the dreadfulness of our condition and end, —were a subject of consideration and solicitude. What a God this is that is unveiled before us here. A God of holiness: a God so holy that even in the abyss of eternity-past He could not rest indifferent to the sin which was only after the lapse of innumerable ages to dawn in this corner of the as yet unexistent universe. A God of justice: a God so just that already His indignation burned against the as yet uncommitted sin of such petty creatures of His will as man. But a God of love: a love so inconceivably vast as already in the profundity of the unlimited past to brood over unimaginable plans of mercy toward these few guilty wretches among the numberless multitudes of His contemplated creatures. When the Psalmist raised his eyes to the heavens above, the work of the fingers of the Almighty, and considered the moon and stars which He had ordained, he was lost in a natural wonder that so great a Creator should concern Himself with so puny a creature: "What is man that Thou art mindful of him? And the son of man that Thou shouldst visit him?" But how much greater a marvel is before us now. It is not man as man,—a weak and puny creature—that we have to consider; but man as sinner,—this weak and puny creature become vile and filthy, offensive and hateful to a holy and just God. It is not in contrast even with the grandeur of the worlds circling about worlds which crowd the depths of the heavens and dwarf the consequence of this speck of earth on the skirts of the universe which is our home, that we are to consider him; but in contrast with the majesty of the increate Triune maker of all that is. It is not simply that God has taken notice of this sinful, puny creature, that we have to consider; but that the All-Holy and All-Blessed God has felt care and solicitude for his fate and looked not at His own things in comparison with his. What indeed is sinful man that God should love him; and before the foundations of the world should prepare to save him by so inconceivable a plan as to give His only-begotten Son as a ransom for his life! My brethren, this is not to the glory of man, but to the glory of God; it is not the expression of our dignity and worth, but raises our wondering hearts to the contemplation of the breadth and length, and height and depth of the love of God that passeth knowledge.

And how our appreciation of the perfection of the work of our Saviour is enhanced by this teaching. As it was upon no sudden caprice that He came into the world, but in execution of a long-cherished and thoroughly laid plan, so it was no partial work which He performed, but the whole work of salvation. "This is a faithful saying, and worthy of all acceptation, That Christ Jesus came into the world to *save* sinners." And this He has accomplished, even to the uttermost. When He cried upon the cross, as His agony went out in the darkness of death,—a death for us—in those words of deepest import and of mighty power, "It is finished!"—when in His great sacerdotal prayer, he proleptically declared that He had "accomplished the work" which the Father "had given Him to do," and was now ready to lay aside His humiliation and re-enter His glory: the precise thing which He published as "finished" and "accomplished" was salvation. All has been done by Him. His saving work neither needs nor admits of supplementary addition by any needy child of man, even to the extent of an iota. When we look to Him we are raising grateful eyes, not to one who invites us to save ourselves; nor merely to one who has broken out a path, in which walking, we may attain to salvation; nor yet merely to one who offers us a salvation wrought out by Him, on a condition; but to one who has *saved* us,—who is at once the beginning and the middle and the end of our salvation, the author and the finisher of our faith.

What can we possibly need that we do not find provided in Him? Do we hopelessly groan under the curse of the broken law, hanging menacingly over us? Christ has "redeemed us from the curse of the law, having been made a curse for us." Do we know that only he that worketh righteousness is acceptable to God, and despair of attaining life on so unachievable a condition; Christ Jesus "hath of God been made unto us righteousness." Do we loathe ourselves in the pollution of our sins, and know that God is greater than we, and that we must be an offence in His holy sight? The blood of Christ cleanseth us from all sin. But do we not need faith, that we may be made one with Him and so secure those benefits? Faith, too, is the gift of God: and that we believe on Him is granted by God in the behalf of Christ. Have we sought to run, and learned by bitter experience that it is not of him that runneth nor of him that willeth? We may learn too by a happy experience that it is of God that showeth mercy and that worketh in us both the willing and the doing. Nothing has been forgotten, nothing neglected, nothing left unprovided. In the person of Jesus Christ, the great God, in His perfect wisdom and unfailing power, has taken our place before the outraged justice of God and under His perfect law, and has wrought out a complete salvation.

What an indefectible certitude of salvation is given by this great teaching. If Christ Jesus came to save and has saved, how can salvation fail? If the free gift of God is eternal life in Christ Jesus our Lord, how can this eternal life thus freely given go out in time, and fail to accord with its very designation as eternal? If Christ has undertaken not merely to open a way of salvation to us, but to save us; if He came into the world for the precise purpose of performing *this* will of God, "that of all that He hath given Him, He should lose nothing, but should raise it up at the last day,"—what possibility lies open of the failure of this great design, framed in eternity by Triune Godhead, and executed in time by none other than the strong Son of God? Therefore our gracious Lord assures us: "All that the Father giveth Me *shall come unto Me*, and him that cometh unto Me I will in no wise cast out." And therefore His servant, condescending to the weakness of our fears, argues with us: "God commendeth His love towards us, in that, while we were yet sinners, Christ died for us. Much more, then, being justified by His blood, shall we be saved from wrath by Him." Oh, the certitude in that "much more." "If God be for us," he argues again, "who can be against us? He that spared not His own Son, but delivered Him up for us all, how shall He not also with Him freely give us all things? . . . Who shall separate us from the love of Christ?" O weak and trembling soul, can you not find, not courage merely, but certitude in this? What matters your weakness? Your salvation rests not on it, but on God's strength. He loves you; He determined to save you; He sent His Son to save you; He has come to do it: He has done it. You are saved: it cannot fail, unless God's set purpose can fail; unless Christ's power to save can fail; unless His promises of love can fail.

What a clear ground of assurance of salvation is furnished by this great teaching. Does some wayward spirit say: "All this is true only of the elect, those whom the Father gave to Christ. And I, alas! how may I know that I am of the elect?" Ah, self-tormenting soul, why expend strength in prying into God's secrets, instead of taking Him at His word? It is true indeed that it is only those whom He has given to

•

Christ that Christ has saved; and the comfort, as the salvation, is for them alone. But it is not true that God requires election of you for salvation, or offers predestination to you as the way of life. He offers you not predestination, but Christ; and He requires of you not election, but faith. Do you make election itself a ground of doubt and despair? This, says an old Puritan, is indeed to gather poison out of the sweetest of herbs. "God layeth it as a duty upon every one to repent and believe, to come to Him and he shall have rest to his soul. . . . If, then, thou believest, thou repentest, this may be a sure testimony unto thee of thy everlasting glory."

Election does indeed lie at the root of our salvation: but faith is the proof of election. Are we saved? The question is resolved in this: Do we believe in Jesus Christ? Christ indeed says, "This is the will of Him who sent Me, that of *all that He hath given Me,* I should lose nothing, but should raise it up at the last day." Here is election the root of the saving work of Christ. But have you failed to note or to remember that He immediately adds: "For this is the will of My Father, that *every one that beholdeth the Son and believeth on Him* should have eternal life, and that I should raise him up at the last day." Here is the work of Christ received in faith the ground of salvation: and here is faith laying hold of Christ the evidence of salvation. And therefore it is not only said, "All that the Father giveth Me shall come unto Me," but it is immediately added: *"And him that cometh to Me I will in no wise cast out."* These words are gracious enough in their broadest sense to send a thrill of joy through the heart. But there lies hidden within them a further delicate grace which is lost in the English translation. The word for "come" is so varied in the two clauses as to lay the stress in the first instance "upon the successful issue of the coming, the arrival," and in the second "on the process of the coming and the welcome." "All that the Father giveth Me shall come unto Me"—shall certainly and unfailingly reach Me. "And him that

cometh unto Me I will in no wise cast out"—"him that is in
the process of coming,"—yea, even though he is but just
begun, with weak and faltering steps, even such an one as this
who is but beginning to come—"I will in no wise cast out."

What a blessed assurance, when faith is made thus not
the ground of salvation, not the condition of salvation, but
its evidence! It is here that the sweet herb of election begins
to pour forth its refreshing cordial. Men may tell us, indeed,
"Believe and you shall be saved," while still making faith the
ground or the condition of salvation. And, then, with what
dreadful solicitude will we pluck up our faith over and over
again by the roots, to examine it with anxious fear. Is it the
right faith? Is it a strong enough faith? Do I believe aright?
Do I believe enough? Shall I abide in my belief until the end?
Dreadful uncertainty! Inexpressible misery of ineradicable
doubt! It is only when we have learned from such words of
our Master as those before us today, that we dare say to our
souls not only, Believe and ye shall be saved! but those other
words of deeper meaning and fuller comfort, caught from the
Master's own blessed lips: Believe and ye *are* saved! "Verily,
verily, I say unto you," says our Saviour in words which sum
up previous teachings, "He that heareth My words and believeth Him that sent Me, *hath* eternal life, and cometh not
into judgment, but *hath* passed out of death into life."
Blessed John, who so caught his Master's words and recorded
them for us. When faith is thus made not the ground or the
condition, but the evidence of salvation, our eternal bliss is
no longer suspended in any sense on aught that we are or do,
but hangs solely on the work of Christ, doing His Father's
will. Faith, even faith, as the ground or condition of salvation, may be also the ground of despair: but faith as the
proof of salvation is the charter of assured though humble
hope. It takes hold of the "strong Son of God, immortal
love," and of the indefectible purpose of Almighty grace
which cannot fail or know any shadow of turning. This we

owe to that doctrine of the eternal covenant which our blessed Saviour reveals to us in the words on which we have meditated today. Because of its blessed provisions we can cry joy to our souls, though they tremble with natural fear and can scarce believe that Christ will save such faithless souls as they. Though they have faith but as a grain of mustard-seed, they *are* saved already. For, this is the will of Him who sent our Redeemer, that of all that He gave Him He should lose nothing, but should raise it up at the last day: for this is the will of the Father, that every one that beholdeth the Son and believeth on Him should have eternal life and He should raise him up at the last day.

Beloved, do not, I beseech you, ground your salvation even in your faith. Ground it only in Jesus Christ who alone is your Saviour. And remember this,—that it is not your faith that saves you but God, and God alone, by whom it is that faith is wrought in your soul, and by whose power it is that you are guarded through your faith unto that salvation which is reserved for you in heaven, and which shall without fail be revealed at the last day. Can your faith fail? Nay, forget your faith. Certainly the power of God, your Almighty Saviour, through which alone you have faith and which is pledged to your guarding, cannot fail!

Philippians ii. 5-8:—Let this mind be in you, which was also in Christ Jesus: who, being in the form of God, thought it not robbery to be equal with God: but made Himself of no reputation, and took upon Him the form of a servant, and was made in the likeness of men: and being found in fashion as a man, He humbled Himself, and became obedient unto death, even the death of the cross.

IMITATING THE INCARNATION

"Christ our Example." After "Christ our Redeemer," no words can more deeply stir the Christian heart than these. Every Christian joyfully recognizes the example of Christ, as, in the admirable words of a great Scotch commentator, a body "of living legislation," as "law, embodied and pictured in a perfect humanity." In Him, in a word, we find the moral ideal historically realized, and we bow before it as sublime and yearn after it with all the assembled desires of our renewed souls.

How lovingly we follow in thought every footstep of the Son of Man, on the rim of hills that shut in the emerald cup of Nazareth, on the blue marge of Gennesaret, over the mountains of Judea, and long to walk in spirit by His side. He came to save every age, says Irenæus, and therefore He came as an infant, a child, a boy, a youth, and a man. And there is no age that cannot find its example in Him. We see Him, the properest child that ever was given to a mother's arms, through all the years of childhood at Nazareth "subjecting Himself to His parents." We see Him a youth, labouring day by day contentedly at His father's bench, in this lower sphere, too, with no other thought than to be "about His father's business." We see Him in His holy manhood, going, "as His custom was," Sabbath by Sabbath, to the synagogue, —God as He was, not too good to worship with His weaker brethren. And then the horizon broadens. We see Him at the banks of Jordan, because it became Him to fulfil every righteousness, meekly receiving the baptism of repentance for us. We see Him in the wilderness, calmly rejecting the subtlest trials of the evil one: refusing to supply His needs by a misuse of His divine power, repelling the confusion of tempting God with trusting God, declining to seek His Father's ends by any other than His Father's means. We see Him among the thousands of Galilee, anointed of God with the Holy Ghost and power, going about doing good: with no pride of birth, though He was a king; with no pride of intellect, though omniscience dwelt within Him; with no pride of power, though all power in heaven and earth was in His hands; or of station, though the fulness of the Godhead dwelt in Him bodily; or of superior goodness or holiness: but in lowliness of mind esteeming every one better than Himself, healing the sick, casting out devils, feeding the hungry, and everywhere breaking to men the bread of life. We see Him everywhere offering to men His life for the salvation of their souls: and when, at last, the forces of evil gathered thick around Him, walking, alike without display and without dismay, the path of suffering appointed for Him, and giving His life at Calvary that through His death the world might live.

"Which of you convinceth Me of sin?" is too low a question. Who can find in all His life a single lack, a single failure to set us a perfect example? In what difficulty of life, in what trial, in what danger or uncertainty, when we turn our eyes to Him, do we fail to find just the example that we need? And if perchance we are, by the grace of God, enabled to walk with Him but a step in the way, how our hearts burn within us with longing to be always with Him,—to be strengthened by the almighty power of God in the inner man, to make every footprint which He has left in the world a stepping-stone to climb upward over His divine path. Do we not rightly say that next to our longing to be in Christ is our corresponding longing to be like Christ; that only second in our hearts to His great act of obedience unto death by which He became our Saviour, stands His holy life in our world of sin, by which He becomes our example?

Of course our text is not singular in calling upon us to make Christ our example. "Be ye imitators of me, even as I also am of Christ Jesus," is rather the whole burden of the ethical side of Paul's teaching. And in this, too, he was but the imitator of his Lord, who pleads with us to "learn of Him because He is meek and lowly in heart." The peculiarity of our present passage is only that it takes us back of Christ's earthly life and bids us imitate Him in the great act of His incarnation itself. Not, of course, as if the implication were that we were equal with Christ and needed to stoop to such service as He performed. "Why art thou proud, O man?" Augustine asks pointedly. "God for thee became low. Thou wouldst perhaps be ashamed to imitate a lowly man; then at least imitate the lowly God. The Son of God came in the character of man and was made low. . . . He, since He was God, became man: do thou, O man, recognize that thou art man. Thy entire humility is to know thyself." The very force of the appeal lies, in a word, in the infinite exaltation of Christ above us: and the mention of the incarnation is the apostle's reminder to us of the ineffable majesty which was by nature His to whom he would raise our admiring eyes. Paul pries at our hearts here with the great lever of the deity of our exemplar. He calls upon us to do nothing less than to be imitators of God. "What encouragement is greater than this?" cries Chrysostom, with his instinctive perception of the motive-springs of the human heart. "Nothing arouses a great soul to the performance of good works so much as learning that in this it is likened to God." And here, too, Paul is but the follower of his Lord: "Be ye merciful, as your Father which is in heaven is merciful," are words which fell from His divine lips, altogether similar in their implication to Paul's words in the text: "Let it be this mind that is in you, which also was in Christ Jesus." It is the spirit which animated our Lord in the act of His incarnation which His apostle would see us imitate. He would have us in all our acts

to be like Christ, as He showed Himself to be in the innermost core of His being, when He became poor, He that was
rich, that we by His poverty might be made rich.

We perceive, then, that the exhortation of the apostle
gathers force for itself from the deity of Christ, and from the
nature of the transaction by which He, being God, was
brought into this sphere of dependent, earthly life in which
we live by nature. It is altogether natural, then, that he
sharpens his appeal by reminding his readers somewhat fully
who Christ was and what He did for our salvation, in order
that, having the facts more vividly before their minds, they
may more acutely feel the spirit by which He was animated.
Thus, in a perfectly natural way, Paul is led, not to inform his
readers but to remind them, in a few quick and lively phrases
which do not interrupt the main lines of discourse but rather
etch them in with a deeper colour, of what we may call the
whole doctrine of the Person of Christ. With such a masterly
hand, or let us rather say with such an eager spirit and such a
loving clearness and firmness of touch, has he done this, that
these few purely incidental words constitute one of the most
complete statements of an essential doctrine to be found
within the whole compass of the Scriptures. Though compressed within the limits of three short verses, it ranks in
fulness of exposition with the already marvellously concise
outline of the same doctrine given in the opening verses of
the Gospel of John. Whenever the subtleties of heresy confuse our minds as we face the problems which have been
raised about the Person of our Lord, it is pre-eminently to
these verses that we flee to have our apprehension purified,
and our thinking corrected. The sharp phrases cut their way
through every error: or, as we may better say, they are like a
flight of swift arrows, each winged to the joints of the
harness.

The golden-mouthed preacher of the ancient Church,
impressed with this fulness of teaching and inspired himself

to one of his loftiest flights by the verve of the apostle's crisp
language, pictures the passage itself as an arena, and the
Truth, as it runs burning through the clauses, as the victori-
ous chariot dashing against and overthrowing its contestants
one after the other, until at last, amid the clamour of ap-
plause which rises from every side to heaven, it springs alone
towards the goal, with coursers winged with joy sweeping like
a single flash over the ground. One by one he points out the
heresies concerning the Person of Christ which had sprung up
in the ancient Church, as clause by clause the text smites and
destroys them; and is not content until he shows how the
knees of all half-truths and whole falsehoods alike concerning
this great matter are made by these searching words to bow
before our Saviour's perfect deity, His complete humanity,
and the unity of His person. The magic of the passage has lost
none of its virtue with the millennium and a half which has
fled by since John Chrysostom electrified Constantinople
with his golden words: this sword of the Spirit is as keen
today as it was then, and happy is the man who knows its
temper and has the arm to wield it. But we must not lose
ourselves in a purely theological interest with such a passage
before us. Rather let us keep our eyes, for this hour, on
Paul's main purpose, and seek to feel the force of the example of Christ as he here advances it, for the government of
our lives. But to do this, as he points it with so full a
reference to the Person of Christ, following him we must
begin by striving to realize who and what our Lord was, who
set us this example.

Let us observe, then, first, that the actor to whose
example Paul would direct our eyes, is declared by him to
have been no other than God Himself. "Who was before in
the form of God," are his words: and they are words than
which no others could be chosen which would more explicitly or with more directness assert the deity of the person who
is here designated by the name of Christ Jesus. After the wear

and tear of two thousand years on the phrases, it would not be surprising if we should fail to feel this as strongly as we ought. Let us remember that the phraseology which Paul here employs was the popular usage of his day, though first given general vogue by the Aristotelian philosophy: and that it was accordingly the most natural language for strongly asserting the deity of Christ which could suggest itself to him. As you know, this mode of speech resolved everything into its matter and its form,—into the bare material out of which it is made, and that body of characterizing qualities which constitute it what it is. "Form," in a word, is equivalent to our phrase "specific character." If we may illustrate great things by small, we may say, in this manner of speech, that the "matter" of a sword, for instance, is steel, while its "form" is that whole body of characterizing qualities which distinguish a sword from all other pieces of steel, and which, therefore, make this particular piece of steel distinctively a sword. In this case, these are, of course, largely matters of shape and contour. But now the steel itself, which constitutes the matter of the sword, has also its "matter" and its "form:" its "matter" being metal, and its "form" being the whole body of qualities that distinguish steel from other metals, and make this metal steel. Going back still a step, metal itself has its "matter" and "form;" its "matter" being material substance and its "form" that body of qualities which distinguish metallic from other kinds of substance. And last of all, matter itself has its "matter," namely, substance, and its "form," namely, the qualities which distinguish material from spiritual substance, and make this substance what we call matter. The same mode of speech is, of course, equally applicable to the spiritual sphere. The "matter" of the human spirit is bare spiritual substance, while its "form" is that body of qualities which constitute this spirit a human spirit, and in the absence of which, or by the change of which, this spirit would cease to be human and become some other kind of spirit. The "matter" of an angel, again, is bare spiritual substance, while the "form" is the body of qualities which make this spirit specifically an angel. So, too, with God: the "matter" of God is bare spiritual substance, and the "form" is that body of qualities which distinguish Him from all other spiritual beings, which constitute Him God, and without which He would not be God. What Paul asserts then, when he says that Christ Jesus existed in the "form of God," is that He had all those characterizing qualities which make God God, the presence of which constitutes God, and in the absence of which God does not exist. He who is "in the form of God," is God.

Nor is it without significance that, out of the possible modes of expression open to him, Paul was led to choose just this mode of asserting the deity of our Lord. His mind in this passage was not on the bare divine essence; it was upon the divine qualities and prerogatives of Christ. It is not the abstract conception that Christ is God that moves us to our deepest admiration for His sublime act of self-sacrifice: but rather our concrete realization that He was all that God is, and had all that God has,—that God's omnipotence was His, His infinite exaltation, His unapproachable blessedness. Therefore Paul is instinctively led to choose an expression which tells us not the bare fact that Christ was God, but that He was "in the form of God,"—that He had in full possession all those characterizing qualities which, taken together, make God that all-holy, perfect, all-blessed being which we call God. Thus the apostle prepares his readers for the great example by quickening their apprehension not only of who, but of what Christ was.

Let us note, then, secondly, that the apostle outlines for us very fully the action which this divine being performed. "He took the form of a servant by coming into the likeness of men; and being found in fashion as a man, He humbled Himself by becoming subject even unto death, and that the death of the cross." There is no metamorphosis of substance asserted here: the "form of God" is not said to have been transmuted into the "form of a servant;" but He who was "in the form of God" is declared to have taken also to Himself "the form of a servant." Nor is there, on the other hand, any deceptive show of an unreal humiliation brought before us here: He took, not the appearance, mere state and circumstances, or mere work and performance, but veritably "the form of a servant,"—all those essential qualities and attributes which belong to, and constitute a being "a servant." The assumption involved the taking of an actually servile nature, as well as of a subordinate station and a servant's work. And therefore it is at once further explained in both its mode and its effects. He took the form of a servant "by coming into the likeness of men:" He did not become merely a man, but by taking the form of a servant He came into a state in which He appeared as man. His humanity was real and complete: but it˙ was not all,—He remained God in assuming humanity, and therefore only appeared as man, not became only man. And by taking the form of a servant and thus being found in fashion as a man, He became subject to obedience,—an obedience pressed so far in its humiliation that it extended even unto death, and that the shameful death of the cross. Words cannot adequately paint the depth of this humiliation. But this it was,—the taking of the form of a servant with its resultant necessity of obedience to such a bitter end,—this it was that He who was by nature in the form of God,—in the full possession and use of all the divine attributes and qualities, powers and prerogatives,—was willing to do for us.

Let us observe, then, thirdly, that the apostle clearly announces to us the spirit in which our Lord performed this great act. "Although He was in the form of God, He yet did not consider His being on an equality with God a precious prize to be eagerly retained, but made no account of Himself, taking the form of a servant." It was then in a spirit of pure

unselfishness and self-sacrifice, that looked not on its own
things but on the things of others, that under the force of
love esteemed others more than Himself,—it was in this mind:
or, in the apostle's own words, it was as not considering His
essential equality with God as a precious possession, but
making no account of Himself,—it was in this mind, that
Christ Jesus who was before in the form of God took the
form of a servant. This was the state of mind that led Him to
so marvellous an act,—no compulsion from His Father, no
desires for Himself, no hope of gain or fear of loss, but
simple, unselfish, self-sacrificing love.

Now it is not to be overlooked that some of the clauses
the meaning of which we have sought to fathom, are differently explained among expositors. Nevertheless, although I
have sought to adduce them so as to bring out the apostle's
exact meaning, and although I believe that his appeal acquires
an additional point and a stronger leverage when they are
thus understood, it remains true that the main drift of the
passage is unaffected by any of the special interpretations
which reasonable expositors have put upon the several
clauses. These divergent expositions do seriously affect our
doctrine of the Person of Christ. In particular, all the forms
of the popular modern doctrine of *kenosis* or *exinanition,*
which teaches that the divine Logos in becoming man "emptied Himself," and thus, that the very God in a more or less
literal sense contracted Himself to the limits of humanity,
find their chief, almost their sole Biblical basis in what
appears to me a gratuitously erroneous interpretation of one
of these clauses,—that one which the Authorized Version
renders, "He made Himself of no reputation," and which I
have ventured to render, "He made no account of Himself,"
that is, in comparison with the needs of others; but which the
theologians in question, followed unfortunately as I think, by
the Revised Version, render with an excessive literality, "He
emptied Himself," thereby resurrecting the literal physical

sense of the word in an unnatural context. We have many
reasons to give why this is an illegitimate rendering; chief
among which are, that the word is commonly employed in its
figurative sense and that the intrusion of the literal sense here
is forbidden by the context. But it is unnecessary to pause to
argue the point. Whatever the conclusion might be, the main
drift of the passage remains the same. No interpretation of
this phrase can destroy the outstanding fact that the passage
at large places before our wondering eyes the two *termini* of
"the form of God" and "the form of a servant," involving
obedience even unto a shameful death; and "measures the
extent of our Lord's self-denying grace by the distance between equality with God and a public execution on a gib-
bet." In any case the emphasis of the passage is thrown upon
the spirit of self-sacrificing unselfishness as the impelling
cause of Christ's humiliation, which the apostle adduces here
in order that the sight of it may impel us also to take no
account of ourselves, but to estimate lightly all that we are or
have in comparison with the claims of others on our love and
devotion. The one subject of the whole passage is Christ's
marvellous self-sacrifice. Its one exhortation is, "Let it be this
mind that is also in you." As we read through the passage we
may, by contact with the full mind and heart of the apostle,
learn much more than this. But let us not fail to grasp this,
his chief message to us here,—that Christ Jesus, though He
was God, yet cared less for His equality with God, cared less
for Himself and His own things, than He did for us, and
therefore gave Himself for us.

Firmly grasping this, then, as the essential content and
special message of the passage, there are some inferences that
flow from it which we cannot afford not to remind ourselves
of.

And first of these is a very great and marvellous one,—
that we have a God who is capable of self-sacrifice for us. It
was although He was in the form of God, that Christ Jesus

did not consider His being on an equality with God so
precious a possession that He could not lay it aside, but
rather made no account of Himself. It was our God who so
loved us that He gave Himself for us. Now, herein is a
wonderful thing. Men tell us that God is, by the very necessity of His nature, incapable of passion, incapable of being
moved by inducements from without; that He dwells in holy
calm and unchangeable blessedness, untouched by human
sufferings or human sorrows for ever,—haunting

> The lucid interspace of world and world,
> Where never creeps a cloud, nor moves a wind,
> Nor ever falls the least white star of snow,
> Nor ever lowest roll of thunder moans,
> Nor sound of human sorrow mounts to mar
> His sacred, everlasting calm.

Let us bless our God that it is not true. God can feel; God
does love. We have Scriptural warrant for believing, as it has
been perhaps somewhat inadequately but not misleadingly
phrased, that moral heroism has a place within the sphere of
the divine nature: we have Scriptural warrant for believing
that, like the old hero of Zurich, God has reached out loving
arms and gathered into His own bosom that forest of spears
which otherwise had pierced ours.

But is not this gross anthropomorphism? We are careless
of names: it is the truth of God. And we decline to yield up
the God of the Bible and the God of our hearts to any
philosophical abstraction. We have and we must have an
ethical God; a God whom we can love, and in whom we can
trust. We may feel awe in the presence of the Absolute, as we
feel awe in the presence of the storm or of the earthquake:
we may feel our dependence in its presence, as we feel our
helplessness before the tornado or the flood. But we cannot
love it; we cannot trust it; and our hearts, which are just as
trustworthy a guide as our dialectics, cry out for a God
whom we may love and trust. We decline once for all to

subject our whole conception of God to the category of the Absolute, which, as has been truly said, "like Pharaoh's lean kine, devours all other attributes." Neither is this an unphilosophical procedure. As has been set forth renewedly by Andrew Seth, "we should be unfaithful to the fundamental principle of the theory of knowledge" "if we did not interpret by means of the highest category within our reach." "We should be false to ourselves, if we denied in God what we recognize as the source of dignity and worth in ourselves." In order to escape an anthropomorphic God, we must not throw ourselves at the feet of a zoomorphic or an amorphic one.

Nevertheless, let us rejoice that our God has not left us by searching to find Him out. Let us rejoice that He has plainly revealed Himself to us in His Word as a God who loves us, and who, because He loves us, has sacrificed Himself for us. Let us remember that it is a fundamental conception in the Christian idea of God that God is love; and that it is the fundamental dogma of the Christian religion that God so loved us that He gave Himself for us. Accordingly, the primary presupposition of our present passage is that our God was capable of, and did actually perform, this amazing act of unselfish self-sacrifice for the good of man.

The second inference that we should draw from our passage consists simply in following the apostle in his application of this divine example to our human life: a life of self-sacrificing unselfishness is the most divinely beautiful life that man can lead. He whom as our Master we have engaged to obey, whom as our Example we are pledged to imitate, is presented to us here as the great model of self-sacrificing unselfishness. "Let this mind be in you, which was also in Christ Jesus," is the apostle's pleading. We need to note carefully, however, that it is not self-depreciation, but self-abnegation, that is thus commended to us. If we would follow Christ, we must, every one of us, not in pride but in humility, yet not in lowness but in lowliness, not degrade ourselves but forget ourselves, and seek every man not his own things but those of others.

Who does not see that in this organism which we call human society, such a mode of life is the condition of all real help and health? There is, no doubt, another ideal of life far more grateful to our fallen human nature, an ideal based on arrogance, assumption, self-assertion, working through strife, and issuing in conquest,—conquest of a place for ourselves, a position, the admiration of man, power over men. We see its working on every side of us: in the competition of business life,—in the struggle for wealth on the one side, forcing a struggle for bare bread on the other; in social life,—in the fierce battle of men and women for leading parts in the farce of social display; even in the Church itself, and among the Churches, where, too, unhappily, arrogant pretension and unchristian self-assertion do not fail to find their temporal reward. But it is clear that this is not Christ's ideal, nor is it to this that He has set us His perfect example. "He made no account of Himself:" though He was in the form of God, He yet looked not upon His equality with God as a possession to be prized when He could by forgetting self rescue those whom He was not ashamed, amid all His glory, to call His brethren.

Are there any whom you and I are ashamed to call our brethren? O that the divine ideal of life as service could take possession of our souls! O that we could remember at all times and in all relations that the Son of Man came into the world to minister, and by His ministry has glorified all ministering for ever. O that we could once for all grasp the meaning of the great fact that self-forgetfulness and self-sacrifice express the divine ideals of life.

And thus we are led to a third inference, which comes to us from the text: that it is difficult to set a limit to the self-sacrifice which the example of Christ calls upon us to be ready to undergo for the good of our brethren. It is comparatively easy to recognize that the ideal of the Christian life is self-sacrificing unselfishness, and to allow that it is required of those who seek to enter into it, to subordinate self and to seek first the kingdom of God. But is it so easy to acknowledge, even to ourselves, that this is to be read not generally merely but in detail, and is to be applied not only to some eminent saints but to all who would be Christ's servants?— that it is required of us, and that what is required of us is not some self-denial but all self-sacrifice? Yet is it not to this that the example of Christ would lead us?—not, of course, to self-degradation, not to self-effacement exactly, but to complete self-abnegation, entire and ungrudging self-sacrifice? Is it to be unto death itself? Christ died. Are we to endure wrongs? What wrongs did He not meekly bear? Are we to surrender our clear and recognized rights? Did Christ stand upon His unquestioned right of retaining His equality with God? Are we to endure unnatural evils, permit ourselves to be driven into inappropriate situations, unresistingly sustain injurious and unjust imputations and attacks? What more unnatural than that the God of the universe should become a servant in the world, ministering not to His Father only, but also to His creatures,—our Lord and Master washing our very feet? What more abhorrent than that God should die? There is no length to which Christ's self-sacrifice did not lead Him. These words are dull and inexpressive; we cannot enter into thoughts so high. He who was in the form of God took such thought for us, that He made no account of Himself. Into the immeasurable calm of the divine blessedness He permitted this thought to enter, "I will die for men!" And so mighty was His love, so colossal the divine purpose to save, that He thought nothing of His divine majesty, nothing of His unsullied blessedness, nothing of His equality with God, but, absorbed in us,—our needs, our misery, our helplessness—He made no account of Himself. If this is to be our example, what limit can we set to our self-sacrifice? Let us remember that we are no longer our own but Christ's, bought with the price of His precious blood, and are henceforth to live, not for ourselves but for Him,—for Him in His creatures, serving Him in serving them. Let all thought of our dignity, our possessions, our rights, perish out of sight, when Christ's service calls to us. Let the mind be in us that was also in Him, when He took no account of Himself, but, God as He was, took the form of a servant and humbled Himself,—He who was Lord,—to lowly obedience even unto death, and that the death of the cross. In such a mind as this, where is the end of unselfishness?

Let us not, however, do the apostle the injustice of fancying that this is a morbid life to which he summons us. The self-sacrifice to which he exhorts us, unlimited as it is, going all lengths and starting back blanched at nothing, is nevertheless not an unnatural life. After all, it issues not in the destruction of self, but only in the destruction of selfishness; it leads us not to a Buddha-like unselfing, but to a Christ-like self-development. It would not make us into

> deedless dreamers lazying out a life
> Of self-suppression, not of selfless love,

but would light the flames of a love within us by which we would literally "ache for souls." The example of Christ and the exhortation of Paul found themselves upon a sense of the unspeakable value of souls. Our Lord took no account of Himself, only because the value of the souls of men pressed upon His heart. And following Him, we are not to consider our own things, but those of others, just because everything earthly that concerns us is as nothing compared with their eternal welfare.

Our self-abnegation is thus not for our own sake, but for the sake of others. And thus it is not to mere self-denial that Christ calls us, but specifically to self-sacrifice: not to unselfing ourselves, but to unselfishing ourselves. Self-denial for its own sake is in its very nature ascetic, monkish. It concentrates our whole attention on self—self-knowledge, self-control—and can therefore eventuate in nothing other than the very apotheosis of selfishness. At best it succeeds only in subjecting the outer self to the inner self, or the lower self to the higher self; and only the more surely falls into the slough of self-seeking, that it partially conceals the selfishness of its goal by refining its ideal of self and excluding its grosser and more outward elements. Self-denial, then, drives to the cloister; narrows and contracts the soul; murders within us all innocent desires, dries up all the springs of sympathy, and nurses and coddles our self-importance until we grow so great in our own esteem as to be careless of the trials and sufferings, the joys and aspirations, the strivings and failures and successes of our fellow-men. Self-denial, thus understood, will make us cold, hard, unsympathetic,—proud, arrogant, self-esteeming,—fanatical, overbearing, cruel. It may make monks and Stoics,—it cannot make Christians.

It is not to this that Christ's example calls us. He did not cultivate self, even His divine self: He took no account of self. He was not led by His divine impulse out of the world, driven back into the recesses of His own soul to brood morbidly over His own needs, until to gain His own seemed worth all sacrifice to Him. He was led by His love for others into the world, to forget Himself in the needs of others, to sacrifice self once for all upon the altar of sympathy. Self-sacrifice brought Christ into the world. And self-sacrifice will lead us, His followers, not away from but into the midst of men. Wherever men suffer, there will we be to comfort. Wherever men strive, there will we be to help. Wherever men fail, there will be we to uplift. Wherever men succeed, there will we be to rejoice. Self-sacrifice means not indifference to our times and our fellows: it means absorption in them. It means forgetfulness of self in others. It means entering into every man's hopes and fears, longings and despairs: it means manysidedness of spirit, multiform activity, multiplicity of sympathies. It means richness of development. It means not that we should live one life, but a thousand lives,—binding ourselves to a thousand souls by the filaments of so loving a sympathy that their lives become ours. It means that all the experiences of men shall smite our souls and shall beat and batter these stubborn hearts of ours into fitness for their heavenly home. It is, after all, then, the path to the highest possible development, by which alone we can be made truly men.

Not that we shall undertake it with this end in view. This were to dry up its springs at their source. We cannot be self-consciously self-forgetful, selfishly unselfish. Only, when we humbly walk this path, seeking truly in it not our own things but those of others, we shall find the promise true, that he who loses his life shall find it. Only, when, like Christ, and in loving obedience to His call and example, we take no account of ourselves, but freely give ourselves to others, we shall find, each in his measure, the saying true of himself also: "Wherefore also God hath highly exalted him." The path of self-sacrifice is the path to glory.

ADDITIONAL SERMONS

The following two sermons originally appeared in
Princeton Sermons
a collection of sermons "chiefly by the professors in
Princeton Theological Seminary

JOHN i. 14:—And the Word was made flesh, and dwelt among us, . . . full of . . . truth.

INCARNATE TRUTH

The obvious resemblance between the prologue to John's Gospel and the proem of Genesis is not a matter of mere phraseology and external form. As the one, in the brief compass of a few verses, paints the whole history of the creation of a universe with a vividness which makes the quickened imagination a witness of the process, so the other in still briefer compass traces the whole history of the re-creation of a dead world into newness of life. In both we are first pointed back into the depths of eternity, when only God was. In both we are bidden to look upon the chaotic darkness of lawless matter or of lawless souls, over which the brooding Spirit was yet to move. In both, as the tremendous pageants are unrolled before our eyes, we are made to see the Living God; and to see him as the Light and the Life of the world, the Destroyer of all darkness, the Author of all good. Here too, however, the Old Testament revelation is the preparation for the better to come. In it we see God as the God of power and of wisdom, the Author and Orderer of all; in this we see him as the God of goodness and mercy, the Restorer and Redeemer of the lost. Law was given through Moses; grace and truth came through Jesus Christ.

Through what a sublime sweep does the Apostle lead our panting thought as he strives to tell us who and what the Word is, and what he has done for men. He lifts the veil of time, that we may peer into the changeless abyss of eternity and see him as he is, in the mystery of his being, along with God and yet one with God—in some deep sense distinct from God, in some higher sense identical with God. Then he shows us the divine work which he has wrought in time. He is the All-Creator—"all things were made by him, and without him was not anything made that hath been made." He is the All-Illuminator—he "was the true Light that lighteth every man that cometh into the world." And now in these last days he has become the All-Redeemer—prepared for by his prophet, he came to his own, and his own received him not; but "as many as received him," without regard to race or previous preparation, "he gave to them the right to become children of God, to them that believe on his name, who were born not of blood, nor of the will of the flesh, nor of the will of man, but of God." Then the climax of this great discourse breaks on us as we are told how the Word, when he came to his own, manifested himself to flesh. It was by himself becoming flesh, and tabernacling among us, full of grace and truth. He came as Creator, as Revealer, as Redeemer: as Creator, preparing a body for his habitation; as Revealer, "trailing clouds of glory as he came;" as Redeemer, heaping grace on grace.

It is clear that it is primarily in its aspect as a revelation of God that John is here contemplating the incarnation. Accordingly, he bears his personal witness to it as such: "The Word was made flesh, and tabernacled among us, and *we beheld his glory,* a glory as of an only-begotten of the Father." Accordingly, too, he summons the prophetic witness of the forerunner. And accordingly, still further, he closes the whole with a declaration of the nature of the revelation made, and its guarantee in the relation of the incarnated Word to the Father: "No man hath seen God at any time; God only-begotten which is in the bosom of the Father, he hath declared him."

In the special verse from which we have taken our text we perceive, then, that John is bearing his personal witness: "And the Word became flesh, and dwelt among us, and *we beheld his glory.* " He is telling us what of his own immediate knowledge he knows—testifying what he had heard, what he had seen with his eyes, what he had beheld and his hands had handled. An eye-witness to Christ's majesty, he had seen his glory and bears his willing witness to it. Nor must we fancy that he gives us merely a subjective opinion of his own, as if he were telling us only that the man Jesus was so full of grace and truth in his daily walk that he, looking upon him admiringly, had been led to conjecture that he was more than man. He testifies not to subjective opinion but to objective fact. We observe that the testimony is made up of three assertions. First, we have the fact, the objective fact, of the incarnation asserted: "And the Word was made flesh, and dwelt among us." Secondly, we have the self-evidencing glory of the incarnation asserted: "And we beheld his glory, a glory as of an only-begotten of the Father." And thirdly, we have the characteristic elements which entered into and constituted the glory which he brought from heaven with him and exhibited to men, asserted: "Full of grace and truth." Jesus Christ was incarnated love and truth. And precisely what John witnesses is, that the Word did become flesh, and dwelt among men, full of grace and truth, and that the blaze of this his glory was manifest to every seeing eye that looked upon him.

Now it seems evident, further, that John had an especial form of the manifestation of love and truth before his mind when he wrote these words. He is thinking of the covenant God, who proclaimed himself to Moses on the mount when he descended on the cloud as "Jehovah, Jehovah, a God full of compassion, and gracious, slow to anger, and plenteous in mercy and truth." He is thinking of David's prayer, "O prepare lovingkindness and truth;" and his heart burns within him as he sees them now prepared. It is the thought of Christ's redeeming work which is filling his mind, and which leads him to sum up the revelation of the incarnation in the revelation of love and truth. Therefore he says, not "love," but "grace"—undeserved love to sinners. And in "truth" he is thinking chiefly of Christ's "faithfulness." The divine glory that rested as a nimbus on the Lord's head was compounded before all else of his ineffable love for the unlovely, of his changeless faithfulness to the unfaithful. For in Christ, God commended his love to us in that, while we were yet sinners, Christ died for us.

Nevertheless, it would be a serious error to confine the words as here used to this single implication. This is rather the culmination and climax of their meaning than the whole extent and impletion of it. Christ is not only love as manifested in grace, but as the God of love manifest in the flesh he is love itself in all its height and breadth. Not only the loftiest reaches of love, love for the undeserving, find their model in him, but all the love that is in the world finds its source and must seek its support in him. His was the love that wept at the grave of a friend and over the earthly sorrows of Jerusalem, that yearned with the bereaved mother at Nain, and took the little children into his arms to bless them; as well as the love that availed to offer himself a sacrifice for sin. In like manner, that John has especially in mind here the highest manifestations of truth—our Lord's trustiness in the great work of salvation—in no way empties the word of its lower connotations. He is still the true Light that lighteth every man that cometh into the world; and all the truth that is in the world comes from him and must seek its strength in him. "We beheld his glory," says the Apostle, *"full"*—complete, perfect—"of grace and truth." And perfection of love and truth avails for all their manifestations. This man, the man Christ Jesus, could not act in any relation otherwise than lovingly, could not speak on any subject otherwise than truly. He is the pure fountain of love and truth.

I. We confine ourselves on the present occasion to the latter of the two characteristics here brought together. And, doing so, the first message which the declaration brings us is one so obvious that, in circumstances other than those in which we are now standing, it would seem an insult to our intelligence to direct attention to it. It is this, that since Jesus Christ our Lord, the manifested Jehovah, was as such the incarnation of truth, no statement which ever fell from his lips can have contained any admixture of error. This is John's testimony. For let us remind ourselves again that he is here bearing his witness, not to the essential truth of the divine nature incarnated in our Lord prior to its incarnation, but to the fullness of truth which dwelt in the God-man: "And the Word became flesh, and dwelt among us, and we beheld his glory, . . . full of . . . truth." More—it is the testimony of our Lord himself. "I," he declared, with his majestic and pregnant brevity, "I am the Truth." Nor dare we fancy that his plenitude of truth is exhausted in his witness to the great and eternal verities of religion, while the pettier affairs of earth and man are beyond its reach. His own norm of judgment is that only he that is faithful in the least may be trusted with the great. And it was testified of him not only that he knew whence he came and whither he went, but equally that he knew all men and needed not that any should bear witness of man, for he himself knew what was in man. He himself suspends his trustworthiness as to earthly things: "Verily, verily, I say unto you, We speak that we do know, and testify that we have seen; and ye receive not our witness. If I told you earthly things and ye believe not, how shall ye believe if I tell you heavenly things?"

Are we beating the air when we remind ourselves of such things? Would that we were! But alas! we are fallen on evil days, when we need to defend the truth of incarnate truth itself against the aspersions of even its professed friends. Oh, the unimaginable lengths to which the intellectual pride of men will carry them! Has one spun out some flimsy fancy as to the origin and composition of certain Old Testament books, which is found to clash with Jesus' testimony to their authorship and trustworthiness? We are coolly told that "as a teacher of spiritual truth sent from God and full of God he is universal," but "as a logician and critic he belongs to his times," and therefore had "a definite, restricted outfit and outlook, which could be only those of his own day and generation." "Why should he be supposed to know the science of the criticism of the Old Testament," we are asked, "which began to exist centuries after his death?" Does another cherish opinions as to the interpretation of certain Old Testament passages which will not square with the use that Christ makes of them? He tells us at once that "interpretation is essentially a scientific function, and one conditioned by the existence of scientific means, which, in relation to the Old Testament, were only imperfectly at the command of Jesus." Has another adopted preconceptions which render our Lord's dealings with the demoniacs distasteful to him? He too reminds us that the habit of ascribing disease to demoniacal influences was universal in Jesus' day, and that we can scarcely expect him to be free from the current errors of his time. Let us cut even deeper. When one desires to break out a "larger hope" for those who die impenitent than Christ's teachings will allow, he suggests that in his efforts to lead his hearers to repentance Jesus spoke habitually as a popular preacher, and far more strongly than he could have permitted himself to do had he been an exact theologian. When another burns with a zeal for moral reform which is certainly not according to knowledge, he suggests that we have reached a stage of ethical development when "new and larger perceptions of truth" have brought "new and larger perceptions of duty" than were attainable in Christ's day, and are accordingly bound to govern our lives by stricter rules than would apply to him in that darker age. Or, to sum up the whole, we have been recently told plainly that "Christ in his manhood was not the equal of Newton in mathematical knowledge," and not "the equal of Wellhausen in literary criticism," because—so we are actually told—the pursuit of such sciences requires "much exercise of mind."

Is, then, the Light that lighteth every man that cometh into the world gone out in darkness? What is left us of the Truth Indeed, who proclaims himself no more the Way and the Life than the Truth, if his testimony cannot be trusted as to the nature, origin, authority, and meaning of the Scriptures of which his own Spirit was the inspirer; as to the constitution of that spiritual world of which he is the Creator and the King; as to the nature of that future state which it is his to determine as Judge; or as to the moral life of which he is the sole author? Yet these are devout men who are propagating such teachings; and each has of course his own way of saving himself from conscious blasphemy in erecting his own thought above the thought of the God-man. The most popular way at present is to suggest that when God became man he so surrendered the attributes of divinity as that, though God, he had shrunk to the capacity of man, and, accepting the weaknesses, become subject also to the limitations of a purely human life in the world. Thus it is sought to save the veracity of the Lord at the expense of his knowledge, his truthfulness at the expense of his truth. But who can fail to see that, were this true, the sorrowing world would be left, like Mary standing weeping in the garden and crying, "They have taken away my Lord"? Where then would be Christ our Prophet? Who could assure us of his trustiness in his witness to his oneness with God, to his mission from God, to the completeness of his work for our salvation? Faith has received a serious wound, as it has been well phrased, if we are to believe that Jesus Christ could have been deceived; if we are to believe that he could—wittingly or unwittingly—deceive, faith has received its death-blow.

Let us bless the Lord, then, that he has left us little excuse for doubting in so important a matter. To the law and the testimony. Is the man Christ Jesus dramatized before us in the length and breadth of that marvelous history which fills these four Gospels, as a child of his times, limited by the intellectual outlook of his times, or rather as a teacher to his times, sent from God as no more the power of God than the wisdom of God? Is he represented to us as learning what he taught us from men, or, as he himself bore witness, from God?—"My teaching is not mine, but his that sent me;" "I am come down out of heaven," and "he that hath sent me is true;" and "the things that I have heard from him, these speak I unto the world." Did he even in his boyhood amaze the Doctors in the temple by his understanding (Luke 2:47)? Did he know even "letters," not having learned them from man (John 7:15)? Did he see Nathanael when, under the fig-tree, he bowed in secret prayer (John 1:47)? Did he know without human informant all things that ever the Samaritan woman did (John 4:29)? Did he so search the heart of man that he saw the thoughts of his enemies (Matt. 9:4); knew that one of the twelve whom he had chosen was a "devil" (John 6:70); led Peter to cry in his adoring distress, "Lord, thou knowest all things, thou knowest that I love thee" (John 20:17); and called out the testimony of John that "he knew all men, and needed not that any should bear witness concerning man, for he himself knew what was in man" (John 2:25); as well as the testimony of all the disciples that they knew that he came from God, because "he knew all things" (John 16:30)?

But why need we go into the details that are spread from one end to the other of these Gospels? In our text itself John bears witness that the fullness of truth which dwelt in the incarnate Word so glorified all his life as to mark him out as the Son of God: "The Word became flesh, and dwelt among us, and we beheld his glory, a glory as of an only-begotten of the Father, full of truth." We surely need not fear to take our stand not only by the truthfulness but by the truth of our Lord. We surely need not shrink from, with the utmost simplicity, embracing, proclaiming, and living by his

views of God and the universe, of man and the world. It was
he that made the world; and without him was not anything
made that hath been made. Who shall teach him how its
beams were laid or how its structure has grown? It was he
that revealed the Word. Who shall teach him how were
written or what is intended by the words which he himself
gave through his servants the prophets? It is he who is at once
the Source and Standard of the moral law, and the Fount and
Origin of all compassion for sinful man. Who shall teach him
what it is right to do, or how it is loving to deal with the
children of men? We need not fear lest we be asked to credit
Jesus against the truth; we may confide wholly in him,
because he is the Truth.

II. Nor let us do this timidly. Trust is never timid. Just
because Jesus is the Truth, while we without reserve accept,
proclaim, and live by every word which he has spoken, not
fearing that after all it may prove to be false, we may with
equal confidence accept, proclaim, and live by every other
truth that may be made known to us, not fearing that after a
while it may prove to contradict the Truth himself. Thus we
may be led to the formulation of a second message which the
text brings us: That since Jesus Christ our Lord, the Founder
of our religion, was the very incarnation of truth, no truth
can be antagonistic to the religion which he founded. John
tells us that he was the true Light that lighteth every man
that cometh into the world; and we may read this as meaning
that as the Word of God, the great Revealer, it is he that leads
man by whatever path to the attainment of whatever truth.
There is, then, no truth in the world which does not come
from him. It matters not through what channel it finds its
struggling way into our consciousness or to our recognition,
—whether our darkened eyes are enabled to catch their
glimpse of it by the light of nature, as we say, by the light of
reason, by the light of history, or by the light of criticism.
These may be but broken lights; but they are broken lights of

that one Light which lighteth every man that cometh into the world. Every fragment of truth which they reveal to us comes from him who is the Truth, and is rendered great and holy as a revelation from and of him.

We must not, then, as Christians, assume an attitude of antagonism toward the truths of reason, or the truths of philosophy, or the truths of science, or the truths of history, or the truths of criticism. As children of the light, we must be careful to keep ourselves open to every ray of light. If it is light, its source must be sought in him who is the true Light; if it is truth, it belongs of right to him who is the plenitude of truth. All natural truths must be—in varying degrees indeed, but all truly—in some sense commentaries on the supernaturally revealed truth; and by them we may be led to fuller and more accurate comprehension of it. Nature is the handiwork of God in space; history marks his pathway through time. And both nature and history are as infallible teachers as revelation itself, could we but skill to read their message aright. It is distressingly easy to misinterpret them; but their employment in the elucidation of Scripture is, in principle, closely analogous to the interpretation of one Scripture by another, though written by another human hand and at an interval of an age of time. God speaks through his instruments. Prediction interprets prediction; doctrine, doctrine; and fact, fact. Wherever a gleam of light is caught, it illuminates. The true Light, from whatsoever reflected, *lighteth.*

Let us, then, cultivate an attitude of courage as over against the investigations of the day. None should be more zealous in them than we. None should be more quick to discern truth in every field, more hospitable to receive it, more loyal to follow it whithersoever it leads. It is not for Christians to be lukewarm in regard to the investigations and discoveries of the time. Rather, the followers of the Truth Indeed can have no safety, in science or in philosophy, save in the arms of truth. It is for us, therefore, as Christians, to push investigation to the utmost; to be leaders in every science; to stand in the van of criticism; to be the first to catch in every field the voice of the Revealer of truth, who is also our Redeemer. The curse of the Church has been her apathy to truth, in which she has too often left to her enemies that study of nature and of history and philosophy, and even that investigation of her own peculiar treasures, the Scriptures of God, which should have been her chief concern. Thus she has often been forced to learn from the inadvertent or unwilling testimony of her foes the facts she has needed to protect herself from their assaults. And thus she has been led to borrow from them false theories of philosophy, science, and criticism, to make unnecessary concessions to them, and to expose herself, as they changed their positions from time to time, to unnecessary disgrace. What has the Church not suffered from her unwillingness to engage in truly scientific work! She has nothing to fear from truth; but she has everything to fear, and she has already suffered nearly everything, from ignorance. All truth belongs to us as followers of Christ, the Truth; let us at length enter into our inheritance.

III. In so speaking, we have already touched somewhat upon a third message which our text brings us: That since Christ Jesus our Lord and Master is incarnate Truth, we as his children must love the truth.

Like him, we must be so single of eye, so steadfast in purpose, so honest in word, that no guile can be found in our mouth. The philosophers have sought variously for the sanction of truth. Kant found it in the respect a man owes to the dignity of his own moral nature: the liar must despise himself because lying is partial suicide—it is the renunciation of what we are and the substitution of a feigned man in our place. Fichte found it in our sense of justice toward our fellowmen: to lie is to lead others astray and subject their freedom to our selfish ends—it is ultimately to destroy society by destroying trust among men. From each of these points of view a

198 THE SAVIOUR OF THE WORLD

powerful motive to truth may be developed. It is unmanly to lie; it is unneighborly to lie. It will destroy both our self-respect and all social life. But for us as Christians no sanction can approach in power that derived from the simple fact that as Christians we are "of the Truth;" that we are not of him who when he speaketh a lie speaketh of his own, who is a liar and the father thereof, but of him who is the fullness of truth—who is light and in whom is no darkness at all. As the children of truth, truth is our essential nature; and to lie is to sin against that incarnate Truth who is also our Lord and Redeemer—in whom, we are told, no liar can have part or share.

Bare avoidance of falsehood is far, however, from fulfilling our whole duty as lovers of truth. There is a positive duty, of course, as well as this negative one beckoning us. We have already noted the impulse which should arise to investigation and research. If all truth is a revelation of our Lord, what zeal we should have to possess it, that we may the better know him! As children of the truth we must love the truth, every truth in its own order, and therefore especially and above all others those truths which have been revealed by God for the salvation of the world. How tenacious we should be in holding them, how persistent in propagating them, how insistent in bearing our witness to them! "To this end was I born," said our Lord himself, "and for this cause came I into the world, that I should bear witness unto the truth." And we too, as his servants, must be, each in his place, witnesses of the truth. This is the high function that has been given us as followers of Jesus: as the Father sent him into the world, so he has sent us into the world, to bear witness of the truth.

We all know in the midst of what dangers, in the midst of what deaths, those who have gone before us have fulfilled this trust. "Martyrs," we call them; and we call them such truly. For "martyrs" means "witnesses;" and they bore their witness despite cross and sword, fire and raging beasts. So constant was their witness, so undismayed, that this proverb has enshrined their eulogy for all time, that "the blood of the martyrs was the seed of the Church." They were our fathers: have we inherited their spirit? If we be Christians at all, must not we too be "martyrs," "witnesses"? must not we too steadfastly bear our witness to the truth assailed in our time? There may be no more fires lighted for our quivering flesh: are there no more temptations to a guilty silence or a weak evasion? Surely there is witness still to be borne, and we are they to bear it. The popular poet of the day sings against "the hard God served in Jerusalem," and all the world goes after him. But we—do we not know him to be the God of our salvation? the God who hath lovingly predestinated us unto the adoption of sons, through Jesus Christ, unto himself, according to the good pleasure of his will, to the praise of the glory of his grace? May God grant that in times like these, when men will not endure the sound doctrine, we may be enabled by his grace to bear unwavering witness to the glory of the Lord God Almighty, who "hath made everything for its own purpose, yea, even the wicked for the day of evil."

Need we pause further to enforce that highest form of the love of the truth, the love of the Gospel of God's grace, which braves all things for the pure joy of making known the riches of his love to fallen men? The missionary spirit is the noblest fruit of the love of truth; the missionary's simple proclamation the highest form of witness-bearing to the truth. This spirit is no stranger among you. And I am persuaded that your hearts are burning within you as you think that to you "this grace has been given, to preach unto the Gentiles the unsearchable riches of Christ, and to make all men see what is the stewardship of the mystery which from all ages hath been hid in God." You need not that I should exhort you to remember that above all else "it is required in stewards that a man be found faithful." May God grant that while you may ask in wonder, as you contemplate the work

of your ministry, Who is sufficient for these things? you may
be able to say, like Paul, "We are not as the many, corrupting
the Word of God; but as of sincerity, but as of God, in the
sight of God, speak we in Christ." May God grant that the
desire which flamed in Paul may burn in you too:

> Oh could I tell ye surely would believe it!
>> Oh could I only say what I have seen!
> How should I tell or how can ye receive it,
>> How till He bringeth you where I have been?
>
> Give me a voice, a cry and a complaining,—
>> Oh let my sound be stormy in their ears!
> Throat that would shout but cannot stay for straining,
>> Eyes that would weep but cannot wait for tears.

2 CORINTHIANS v. 1-10:—For we know that if the earthly house of our tabernacle be dissolved, we have a building from God, a house not made with hands, eternal in the heavens. For verily in this we groan, longing to be clothed upon with our habitation which is from heaven: if so be that being clothed we shall not be found naked. For indeed, we that are in this tabernacle do groan, being burdened: not for that we would be unclothed, but that we would be clothed upon, that what is mortal may be swallowed up in life. Now he that wrought us for this very thing is God, who gave unto us the earnest of the Spirit. Being therefore always of good courage, and knowing that, whilst we are at home in the body, we are absent from the Lord (for we walk by faith, not by sight): we are of good courage, I say, and are willing rather to be absent from the body, and to be at home with the Lord. Wherefore also we make it our aim, whether at home or absent, to be well-pleasing unto him. For we must all be made manifest before the judgment seat of Christ; that each one may receive the things done in the body, according to what he hath done, whether it be good or bad.

THE CHRISTIAN'S ATTITUDE TOWARD DEATH

Nowhere more fully than in the opening chapters of the Second Epistle to the Corinthians does Paul describe the trials and distresses of the life that he was living as ambassador of Christ. He had been lately thrown to the beasts at Ephesus, and had escaped, almost miraculously as we may well believe, with bare life. While recovering, perhaps slowly, from the deadly injuries thus received, the news reached him of the threatening defection of the churches of Galatia, and of the danger of that in Corinth, and added mental to his physical distress. For the good of his children in the Lord he controlled the expression of his sorrows, and sent to each of these churches a letter of admonition and instruction, only venturing in that to the Galatians on the pathetic appeal which consisted in calling their attention to the large, misshapen, and painfully formed characters in which alone he could now scrawl the accustomed line or two which he added with his own hand at the end of his letters. Meanwhile things came once more to a climax at Ephesus. Under the leadership of one Demetrius, the craftsmen who made profit out of the service of Diana raised a tumult against the Apostle's preaching; and assembling in the theater, "all with one voice about the space of two hours cried out, 'Great is Diana of the Ephesians!' "—not the first instance in history, nor likely to be the last, when volume and continuance of sound are made to do duty for argument.

Warned by this that the public mind in Ephesus was no longer in a condition to profit by his preaching, Paul departs for Macedonia, apparently before the time appointed for the return of his messengers from Corinth, hoping to meet them on the road. But Titus does not come even at Troas (II Cor. 2:13); and torn with anxiety the Apostle pushes on into Macedonia. There at length his returning messengers meet him, and, better than that, bring him good news. The Corinthians allow his authority, and have humbled themselves to his rebukes; and that beloved church at least has ridden safely over the crest of the wave that threatened to submerge it. The burdened heart of the Apostle overflows, and he writes to the Corinthians out of his very soul. For once we see within him, and learn how the stupendous trials which pressed upon him affected his thought and feelings.

Amid all these sufferings, the mere allusions to which, lightly touched as they are, appall us, he is upheld by his sense of the greatness of his work and of the greatness of his hope. Though his outward man is being literally worn away, he need not faint; for his inward man is being renewed day by day, and all this affliction, terrible as it is, is light compared with the eternal weight of glory which it is working for him. His courage draws its force, thus, from his confidence in his future reward. It is because he looks not at the things that are seen, which are temporal, but at those that are not seen, which are eternal, that he can bear all things. Like Moses, he looks unto the recompense of reward, and endures as seeing the Invisible One. Like Abraham, he is content to dwell in tents for a season, because he looks for the city which hath the foundations, whose builder and maker is God. It is, indeed, with just this last figure that the Apostle expresses his feeling here. The reason of his strength, he tells us, is because "we know that if our earthly tent-dwelling be destroyed, we have a house from God, a dwelling not made with hands, eternal, in the heavens." What are earthly sufferings to one who looks upon his very bodily frame as but a tent, in which he sojourns for a time, and expects the laying of it aside to be merely a step toward entering into a mansion prepared for him by God himself?

The Apostle then contemplates the wearing away of his present body with patience. But we must observe that it is not exactly death that he longs for. He is burdened here, and sighs for relief from the burdens of this life, that somehow mortality may be swallowed up by life. But he shrinks from death. He could wish to be alive to greet the Lord when he comes, and so put on the habitation which is from heaven over this earthly tent, rather than be found naked on the coming of that glad day. Not that he expects to live until the Advent; he only could find it in his heart to wish it; he is in entire uncertainty as to the issue, and accordingly adds, "That is, of course, if, when we do put on" (or "when the putting-on time comes") "we shall be found not naked." How instructive meanwhile it is to observe this great soldier of the cross, who was "in deaths oft" and "died daily," shrinking with purely human feeling from the act of death; how magnificent must have been his courage, a courage rooted in nothing human, but in a divine faith and hope. For scarcely has this cry of human nature escaped from him before he proceeds, as if quietly reasoning with himself, to declare that God has wrought us for the very purpose of swallowing up our mortality in life, and given us even here his Spirit as earnest of his intention. And his contemplation being thus withdrawn from self and cast on God, his shrinking from death disappears too. "Being, then, of good courage always," he declares, "and knowing that while we are at home in the body we are away from home from the Lord (for it is by faith that we are walking, not by appearance), we are of good courage, I say, and are well pleased rather to go away from home from the body and go home to the Lord." Thus faith conquers the natural fear of death. As much as he fears it, he longs for the Lord more, and the most direct path that leads to his side, however painful or even unnatural it may be, he will joyfully take.

Paul's whole heart is now before us. He is burdened in this life and longs to be with his Lord. He could wish that the Lord would hasten his coming, and thus "clothe him upon" with immortality; but if this is not to be he earnestly desires even in nakedness of soul to be with him, and welcomes the fearful and unnatural portal of death as access to him. It is the model of the Christian's attitude toward life and death and the life that lies beyond death. Let us seek to make it such for our bruised hearts today,* and endeavor to understand from the Apostle's uncovered soul what should be the attitude of our souls toward these great mysteries.

I. First of all, then, we may learn that this life which we are living here cannot be a satisfactory living to a Christian. "In this tent-dwelling," says Paul, "we groan, longing to be clothed upon with our habitation which is from heaven." "We that are in the tent," he repeats, "groan, being burdened, with a view to the swallowing up of mortality in life." And lest we should think this a state of mind peculiar to himself, as one "in labors more abundant," let us remind ourselves that he elsewhere represents it as characteristic of Christians, broadly declaring that they "who have the first-fruits of the Spirit, even we ourselves, groan within ourselves, waiting for our adoption, to wit, the redemption of our body." This is indeed the whole drift of that great chapter, the seventh of Romans, in which the conflict of the Christian life, that ineradicable strife between the implanted good and the natural evil within us, is vividly portrayed, ending with the heart-rending cry, "O wretched man that I am! who shall deliver me out of this body of death?" It is a body of humiliation, as the Apostle elsewhere calls it, a body of death, a body of sin, with which our spirits are now clothed. How can we fail to long for deliverance from it?

*This sermon was preached on January 17, 1892, the first Sabbath after the death of Prof. Charles Augustus Aiken, Ph.D., D.D.

One of the characteristics of the true Christian attitude, then, is that we should be dissatisfied with the life which we are now living in the flesh. This is, of course, not inconsistent with the contentment which is equally a mark of the Christian attitude. The contentment with his lot which the follower of Jesus is called upon to feel and to exhibit, is, at bottom, contentment with Christ and his provision for us, with God and his providential direction of us; so that whatever our Father in heaven sends us we are well content to receive, and whatever hardness he desires us to experience we are glad for his sake to endure. Paul longed to be delivered from this body of death, but he was not stranger to a Christian's content. Years after this he writes to the Philippians that he still cherished his "desire to depart and be with Christ," yet since living in the flesh meant fruit of his work and was needful for them, he was glad to forego what for him was "very far better," and abide with them all for their progress and joy in faith. To be content to fill the place which God assigns us and to do the work which our Lord requires of us is quite consistent with the deepest dissatisfaction with our own Christian attainment and the most passionate longing to perfect our course. To speak of consistency here is indeed short of the mark. The very ground of our dissatisfaction with self is, that we are not what Christ would have us be and fall sadly behind filling the place for which God designs us. Just because we are content with him, we cannot be content with ourselves. And just so long as to us "who would do good, evil is present," as, though we "delight in the law of God after the inward man," we "see a different law in our members bringing us into captivity under the law of sin which is in our members," we must cry, "O wretched man that I am! who shall deliver me out of the body of this death?"

It is for us to ask our souls seriously this day whether this is the case with us. The human heart is very subtle; and it may be that some of us who would fain reply with a hasty "yes" may find cause, on consideration, to doubt whether our dissatisfaction is with self or with God—dissatisfaction with the dispensations of his providence, by which some messenger of sickness or sorrow or failure has visited us. In the bitterness of the moment we may feel glad to leave this world of our misery or our shame, not knowing that the long-suffering of God leadeth us to repentance. The truly Christian dissatisfaction is not such. It is with self and the meagerness of our Christian attainment. And it shows itself in an eager desire not so much to depart from the world as to depart from sin and to sit down in the heavenly places with Christ.

II. We cannot help observing, as a second important truth which we may learn from this unique record of Paul's inner experience, that even to the Christian death remains an undesired guest. Although the Apostle groaned under the burden of his body of sin, and therefore eagerly wished to pass out of this bodily life, yet he expresses a strong desire not to die. He longed rather for the coming of his Lord, that he might go to him without dying. He shrank from death; and it cannot be wrong for other Christians like him to shrink from death. We learn from this at once that though this bodily life which we are now living in the flesh is an evil, and every truly Christian soul will long to be delivered from it, a bodily life in itself considered is not an evil, but a good, and every rightly constituted man must cling instinctively to it. Death is unnatural and rightly terrifies its victims. Even more—death is evil, sin's offspring, Christ's enemy, Satan's servant; and every Christian heart must stand aghast before it. It is only because our Lord and Saviour lies now behind death that we can tolerate the thought of it. To whom of us has this dread presence not come to snatch from our arms one we loved better than life? It has been our comfort and joy that we were surrendering him to the even more loving arms of our Saviour. Since Christ has died, how much of the terror of death has departed! He has broken its sting, which is sin, by removing its strength, which is the curse of the broken law. Since he has lain in it, how much of the gloom of the tomb has gone! But have we not needed all this comfort which we could gain? The gloom of the tomb still overhangs it; it must, it ought to do so. And terrible death remains terrible still; it bears on its front still the dreadful legend which marks it as God's threatened punishment of sin.

III. In its closest analysis, the horror which we have of death turns on the unnatural separation which it brings about between those life-long companions, the soul and the body. And this leads us to the third great truth which is here brought before us. It is plain that the state of the blessed dead between death and the resurrection, when considered in itself alone as a condition—apart from their case, circumstances, and situation—is an undesirable state, because a state of unnatural separation between soul and body induced by and the fruit of sin. We are apt to think more of the body bereft of its animating and informing principle: even the bodies of our beloved are dear to us. But it is observable that Paul's solicitude seems to be less for the deserted body than for the naked soul. It is its unnatural and sin-born nakedness at death which appalls him; and in this unclothing of the soul he finds the horror of death.

In this sense the state of the blessed dead while awaiting the resurrection, as it is not their final state, is an imperfect state and therefore an undesirable state. In no other sense, however. It is a state of entire happiness; the soul is with the Lord. It is a state of, so far as the soul is concerned, completed salvation, finished sanctification, entire holiness. The Romish invention of purgatory, by which for the great majority of the saved a period of purification of longer or shorter duration and of greater or less suffering is interposed between death and "the going home to the Lord," is not only

a baseless but a wicked invention, at war with every statement of Scripture in the premises, and with every dictate of
the truly Christian consciousness alike. The same is true, of
course, of all the fancies of the so-called ethical theology of
our day which agree in supposing the saved soul to carry
remainders of sin with it into the other world, because in its
subtle and often only half-conscious antagonism to the supernatural this school of thought finds difficulty in believing
that God cleanses the soul at death from its remaining sin,
according to his Word; and looks only for a self-cleansing by
the soul itself in its own activity, which of course would be,
however aided by the Spirit, gradual and slow. It is not only
the Westminster Confession, but also the Scripture, which
teaches in every form of language, and with every circumstance of emphasis possible, that "the souls of the righteous
are at their death made perfect in holiness, and are received
into the highest heavens, where they behold the face of God
in light and glory, waiting for the full redemption of their
bodies."

The sole element of truth in the teachings just adverted
to lies in the one fact that redemption is incomplete until the
resurrection. It is the soul alone which is immediately trans-
ferred into holy bliss. The body lies moldering in the grave;
and though "even in death," in the beautiful language of the
Westminster Larger Catechism, the bodies of Christ's members "continue united to Christ, and rest in their graves *as in
their beds,* till at the last day they be again united to their
souls," their redemption is not "full" until the resurrection.
The salvation is complete, but it is as yet only an incomplete
man that is saved. As the separation between soul and body is
not natural to man, as God made man's nature, but is the
fruit of sin and the penalty specifically threatened to sin, the
work of redemption is not "full" until Christ conquers his
last enemy, Death, and comes again in triumph, reuniting the
souls and bodies of all his saints.

It is not, indeed, a pleasant thought that Christ's enemy, dreadful Death, retains dominion over even this lower element in our nature after death and on through what may well prove to be countless ages, until the Lord comes again in the epiphany of his glory, and in visible conquest over the last of his foes. Do we wonder, in view of such a fact, that the Old Testament saints, in the comparative twilight of revelation, sitting, if not in darkness, yet not yet in the full illumination of the day of salvation, could scarcely speak of death without a shudder, or of the land beyond death except as "a land of darkness and the shadow of death"? Or do we wonder that in the fullness of New Testament light the apostles teach us to long rather for Christ's coming than for death, to wait for that rather than for this, with expectant patience indeed, but also with strong desire? Have we not, indeed, uncovered here the one secret of the gloom that hangs over the Old Testament allusions to the other world, and as well, of that strong emphasis that is placed in the New Testament on the Second Advent which has puzzled many, and which, being misunderstood, has given birth to much Chiliastic error? It was important in the period of preparation that men's minds should not escape from the conception of death as the penalty of sin; and only when life and immortality were ready to be brought fully to light was it safe to make them fully understand the bliss that lay behind death. And now, when preparation has passed into the glorious reality of a completed sacrifice for sin, it is equally important that we should keep in mind that we do not obtain our entire salvation, that all the terrible harvest which springs from sin is not fully garnered by any one of us, until our enraptured eyes behold him who is the Redeemer from sin descending from heaven in like manner as he went into heaven. We are still reaping fruitage from our sin, even after we go abroad from the body and go home to the Lord, or, better, just because in order to go home to the Lord we must needs go abroad from the body.

Let us praise God that he saves the soul at once utterly; and, naked as it may be, takes it home to himself and grants it continual fruition of his favor, while it awaits in his sheltering arms the perfecting of its old companion the body. How great a mercy that our Lord enables us to know that our dead are perfectly holy and happy at once, and that it is only the insensate body that awaits in the disgrace of the tomb the great day when he shall come to be glorified in all his saints. But it is equally important to keep ourselves reminded that they gravely err who speak with scant respect of the body which has also in its measure been a habitation of the Spirit, and is also joined to the Lord, referring to the soul as released from a prison when it is freed from what they are pleased to term the clog of clay. We cannot emphasize too strongly that human souls were not created to exist apart from matter, and so far from needing to be separated from their bodies for their completest freedom, are incomplete and naked things away from their dwelling-houses of clay. It is the glory of Christianity to provide a salvation adequate to the whole man; and though it be only gradually realized, and the soul be taken to bliss long before the renewed and glorified body is prepared for it, yet it is accomplished in the end, and the complete man stands before his God, justified, sanctified, glorified. The saints of God have prelibations of their glory. Even in this world they are received into the number of his sons, and are made temples of the Holy Ghost. When their period of service below is accomplished, their spirits are cleansed from remainders of sin and received into the presence of God. But the day that marks the beginning of their heavenly perfection and of their completed bliss is not the day in which they believed, although in that act their whole salvation was in principle involved; nor yet is it the day in which they depart to be with Christ, although in that they enter into glory; but it is to be the day of Christ's glorious coming and of the resurrection of the saints. And this is the reason of the emphasis on the Day of Judgment in the Bible; it is the day in which the inheritance, incorruptible and undefiled, and that fadeth not away, reserved in heaven for Christ's people, shall be fully revealed.

IV. It is time that we were throwing stress, however, on a further blessed truth brought to us by this passage, and indeed underlying it as one of its foundations; and that is that this intermediate state of the blessed dead, although imperfect when compared with their final state, when the whole man shall partake of the divine glory, is, apart from that comparison, unspeakably blissful, and to be infinitely desired and longed for by every Christian soul. We remember that Paul, with a clear sense of all the unnaturalness of a separation of the soul from the body, yet wished rather to be absent from the body and to be at home with the Lord, and declared to depart and be with Christ to be "very far better." Just so soon as he remembered that while we are at home in the body we are absent from the Lord, he desired to go away from home from the body that he might go home to the Lord. Perhaps no clearer insight could be given of the infinite bliss of the saved soul in heaven than is afforded by the fact that it is so great as to make it intensely to be desired even at the expense of so unnatural a mutilation. Paul does not conceal from his readers that he would rather, for himself, that the coming of Christ should be hastened, so that the conquest of Death, the last enemy, might be completed, and he be glorified, soul and body, without death. But presence with the Lord was so to be yearned for, that, if this was not to be, he was well pleased to depart from the body itself and go to the Lord. It is well to let our hearts dwell on this revelation of bliss. What comfort it brings us for those who have died in the Lord! And perhaps it may entice our own hearts to long to lay aside our body of sin and enter into the inheritance of the saints beyond the grave.

Let us note the superiority of their state to ours here.

The evil of our present life is positive evil; all that can be called an evil in the soul-life in heaven is negative only. By which it is intended to say that the holiness and bliss of the disembodied soul in heaven is perfect of its kind; it has only not yet been made a sharer in so complete a glorification of human nature as is destined for it. While, on the other hand, in this life not only do we lag behind the positive attainment there and thus live on a lower plane, but there is a weight of positive evil upon us, a law of sin reigning in our members. Ah, if we could only catch a glimpse of what perfect holiness really is, how would we long to be separated from this body of sin and enter into it at any cost! We observe, therefore, that though the separation of soul and body is in itself an unnatural thing, the separation of our redeemed and sanctifying soul from this body of humiliation in which we now live is a thing to be greatly desired, not because it is a body, but because it is a body of sin. The bliss of the intermediate state is thus infinitely more to be desired than anything that can come to us on earth; it is only less desirable than the completed redemption which is yet to come.

And of this complete redemption it is the earnest and pledge. It is the completion of the salvation of the higher element of our nature, and bears in itself the prophecy and promise of the completion of the salvation of the whole man. It is to be desired, then, as the storm-tossed mariner desires the haven which his vessel has long sought to win through the tossing waves and adverse winds—gate only though it be of the country which he calls home, and long though he may need to wait until all his goods are landed. It is the end of the journey, when the friends come out to meet us. It is within the Father's house, where the greeting rings, "Bring forth the best robe and put it on him." Should the prodigal be impatient for the coming of the robe? The bliss of the holy, happy dwelling with the Lord is such that even were there nothing beyond we should joyfully seek it; and it is the promise and the surety of a yet grander future.

But the Apostle throws his emphasis on the chief joy of the intermediate state. Christ is there. To go abroad from the body is to go home to the Lord. No wonder he prefers nakedness of soul with Christ to personal completeness away from Christ. And no wonder since his day many a bed of suffering has been smoothed, and many a soul has gone forth brightening the face of even the deserted body with its smile of joy as it hears the words of its Saviour, "Today thou shalt be with me in Paradise." No wonder Christian song is vocal with the sigh

"O mother dear, Jerusalem!
　　When shall I come to thee?
When shall my sorrows have an end,
　　Thy joys when shall I see?
O happy harbor of God's saints,
　　O sweet and pleasant soil,
In thee no sorrows can be found,
　　No grief, no care, no toil!

"Jerusalem the city is
　　Of God our King alone;
The Lamb of God, the light thereof,
　　Sits there upon his throne.
Ah, God! that I Jerusalem
　　With speed may go and see,—
Jerusalem! Jerusalem!
　　Would God I were in thee!"

V. Do we not share these yearnings? May God grant that in his own good time each of us may indeed be permitted to join the innumerable throng of praising saints about his throne. Dare we confront the possibility that it may not be so? The Apostle seems to confront it. For, on reaching this point in his statement, he makes a sudden and strange transition. He had reached the climax: "We are of good courage, I say, and are well pleased rather to go away from home from the body, and go home to the Lord." Here he might be expected to pause. But he continues; and the words which he adds demand our serious attention: *"Wherefore also we make it our aim, whether at home or away from home, to be well-pleasing unto him. For we must all be made manifest before the judgment seat of Christ, that each one may receive the things done in the body, according to what he hath done, whether it be good or bad."* Thus he turns from the glories of his inheritance in Christ in heaven to the duties which he owes him on earth; from the consideration of what he may attain in him to the danger of losing it all; from the bliss of dwelling with Christ to the dread of standing before his judgment-seat. His purpose is obvious, and the addition of these solemn words ceases to be strange. It is not enough to contemplate the glories of heaven; we must seek to make those glories ours. They are given to whom they justly belong; we must all stand before the judgment-seat of Christ and receive according to the deeds done in the body, whether good or bad. And note the finality of this judgment. The Apostle plainly does not contemplate the possibility of any reversal or of any change; the verdict upon what is done here is the irreversible doom of all the future. And therefore it behoves us to be well-pleasing to him.

Oh, the troops upon troops that have laid aside the trials and labors of earth, well-pleasing to their Lord, and entered into their rest with him!

> "Death's wings beat round about us day and night;
> Their wind is on our faces now."

While yet our farewell to them on this side of the separating gulf was sounding in their ears, the glad "Hail!" of their Lord was welcoming them there. May God grant to each of us to follow them. May he give us his Holy Spirit to sanctify us wholly and enable us when we close our eyes in our long sleep to open them at once, not in terrified pain in torment, but in the soft, sweet light of Paradise, safe in the arms of Jesus!

APPENDIX

The following are two short articles and one lecture by Dr. Warfield which have not recently appeared in print. The publisher is of the opinion that this material is of sufficient importance to those seriously aspiring to the ministry of the Gospel to warrant its inclusion in this volume.

The reason for the inclusion of the article entitled *The Indispensableness of Systematic Theology to the Preacher* and the lecture *Spiritual Culture in the Theological Seminary* in a volume of sermons will be readily obvious. There are those would-be preachers (who are in great abundance in Fundamentalist circles) who scoff at the need for an abundance of theological knowledge in order for one to be equipped to preach the Gospel effectively. Warfield deals most directly with this oft-occuring attitude. On the other hand, there are those seeking the ministry who, while they see the need for a sound theological education in order to be properly prepared to preach the mysteries of Christ, fail to sufficiently ground themselves in the practical and experimental aspects of a true Christian life. To this pressing need Dr. Warfield also directs himself with great spiritual insight. To those who turn to this volume for instruction in how to better preach the Biblical Gospel from one so capable in homiletics as Dr. Warfield, may God bless also this material in the Appendix in order better to prepare the *man* as well as the *message*.

Finally, the reason for the inclusion of the short article *Paul on Women Speaking in Church* is to be found in the fact that this article has not been included recently in other volumes of Warfield's writings although the feminist movement is at high pitch and is making great inroads in the Church of Jesus Christ. Dr. Warfield's incisive exegesis on this question of "What women may *not* do in the church" should be most helpful to those seeking to follow Biblical instruction in this area. It should also be noticed that we at *Mack Publishing Company* have recently published a small book entitled *The Role of Women in the Church* by Wayne Mack which deals in an excellent manner with all the facets of this issue—the positive as well as the negative side to the question. It is to that book that we would direct anyone seeking more help in this area—certainly Pastor Mack has dealt with the issues involved in a way which effectively complements the fruits of Warfield's exegesis in the short article contained herein.

Dave Mack

THE INDISPENSABLENESS OF SYSTEMATIC THEOLOGY TO THE PREACHER[1]

Professor Flint, of Edinburgh, in closing his opening lecture to his class a few years ago,[2] took occasion to warn his students of what he spoke of as an imminent danger. This was a growing tendency to "deem it of prime importance that they should enter upon their ministry accomplished preachers, and of only secondary importance that they should be scholars, thinkers, theologians." "It is not so," he is reported as saying, "that great or even good preachers are formed. They form themselves before they form their style of preaching. Substance with them precedes appearance, instead of appearance being a substitute for substance. They learn to know truth before they think of presenting it. . . . . They acquire a solid basis for the manifestation of their love of souls through a loving, comprehensive, absorbing study of the truth which saves souls." In these winged words is outlined the case for the indispensableness of Systematic Theology for the preacher. It is summed up in the propositions that it is through the truth that souls are saved, that it is accordingly the prime business of the preacher to present this truth to men, and that it is consequently his fundamental duty to become himself possessed of this truth, that he may present it to men and so save their souls. It would not be easy to overstate, of course, the importance to a preacher of those gifts and graces which qualify him to present this truth to men in a winning way—of all, in a word, that goes to make him an "accomplished preacher." But it is obviously even more important to him that he should have a clear apprehen-

sion and firm grasp of that truth which he is to commend to
men by means of these gifts and graces. For this clear
apprehension and firm grasp of the truth its systematic study
would seem certainly to be indispensable. And Systematic
Theology is nothing other than the saving truth of God
presented in systematic form.

The necessity of systematic study of any body of truth
which we need really to master will scarcely be doubted. Nor
will it be doubted that he who would indoctrinate men with
a given body of truth must needs begin by acquiring a
mastery of it himself. What has been made matter of controversy is whether Christian truth does lie so at the basis of the
Christian hope and the Christian life that it is the prime duty
of the preacher to possess himself of it and to teach it. It has
been argued that the business of the preacher is to make
Christians, not theologians; and that for this he needs not a
thorough, systematic knowledge of the whole circle of what
is called Christian doctrine, but chiefly a firm faith in Jesus
Christ as Savior and a warm love toward Him as Lord. His
function is a practical, not a theoretical one; and it matters
little how ignorant he may be or may leave his hearers, so
only he communicates to them the faith and love that burn
in his own heart. Not learning but fervor is what is required;
nay, too much learning is (so it is often said) distinctly
unfavorable to his best efficiency. Engagement of the mind
with the subtleties of theological construction excludes that
absorption in heart-devotion and in the practical work of the
ministry, which on its two sides forms the glory of the
minister's inner life and the crown of his outer activity. Give
us not scholars, it is said, but plain, practical men in our
pulpits—men whose simple hearts are on fire with love to
Christ and whose whole energy is exhausted in the rescue of
souls.

Surely, if the antithesis were as is here implied, no voice
would be raised in opposition to these demands. If we are to

choose between a chilly intellectualistic and a warmly evangelistic ministry, give us the latter by all means. A comparatively ignorant ministry burning with zeal for souls is infinitely to be preferred to a ministry entirely absorbed in a purely intellectual interest in the relations of truths which are permitted to exercise no influence on their own lives and which quicken in them no fervor of missionary love. But the matter can not be settled by fixing the eye on this extreme only. What should we do with a ministry which was absolutely and blankly ignorant of the whole compass of Christian truth? Obviously it would not be a Christian ministry at all. Let it be admitted, then, that it is possible for men to become so occupied with the purely intellectual aspects of Christian truth as to be entirely unfitted for the prosecution of the Christian ministry. It must be equally allowed that they must have a sound knowledge of Christian truth in order to be qualified to undertake the functions of the Christian ministry at all. The possibility of the abuse of Systematic Theology has no tendency to arraign its usefulness or even its indispensableness to the preacher. A high capacity and love for mathematics may live in a sadly unpractical brain, and, for aught I know, the world may be full of pure mathematicians who are absolutely useless to it; but it does not follow that the practical worker in applied mathematics can get on just as well without any mathematics at all. In like manner, though there may be such a thing as a barren knowledge of even such vital truth as the Christian verities, there is not and can not be such a thing as a fruitful Christian ministry without a sound and living knowledge of these verities. And it is very much to be deprecated that men should sometimes permit themselves to be driven, through their keen sense of the valuelessness of an inoperative knowledge, to speak as if no importance attached to that vitalizing knowledge of divine truth without which any true ministry is impossible. The warning given us by the lamented Aubrey Moore is sorely needed in our times. He says:

> "There are many earnest-minded Christians who are so morbidly afraid of a barren belief that they sometimes allow themselves to talk as if to hold fast to any form of sound words must be formalism; as if, in fact, the belief in a creed were rather dangerous than helpful. It is true, of course, as we all know well, that a right creed can not save a man, and that when the bridegroom comes many may be found with lamps that have no oil; but surely if we discard our lamps, much of the precious oil we have may be lost."[3]

The fundamental principle on which the indispensableness to the preacher of a sound knowledge of Christian truth rests is not more surely rooted in a true psychology than it is illustrated by universal experience. That "conduct in the long run corresponds with belief," as Bishop Westcott puts it, "all experience goes to show." And certainly he is entitled to add that "this unquestionable principle carries with it momentous consequences." "Patient investigation," he continues, "will show that no doctrine can be without a bearing on action. . . . The influence of a dogma will be good or bad—that is an important criterion of dogma, with which we are not now concerned,—but if the dogma be truly maintained, it will have a moral value of some kind. Every religion, and every sect of every religion, has its characteristic form of life; and if the peculiarities of these forms of life are smoothed away by time, it is only because the type of belief to which they correspond has ceased to retain its integrity and sharpness."[4] It is therefore that Principal Wace rebukes the "tendency of some modern historians to undervalue the influence upon human nature of variations in religious and moral principles," as "strangely at variance with the evidence before them."[5] "The history of the world," he adds, "would appear to be in great measure a history of the manner in which religious ideas, often of an apparently abstract and subtle character, can determine the future of whole races and of vast regions of the earth. . . . The facts of history thus afford conclusive evidence that the instinct of the Christian world, or rather the instinct of mankind, has not been mistaken in attributing extreme importance to those variations in faith, even on points apparently secondary, by which Christendom has been and is still so grievously divided." The whole case is most concisely put in a comprehensive passage in the "Systematic Theology" of the late Prof. John Miley:[6]

> "A religious movement with power to lift up souls into a true spiritual life must have its inception and progress in a clear and earnest presentation of the vital doctrines of religion. The order of facts in every such movement in the history of Christianity has been, first, a reformation of doctrine, and then, through the truer doctrine, a higher and better moral and spiritual life. . . . Such has ever been and must forever be the chronological order of these facts, because it is the logical order. When souls move up from a sinful life or a dead formalism into a true spiritual life they must have the necessary reasons and motives for such action. . . . If we should be consecrated to God in a life of holy obedience and love, it must be for reasons of duty and motives of spiritual well-being which are complete only in the distinctive doctrines of Christianity. These doctrines are not mere intellectual principles or dry abstractions, but living truths which embody all the practical forces of Christianity. The spiritual life takes a higher form under evangelical Christianity than is possible under any other form, whether ritualistic or rationalistic, because therein the great doctrines of Christianity are apprehended in a living faith and act with their transcendent practical force upon all that enters into this life."

If there be any validity at all in these remarks, the indispensableness of Systematic Theology to the preacher is obvious. For they make it clear not only that some knowledge of Christian truth is essential to him who essays to teach that truth, but that the type of life which is produced by his preaching, so far as his preaching is effective, will vary in direct relation to the apprehension he has of Christian truth and the type and proportion of truth he presents in his preaching. As Bishop Westcott puts it:[7] "Error and imperfection in such a case must result in lives which are faulty and maimed where they might have been nobler and more complete;" and, on the other hand, "right doctrine is an inexhaustible spring of strength, if it be translated into deed." In directly the same line or remark that saint of God, Dr. Horatius Bonar, urges[8] that: "All wrong thoughts of God, whether of Father, Son, or Spirit, must cast a shadow over the soul that entertains them. In some cases the shadow may not be so deep and cold as in others; but never can it be a trifle. And it is this that furnishes the proper answer to the flippant question so often asked: Does it really matter what a man believes? All defective views of God's character tell upon the life of the soul and the peace of the conscience. We must think right thoughts of God if we would worship Him as He desires to be worshiped, if we would live the life He wishes us to live, and enjoy the peace which He has provided for us." And what is true of the doctrine of God is true of every other doctrine about His ways and works; as Dr. Westcott phrases it: "The same law which holds good of the effect of the ideas of God and of a future and of the Incarnation in their most general form, holds good also of the details of the view upon which they are realized."[9]

Accordingly Dr. Alexander Whyte testifies to the relation of right belief and all the highest devotion, in a striking passage which we can not forbear quoting somewhat in full.[10] He writes:

"One of the acknowledged masters of the spiritual life warns us against 'an untheological devotion.' 'True spirituality,' he insists, 'has always been orthodox.' And the readers of the 'Grammar of Assent' will remember with what masterly power and with what equal eloquence it is there set forth that the theology of the Creeds and Catechisms, when it is rightly understood and properly employed, appeals to the heart quite as much as to the head, to the imagination quite as much as to the understanding. And we can not study Andrewes's book [his 'Private Devotions'], his closet confession of faith especially, without discovering what a majesty, what a massiveness, what a depth, and what a strength, as well as what an evangelical fervor and heartsomeness, his theology has given to his devotional life. . . . In the 'Grammar' its author says that for himself he has ever felt the Athanasian Creed to be the most devotional formulary to which Christianity has given birth. We certainly feel something not unlike that when Andrewes takes up the Apostles' Creed, or the Nicene Creed, or the Life of our Lord, or His Names, or His Titles, or His Offices. When Andrewes takes up any of these things into his intellect, imagination, and heart, he has already provided himself and his readers with another great prayer and another great psalm. So true is it that all true theology is directly and richly and evangelically devotional "

Readers of Dr. Palmer's "Life of Thornwell" will recall a parallel testimony to what the reading of the Westminster Confession did for Thornwell's soul; and we can ourselves testify from experience to the power of the Westminster Confession to quicken religious emotion, and to form and guide a deeply devotional life. "So true is it," to repeat Dr. Whyte's words, that "all true theology is directly and richly and evangelically devotional."

It can not be a matter of indifference, therefore, what doctrines we preach or whether we preach any doctrines at all. We can not preach at all without preaching doctrine; and the type of religious life which grows up under our preaching will be determined by the nature of the doctrines which we

preach. We deceive ourselves if we fancy that because we
scout the doctrines of the creeds and assume an attitude of
studied indifference to the chief tenets of Christianity we
escape teaching a system of belief. Even the extremest doctrinal indifferentism, when it ascends the pulpit, becomes
necessarily a scheme of faith. As a bright writer in *The
Atlantic Monthly*[11] puts it, men are always found believers
in either the head or the tail of the coin. Even "Renan's
followers have their pockets crammed with beliefs of their
own, bawling to the public to try them; they trundle their
push-carts down the boulevard, hawking new creeds: *'Par ici,
mes amis, par ici! Voici des croyance neuves, voici la Ver-
ité!' "* Beliefs old or beliefs new, we all have them; and
when we take our place in the rostrum in their behalf we
perforce become their teachers. There may be Christian
truths of which we speak as if they were of infinitesimally
little importance, because, as Aubrey Moore caustically puts
it, "from first to last we know infinitesimally little about
them;"[12] but we need not fancy that we are teaching nothing in so speaking of them, or are failing to preach a dogmatic
faith or by it mold lives in essaying to occupy a position of
indifference. To withold these truths from our hearers is not
merely a negative act, nor can their loss act merely negatively
upon their spiritual development. A mutilated Gospel pro-
duces mutilated lives, and mutilated lives are positive evils.
Whatever the preacher may do, the hearers will not do
without a system of belief; and in their attempt to frame one
for the government of their lives out of the fragments of
truth which such an one will grant to them, is it any wonder
if they should go fatally astray? At the best, men will be
"driven to a king of empirical theologizing, attempting with
necessarily imperfect knowledge to coordinate for themselves
the truths of religion and those which follow as consequences
from them;"[13] and so will build up an erroneous system of
belief which will mar their lives. At the worst, they will be

led to discard the neglected or discredited truths, and with them the whole system of Christianity—which they see, even though the preacher does not see, to be necessarily correlated with them; and so will lapse into unbelief. In either case, they may rightly lay their marred or ruined lives at the preacher's door. It is not given to one who stands in the pulpit to decide whether or no he shall teach, whether or no he shall communicate to others a system of belief which will form lives and determine destinies. It is in his power only to determine what he shall teach, what system of doctrine he shall press upon the acceptance of men, by what body of tenets he will seek to mold their lives and to inform their devotions.

By as much, however, as the communication of a system of belief is the inevitable consequence of preaching, by so much is the careful formation of his system of belief the indispensable duty of the preacher. And this is but another way of saying that the systematic study of divine truth, or the study of Systematic Theology, is the most indispensable preparation for the pulpit. Only as the several truths to be presented are known in their relations can they be proclaimed in their right proportions and so taught as to produce their right effects on the soul's life and growth. Systematic Theology is, in other words, the preacher's true text-book. Its study may be undertaken, no doubt, in a cold and unloving spirit, with the mind intent on merely scholastic or controversial ends. In that case it may be for the preacher an unfruitful occupation. But so undertaken it has also lost its true character. It exists not for these ends, but to "make wise unto salvation." And when undertaken as the means of acquiring a thorough and precise knowledge of those truths which are fitted to "make wise unto salvation," it will assuredly bear its fruit in the preacher's own heart in a fine skill in rightly dividing the word of truth, and in the lives of the hearers as a power within them working a right attitude before God and building them up into the fulness of the stature of symmetrical manhood in Christ.

FOOTNOTES

[1]Reprinted from *The Homiletic Review,* Vol. XXXIII, Feb., 1897.

[2]As reported in *The Scotsman* for Nov. 13, 1888.

[3]"Some Aspects of Sin," p. 20.

[4]"The Gospel of Life," pp. 48, 57.

[5]"The Foundations of Faith," pp. 194–198.

[6]Vol. i., pp. 48–49. *Cf.* also p. 40.

[7]*Op. cit.,* p. 58.

[8]"The Gospel of the Spirit's Love," p. 22.

[9]*Op. cit.,* p. 55.

[10]"Lancelot Andrewes and His Private Devotions," pp. 49–51.

[11]Henry T. Sedgwick, Jr., in *The Atlantic Monthly,* August 1896, p. 188.

[12]*Op. cit.,* p. 26.

[13]Aubrey Moore, *loc. cit.,* p. 25.

SPIRITUAL CULTURE IN THE THEOLOGICAL SEMINARY[1]

It is natural that at the opening of a new Session the minds of both Professors and Students, especially of those Students who are with us for the first time, should be bent somewhat anxiously upon the matter which has brought us together. How are we who teach best to fulfill the trust committed to us, of guiding others in their preparation for the high office of Minister of Grace? How are you who are here to make this preparation, so to employ your time and opportunities as to become in the highest sense true stewards of the mysteries of Christ? Standing as you do at the close of your University work and at the beginning of three years more of mental labor—looking back at the conquests you have already made and forward at unconquered realms still lying before you—it would not be strange if your thoughts as they busy themselves with the preparation you require for your ministerial work should be predominately occupied with intellectual training. It is the more important that we should pause to remind ourselves that intellectual training alone will never make a true minister; that the heart has rights which the head must respect; and that it behooves us above everything to remember that the ministry is a spiritual office.

I should be sorry to leave the impression that it is questionable whether the Church may not have laid too strong an emphasis on the intellectual outfit that is needed for her ministry. I must profess, indeed, that I am incapable of understanding the standpoint of those (for such there seem to be) who talk of the over-intellectualization of the ministry. The late Dr. Joseph T. Duryea spoke strongly, but with substantial justice, when he declared it to be "high time that the question whether culture and learning do not unfit preachers for the preaching of the Gospel to ordinary men and women, were referred back without response to the stupidity that inspires it." It is not to be denied, of course, that there are learned men who are perfectly useless in the ministry; and even, what is more surprising, that there are men of broad and varied and, one would have thought, humanizing culture, who seem to be unable to turn their culture to any practical use. But it is yet to be shown that these same men, without knowledge and destitute of the culture which might have been expected to humanize them, would have been any more useful. Are there no ignorant men, no men innocent of all culture, who are unpractical and of no possible use in the ministry? The fact is that when our Lord decreed that the religion He founded should be propagated by preaching, or, to put it more broadly, when He placed it in the world with the commission to reason its way to the hearts of men, He put a premium on intellectual endowments, and laid at the basis of ministerial equipment a demand for intellectual training, which no sophistry can cloud. The minister must have good tools with which to work, and must keep these tools in good condition.

You will find nothing in the curriculum which will be offered to you in this Seminary, the mastery of which is not essential to your highest efficiency in your ministry. The intellectual training at present provided for candidates for the ministry is not above either their prospective needs or the easy possibilities of their present powers. You will be wise to give yourselves diligently to making full account of it. It would not be easy to exaggerate the intimacy of the relation between sound knowledge and sound religious feeling: and the connection between sound knowledge and success in ministerial work is equally close. "Without study," says an experienced bishop of the Church of England, with his eye on the daily life of the minister it is true, but no less applicably to his preparation—"without study we shall not only fail to bring to our people all the blessings which God intends for them, but we shall gradually become feeble and perfunctory in our ministrations: our life may apparently be a busy one, and our time incessantly occupied, but our work will be comparatively fruitless: we shall be fighting as one that beateth the air."

So intimate is the connection between the head and the heart and hand, indeed, that it is not unfair to say broadly that if undue intellectualism exhibits itself in those preparing for the ministry, the fault is relative, not absolute: that, in a word, there is not a too muchness in the case at all, but a too littleness somewhere else. The trouble with those whom a certain part of the world persists in speaking of as over-educated for an effective ministry is not that they are too highly trained intellectually, but that they are sadly undertrained spiritually; not that their head has received too much attention, but that their heart has received too little. Of course I shall not deny that it is possible to find men who are naturally lacking in sufficient mental power to pursue a Seminary course profitably: and I am far from saying that there are none of these "unlearned and ignorant men" who have been so baptized with the Holy Spirit that the Church may profitably induct them into the ministry to which God has obviously called them. But these are rare exceptions; and I do not think it characteristic of this humble but honorable class that they refuse to make the best use possible of the mental powers that have been vouchsafed to them. Certainly it would be perilous for us to make the existence of such a class the excuse for neglecting to stir up the gift that is in us. Rather I think it may be fairly inferred that when students for the ministry fail to take full advantage of the opportuni-

ties for intellectual culture offered them, the fault is usually
to be found in the heart itself. When too much blood seems
to have gone to the head, we may ordinarily justly presume
that this is only because too little has gone to the heart; and
similarly when little or none is thrown to the head, we may
quite generally suspect it is because the heart has too little
within it to supply the needs of any organ.

I.

I have missed my mark in what I have been saying if,
while insisting on the need of a strenuous intellectual preparation for the ministry, I have not also suggested that the
deepest need is a profound spiritual preparation. An adequate
preparation for the Gospel ministry certainly embraces much
more than merely the study of certain branches of learning.
When Bishop Wilberforce opened Cuddesden College in 1854,
he wrote: "Threefold object of residence here: 1. Devotion;
2. Parochial Work; 3. Theological Reading." The special circumstances of "candidates for holy orders" in the Church of
England suggested, as we shall subsequently see, the order in
which these three elements in their preparation are men-
tioned. In our special circumstances a different order might
be suggested. But does it not, even on first sight, commend
itself to you with clear convincingness, that any proper
preparation for the ministry must include these three chief
parts—a training of the heart, a training of the hand, a
training of the head—a devotional, a practical and an intellectual training? Such a training, in a word, as that we may learn
first to know Jesus, then to grasp the message He would have
us deliver to men, and then how He would have us work for
Him in His vineyard. We are told by the Evangelist Mark
(3:14) that when Jesus appointed His twelve apostles, it was
first that they might be with Him, and then that He might
send them forth to preach. And surely we may believe that

we who are the successors of the apostles as the evangelizers of the world have been called like them first of all to be with Jesus and only then to go forth to preach. It may not be without significance that out of the fourteen or fifteen qualifications which, according to the Apostle Paul, must unite in order to fit a man to be a bishop, only one requires an intellectual preparation. The bishop must be "apt to teach." But aptness to teach is only the beginning of his fitting. All the other requirements are rooted in his moral or spiritual fitness.

I am not going to lose myself in a vain—perhaps worse than vain—inquiry as to which of the three lines of preparation I have hinted at is the most essential. Why raise a question between three lines of training, each of which is essential both in itself and to the proper prosecution of the others? If intellectual acuteness will not of itself make a man an acceptable minister of Christ, neither will facility and energy in practical affairs by themselves, nor yet piety and devotion alone. The three must be twisted together into a single three-ply cord. We are not to ask whether we will cultivate the one or the other; or whether we will give our chief attention to the one or the other. We must simultaneously push our forces over all three lines of approach, if we are to capture the stronghold of a successful ministry at all. Doing so, they will interact, as we have suggested, each to secure the others. Do we wish to grow in grace? It is the knowledge of God's truth that sanctifies the heart. Do we desire a key to the depths of God's truth? It is the Spirit-led man who discerns all things. Are our souls in travail for the dying thousands about us? How eager, then, will be our search in the fountain of life for the waters of healing? Is the way weary? Do we not know whence alone can be derived our strength for the journey of life? There is no way so surely to stimulate the appetite for knowledge as to quicken the sense of the need of it in the wants of our own spiritual life or in the calls of practical work for others. There is no way so potent for awakening a craving for personal holiness or for arousing a love of souls in our hearts, as to fill the mind with a knowledge of God's love to man as revealed in His Holy Book.

The reciprocal relation in which the several lines of preparation for the ministry stand to one another, supplies me with my first remark as I address myself to the task immediately before me—of attempting to outline in a practical way some account of how your spiritual training may be advanced during your stay in the Seminary. This remark takes a negative form and amounts to saying with some emphasis that your spiritual growth will not be advanced by the neglect of the very work for which you resort to the Seminary. Such a remark may seem to some of you out of place: it is perhaps not so entirely unnecessary as it may appear. There is a valuable bit from his own personal experience given us by the late Phillips Brooks in his Yale Lectures,[2] which I shall repeat here for our admonition also. He is impressing on his readers the important truth that the first and most evident element in a true preparation for the ministry consists in a mastery of the professional studies leading up to it. He writes as follows:

"Most men begin really to study when they enter on the preparation for their professions. Men whose college life, with its general culture, has been very idle, begin to work when at the door of the professional school the work of their life comes into sight before them. It is the way in which a bird who has been wheeling vaguely hither and thither sees at last its home in the distance and flies toward it like an arrow. But shall I say to you how often I have thought that the very transcendent motives of the young minister's study have a certain tendency to bewilder him and make his study less faithful than that of men seeking other professions from lower motives? The highest motive often dazzles before it illuminates. It is one of the ways in which the light within us becomes darkness. I never shall forget my first experience of a divinity school. I had come from a college where men studied hard but said nothing about faith. I had never been at a prayer-meeting in my life. The first place I was taken to at the Seminary was the prayer-meeting; and never shall I lose the impression of the devoutness with which those men prayed and exhorted one another. Their whole souls seemed exalted and their natures were on fire. I sat bewildered and ashamed and went away depressed. On the next day I met some of these same men at a Greek recitation. It would be little to say of some of the devoutest of them that they had not learnt their lesson. Their whole way showed that they had never learnt their lessons; that they had not got hold of the first principles of hard, faithful, conscientious study. The boiler had no connection with the engine. The devotion did not touch the work which then and there was the work, and the only work, for them to do. By and by I found something of where the steam did escape to. A sort of amateur, premature preaching was much in vogue among us. We were in haste to be at what we called 'our work!' A feeble twilight of the coming ministry we lived in. The people in the neighborhood dubbed us 'parsonettes.' Oh, my fellow-students, the special study of theology and all that appertains to it, that is what the preacher must be doing always; but he can never do it afterward as he can in the blessed days of quiet in Arabia, after Christ has called him, and before the apostles lay their hands upon him. In many respects an ignorant clergy, however pious it may be, is worse than none at all. The more the empty head glows and burns, the more hollow and thin and dry it grows. 'The knowledge of the priest,' said St. Francis de Sales, 'is the eighth sacrament of the Church.' "

Well, it was not at Princeton Seminary that Dr. Brooks saw these evils. Perhaps they do not exist here: let us hope that they do not, at least in the measure in which he portrays them. Nevertheless his experience may fitly be laid to heart by us for our warning. The religious training which a minister needs to get in his days of preparation assuredly cannot be had by neglecting the very work he is set to do, in favor of any show of zeal in another work which it is not yet his to do.

Of course there is another side to it. This religious training is not already obtained by the mere refusal to be led away from our primary work at the Seminary by practical calls upon our energies. Our primary business at the Seminary is, no doubt, to obtain the intellectual fitting for our ministerial work, and nothing must be allowed to supersede that in our efforts. But neither must the collateral prosecution of the requisite training of the heart and hand be neglected, as opportunity offers. Nor will a properly guarded attention to these injure the discharge of our scholastic duties; it will, on the contrary, powerfully advance their successful performace. The student cannot too sedulously cultivate devoutness of spirit. The maxim has been often verified in the experience of us all: *bene orasse est bene studuisse.* When the heart is thoroughly aroused, the slowest mind starts into motion and an impulse is given it which carries it triumphantly over intellectual difficulties before which it quailed afraid. And equally a proper taste of the practical work of the ministry is a great quickener of the mind for the intellectual preparation. We cannot do without these things. And the student must be very careful, therefore—even on this somewhat low ground—while not permitting any distractions to divert him from his primary task as a student, yet to take full advantage of all proper opportunities that may arise to train his heart and hand also. Preparation for ministerial service is very much like building a machine—say a locomotive. The intellectual work may have been accomplished and the machine may stand perfect before us. But it will not go unless the vital force of devotion is throbbing through it. Knowledge is a powerful thing: and practical tact is a powerful thing. And so is a locomotive a powerful thing—provided it has steam in it! Though I know all mysteries and all knowledge, and though I bestow all my goods to feed the poor, if I have not the love of God and man welling up in invincible power beneath it all and lifting it all and transmuting it all into effective working force—it profits me nothing.

II.

But the question comes back to us, How are we to obtain this spiritual culture in the Seminary? Well, theological students, in becoming theological students, have not ceased to be men; and there is no other way for them to become devout men than that which is common to man. There is but one way, brethren, to become strong in the Lord. That way is to feed on the Bread of Life! This is the way other men who would fain be devout take, and it is the way we, if we would fain be devout, must take. We are simply asking ourselves then, as theological students, what opportunities are offered us by our residence in the Seminary for the cultivation of faith in Jesus Christ and obedience to Him. What we are eager to know is how we can, not merely keep alive, but fan into a brighter flame, the fires of our love for our Lord and Saviour. I desire to be perfectly plain and simple in attempting to suggest an answer to this question. I shall, therefore, only enumerate in the barest manner some of the ways in which the devout life may be assisted in the conditions in which we live in the Seminary.

First of all, I must point you to the importance of a diligent use of the public means of grace. Public means of grace abound in the Seminary. There is the stated Sabbath-morning service in the chapel; and no student who is not prevented from attending it by some imperative duty should fail to be in his seat at that service, adding whatever his presence and his prayers can bring to the spiritual forces at work there. Then there is our weekly Conference on Sabbath afternoon, in which we talk over together the blessed promises of our God and seek to learn better His will for the ordering of our lives. There have been those in times past whose hearts have been stirred within them at these Conferences; and they may be made by the seeking spirit very precious seasons of social meditation and prayer. Then, Faculty and Students meet daily, at the close of the day's work, to listen to a fragment of God's Word, mingle their voices in praise to God, and ask His blessing on the labor of the day. Indeed, we proceed to no one of our classroom exercises without pausing a moment to lift up our hearts to God in prayer. And every effort is made by all of us who teach, I know, in all our teaching—however it may appear from moment to moment to be concerned with mere parts of speech, or the signification of words, or the details of history, or the syllogisms of formal logic—to preserve a devout spirit and a reverent heart, as becomes those who are dealing even with the outer coverings that protect the mysteries of God. I need not stay to speak with particularity of the more rarely occurring stated services, such as the monthly concert of prayer for missions and the like. Enough has been said to suggest the richness of provision made in the Seminary for public worship: and assuredly amid such abounding opportunities for the quickening of the religious life it ought to be a comparatively easy thing to cultivate devoutness of spirit.

You will doubtless observe that I have said nothing, so far, of additional opportunities for social worship afforded by public services open to the attendance of the students outside the boundaries of the Seminary, or by voluntary associations for religious culture among the students themselves. These also are abundant, and have their parts to play in your edification. They may be justly accounted supplementary means of grace, useful to you, each in its own place and order. But what I am insisting on now is something which no such services, whether without or within the Seminary walls, can supply: something which by the grace of God can go much deeper into the bases of your religious nature and lay much broader foundations for the building up of a firm and consistent and abiding Christian character. I am exhorting you to give diligence to the cultivation of the stated means of grace provided by the Seminary, to live in them and make them the full and rich expression of the organic religious life of the institution. I am touching on something here that seems to me to be of the utmost importance and which does not seem to me to have received the attention from the students which it deserves. Every body of men bound together in as close and intimate association as we are, must have an organic life: and if the bonds that bind them together are fundamentally of a religious character, this organic life must be fundamentally a religious one. We do not live on the top of our privileges in such circumstances unless we succeed in giving this organic religious life full power in our own lives and full expression in the stated means provided for its expression. No richness of private religious life, no abundance of voluntary religious services on the part of members of the organism, can take the place of or supersede the necessity for the fullest, richest and most fervent expression of this organic religious life through its appropriate channels. I exhort you, therefore, brethren, with the utmost seriousness, to utilize the public means of grace afforded by the Seminary, and to make them instruments for the cultivation and expression of the organic religious life of the institution. We shall not have done our duty by our own souls until we find in these public services the joy of our hearts and the inspiration of our conduct.

Let me go a step further and put into plain words a thought that is floating in my mind. The entire work of the

Seminary deserves to be classed in the category of means of grace; and the whole routine of work done here may be made a very powerful means of grace if we will only prosecute it in a right spirit and with due regard to its religious value. For what are we engaging ourselves with in our daily studies but just the Word of God, the history of God's dealings with His people, the great truths that He has revealed to us for the salvation of our souls? And what are we doing when we engage ourselves day after day with these topics of study and meditation, but just what every Christian man strives to do when he is seeking nutriment for his soul? The only difference is that what he does sporadically, at intervals, and somewhat primarily, it is your privilege to give yourselves to unbrokenly for a space of three whole years! Precious years these ought to be to you, brethren, in the culture of the spiritual life. If such contact as we in the Seminary have the privilege of enjoying with Divine truth does not sanctify our souls, should we not infer either that it is a mistake to pray in Christ's own words, "Sanctify us in the truth; Thy word is truth," or else that our hearts are so indurated as no longer to be capable of reaction even to so powerful a reagent as the very truth of God?

I beseech you, brethren, take every item of your Seminary work as a religious duty. I am emphasizing the adjective in this. I mean do all your work religiously—that is, with a religious end in view, in a religious spirit, and with the religious side of it dominant in your mind. Do not lose such an opportunity as this to enlighten, deepen and strengthen your devotion. Let nothing pass by you without sucking the honey from it. If you learn a Hebrew word, let not the merely philological interest absorb your attention: remember that it is a word which occurs in God's holy Book, recall the passages in which it stands, remind yourselves what great religious truths it has been given to it to have a part in recording for the saving health of men. Every Biblical text whose meaning you investigate treat as a Biblical text, a part of God's holy Word, before which you should stand in awe. It is wonderful how even the strictest grammatical study can be informed with reverence. You cannot read six lines of Bishop Ellicott's *Commentaries, Critical and Grammatical,* on Paul's epistles without feeling through and through that here is a man of God studying the Word of God. *O si sic omnes!* Let us make such commentators our models in our study of the Word, and learn like them to keep in mind Whose word it is we are dealing with, even when we are merely analyzing its grammatical expression. And when, done with grammar, we begin to weigh the meaning, O let us remember what meaning it has *to us!* Apply every word to your own souls as you go on, and never rest satisfied until you feel as well as understand. Every item of God's dealing with His Church to which your attention is directed, contemplate reverently as an act of God and search out the revelation it carries of God and His ways with man. And the doctrines—need I beg you to consider these doctrines not as so many propositions to be analyzed by your logical understanding, but as rather so many precious truths revealing to you God and God's modes of dealing with sinful man? John Owen, in his great work on Justification, insists and insists again that no man can ever penetrate the significance of this great doctrine unless he persistently studies it, not in the abstract light of the question, How can man be just with God? but in the searching light of the great personal question, How can *I,* sinner as I am, be accepted of God? It is wonderful how inadequacies in conceiving what is involved in Justification fall away under the illumination of this personal attitude toward it. And is it conceivable that it can be so studied and the heart remain cold and unmoved? Treat, I beg you, the whole work of the Seminary as a unique opportunity offered you to learn about God, or rather, to put it at the height of its significance, to learn God—to come to know Him whom to know is life everlasting. If the work of the Seminary shall be so prosecuted, it will prove itself to be the chief means of grace in all your lives. I have heard it said that some men love theology more than they love God. Do not let it be possible to say that of you. Love theology, of course: but love theology for no other reason than that it is THEOLOGY—the knowledge of GOD, and because it is your meat and drink to know God, to know Him truly, and as far as it is given to mortals, to know Him whole.

There is yet another aspect of the Seminary life the value of which as a means of spiritual development cannot easily be over-estimated. I do not know how better to express what I mean than by calling the Seminary a three years' retreat. The word "retreat" may strike somewhat strangely upon our Protestant ears: though even our Presbyterian ministry has been learning of late what a "retreat" is. Well, that is what a Seminary life very largely is—a period of three years' duration during which the prospective minister withdraws from the world and gives his time exclusively to study and meditation on God's Word, in company with a select body of godly companions.

> Here man more purely lives, less oft doth fall,
> More promptly rises, walks with stricter heed.

Possibly with our natural Protestant objection to all that in the remotest way savors of the monastery, we may be prone to take little account of this feature of Seminary life—much to our hurt. Much to our hurt, I say; for a "retreat" is what a Seminary life is, and it will have its effect on us as such—one way or another, according as we do or do not prepare for it, and are or are not receptive of it.

Our brethren of the Church of England, who have only comparatively lately taken to multiplying distinctively theological colleges, because they look to the universities as the places where their candidates are to be educated for the holy office, consider this element in the life at a theological college one of its most characteristic and helpful features. It was because he viewed it thus that Bishop Wilberforce declared the three objects of residence at Cuddesden to be: 1. Devotion; 2. Parochial Work; and 3. Theological Reading. It is as a matter of fact inevitable that the practical withdrawal from the world and the congregation together of a hundred or two young men, all consecrated to the work of the Lord, and living in that closeness of intimacy which only community-life can induce, should have a very powerful effect on their religious development. What, brethren, can you draw coals together without creating a blaze? I beseech you, esteem very highly and cultivate with jealous eagerness this unique privilege of long and intimate association with so many of God's ch. lren. No such opportunities of interaction of devout lives upon one another can ever come to you again in all your life. If no fire of Christian love breaks out among you, look well to yourselves: you may justly suspect there is something wrong with your souls. In the daily intercourse of scores of Christian men there must arise innumerable opportunities of giving and receiving spiritual impressions. See to it that all you give shall conduce to the quickening of the religious life, and that all you receive shall be food on which your own hearts feed and grow strong in the Lord. When you leave the Seminary you will miss this intercourse sorely: but by God's help you may so use it while here that in the strength derived from it you may go many days.

III.

But we must penetrate beneath even such means of grace as those I have enumerated before we reach the centre of our subject. It is not to the public ordinances, not to your Professors, and not even to your companions, that you can look for the sources of your growth in religious power. As no one can give you intellectual training except at the cost of your own strenuous effort, so no one can communicate to you spiritual advancement apart from the activities of your own eager souls. True devoutness is a plant that grows best in seclusion and the darkness of the closet; and we cannot reach the springs of our devout life until we penetrate into the sanctuary where the soul meets habitually with its God. If association with God's children powerfully quickens our spiritual life, how much more intimate communion with God Himself. Let us then make it our chief concern in our preparation for the ministry to institute between our hearts and God our Maker, Redeemer and Sanctifier such an intimacy of communion that we may realize in our lives the command of Paul to pray without ceasing and in everything to give thanks, and that we may see fulfilled in our own experience our Lord's promise not only to enter into our hearts, but unbrokenly to abide in them and to unite them to Himself in an intimacy comparable to the union of the Father and the Son.

Lectio, meditatio, oratio, the old Doctors used to say, *faciunt theologum.* They were right. Take the terms in the highest senses they will bear, and we shall have an admirable prescription of what we must do would we cultivate to its height the Christian life that is in us.

Above all else that you strive after, cultivate the grace of private prayer. It is a grace that is capable of cultivation and that responds kindly to cultivation; as it can be, on the other hand, atrophied by neglect. Be not of those that neglect it, but in constant prayer be a follower of Paul, or rather of our Lord Himself; for, God as He was, our blessed Lord was a man of prayer, and found prayer His ceaseless joy and His constant need. Of course the spirit of prayer is the main thing here, and the habit of "praying without ceasing," of living in a prayerful frame, is above all what is to be striven for. But let us not fall into the grave error of supposing this prayerful habit of mind enough, or that we can safely intermit the custom of setting apart seasons for formal prayer. Let me

read you a few appropriate words here from one of Dr. H. C.
G. Moule's delightful devotional treatises:

"To speak in terms of the simplest practicality," he
says,[3] "the living Christian will do anything rather than
make his 'life' an excuse for indolence, and for want of
method and self-discipline, in secret devotion; or for
want of adoring reverence in the manner of it; or for
neglect of the Written Word as a vital element in it, and
as the one sure guide and guard of it all along. He will
most specially take care that Christ is thus 'in his life,' in
respect of *morning* intercourse with Him. His 'morning
watch' will be a time of sacred necessity and blessed
benefit. He will not merely confess the duty of 'meeting
God before he meets man.' He will understand that he
cannot do without it, if indeed he would deal with the
unfolding day as it should be dealt with by one whose
'life is hid with Christ in God;' one who possesses the
priceless treasure of the blessed Union, 'joined to the
Lord, one Spirit,' and who has his treasure at hand, in
hand for use. And he will be not less watchful over his
evening interview with Him who is at once his Master
and his Life; coming with punctual reverence *to* Him
who meanwhile liveth *in* Him, to report the day's bond-
service, to confess the day's sins in contrite simplicity,
to look again deliberately upon his Master's face mir-
rored in His Word, to feel again the bond of the Union,
tested and handled through the promises and then to lie
down in the peace of God. And will he not see whether
some *midday* interval, if but for a few brief minutes,
cannot be found and kept sacred, for a special prayer
and watch half-way? Such stated times are not substi-
tutes for the spiritual attitude in which the 'eyes are
ever toward the Lord,' but they are, I believe, quite
necessary in order to the proper preparedness of the
soul for that attitude, and for the right use, too, of all
public and social ordinances. Nothing can annul the vital
need of secret and deliberate communion with Him in

whom we live, by whom we move."

Next to the prayerful spirit, the habit of reverent meditation on God's truth is useful in cultivating devoutness of life. It is commonly said around us that the old gift of meditation has perished out of the earth. And certainly there is much in our nervous, fussy times which does not take kindly to it. Those who read nowadays like to do it running. It is assuredly worth our while, however, to bring back the gracious habit of devout meditation. Says Jeremy Taylor in the opening page of his *Holy Living,* in his quaint, old-world words:

"The counsels of religion are not to be applied to the distempers of the soul as men used to take hellebore; but they must dwell together with the spirit of a man, and be twisted about his understanding for ever: they must be used like nourishment, that is, by a daily care and meditation; not like a single medicine, and upon the actual pressure of a present necessity."

It is the same lesson that Mr. Spurgeon expounds in his illuminating way in a passage like the following:

"We ought to muse upon the things of God, because we thus get the real nutriment out of them. Truth is something like the cluster of the vine: if we would have wine from it, we must bruise it; we must press and squeeze it many times. The bruisers' feet must come down joyfully upon the bunches, or else the juice will not flow; and they must well tread the grapes, or else much of the precious liquid will be wasted. So we must by meditation tread the clusters of truth, if we would get the wine of consolation therefrom. Our bodies are not supported merely by taking food into the mouth, but the process which really supplies the muscles and the nerve and the sinew and the bone is the process of digestion. It is by digestion that the outer food becomes assimilated with the inner life. Our souls are not nourished merely by listening awhile to this, and then to that, and then to the other part of divine truth. Hearing, reading, marking, and learning all require inwardly digesting to complete their usefulness, and the inward digesting of the truth lies for the most part in meditating upon it. Why is it that some Christians, although they hear many sermons, make but slow advances in the divine life? Because they neglect their closets, and do not thoughtfully meditate on God's Word. They love the wheat,but they do not grind it; they would have the corn, but they will not go forth into the fields to gather it; the fruit hangs upon the tree, but they will not pluck it; the water flows at their feet, but they will not stoop to drink it. From such folly deliver us, O Lord, and be this our resolve this day, 'I will meditate on Thy precepts.' "4

Meditation is an exercise which stands somewhere between thought and prayer. It must not be confounded with mere reasoning; it is reasoning transfigured by devout feeling; and it proceeds by broodingly dissolving rather than by logically analyzing the thought. But it must be guarded from degenerating into mere day-dreaming on sacred themes; and it will be wise in order to secure ourselves from this fault to meditate chiefly with the Bible in our hands and always on its truths. As meditation, then, on the one side takes hold upon prayer, so, on the other, it shades off into devotional Bible-reading, the highest exercise of which, indeed, it is. Life close to God's Word, is life close to God. When I urge you to make very much while you are in the Seminary of this kind of devotional Bible study, running up into meditation, pure and simple, I am but repeating what the General Assembly specifically requires of you. "It is expected," says the *Plan of the Seminary,* framed by the Assembly as our organic law, "that every student will spend a portion of time, every morning and evening, in devout meditation and self-recollection and examination; in reading the Holy Scriptures solely with a view to a personal and practical application of the passage read to his own heart, character and circumstances; and in humble, fervent prayer and praise to God in secret."

And do we not find in the practice here recommended the remedy for that lamentable lack of familiarity with "the English Bible"—as it is fashionable now to speak of it—which is distressing us all in candidates for the ministry? Brethren, you deceive yourselves if you fancy any one can *teach* you "the English Bible" in the sense in which knowledge of it is desiderated. As well expect some one to digest your food for you. You must taste its preciousness for yourselves, before you can apply its preciousness to others' needs. You must assimilate the Bible and make it your own, in that intimate sense which will fix its words fast in your hearts, if you would have those words rise spontaneously to your lips in your times of need, or in the times of the need of others. Read, study, meditate on your Bible: take time to it—much time; spend effort, strength, yourselves on it; until the Bible is in you. Then the Bible will well up in you and come out from you in every season of need.

It is idle to seek aids for such reading and meditation. The devout and prayerful spirit is the only key to it. Nevertheless there are helps which may be temporarily used as crutches if the legs halt too much to go. Dean Alford has a couple of little books on *How to Study the Scriptures,* and Dean Goulburn has a little volume on *The Practical Study of the Bible* which may be profitably consulted for general direction. Our fathers used to read their Bibles with Thomas Scott's *Family Bible with Notes,* or Matthew Henry's *Expository Notes on the New Testament* (which turns every passage into a prayer) on their knee; and a worse practice can be conceived. The pungent quaintness of Henry especially remains until today without a rival: and no one can read his comments with his heart set on learning of God without deriving from them perennial profit. Direction for your thoughts in meditating on Divine truth may be sought also in the numerous books now in such general use for morning and evening religious reading. Bogatzky's *Golden Treasury* is the book of this sort our grandfathers used. William Jay's *Morning and Evening Exercises* is still one of the most useful of them. By its side may be fairly placed at least Mr. Spurgeon's *Checkbook on the Bank of Faith.* And the little books of Frances Ridley Havergal have won for themselves a good report. In the use of such aids it is wise to be constantly on guard lest, on the one side, we permit the aid to supplant the direct use of the Word of God as the basis of our meditation, and, on the other, we grow so accustomed to the crutch that we never learn to walk alone. Let neither Matthew Henry nor Charles Spurgeon supplant either the Word of God or the Spirit of God as the teacher of your soul.

IV.

In speaking of such aids to the devotional study of Scripture and prayerful meditation, we are already making the transition to a further class of helps to which I must advert before closing. "Every student," says the *Plan of the Seminary,* "at the close of his course . . . must" (I beg you to observe that "must") "have read a considerable number of the best practical writers on the subject of religion." Even without such admonition we certainly could not have failed to recognize this source of quickening for the religious life. The question that is pressing is, Which are "the best practical writers on the subject of religion?" In the multitude clamoring for our attention, some good, many bad and not a few indifferent, the need of guidance in the choice of our practical reading becomes very acute.

Four great movements have been especially prolific in books of edification, each, of course, after its own fashion and with peculiarities of its own. These are the great mystical movement which runs through all ages of the Church; the

Puritan movement of the seventeenth century; the Evangelical movement in the latter part of the eighteenth and early nineteenth centuries; and more lately and to a less extent the Anglican revival of the nineteenth century. The characteristic mark of the works which have emanated from the mystical writers is a certain aloofness combined with a clear and piercing note of adoration. The Puritan literature is marked by intense devotion to duty and strong insistence on personal holiness. Its message is apt to be couched in a somewhat unadorned literary style. But when the graces of style happen to be added to its clear good sense and profound piety, nothing could be more charming. I can never forget my "discovery" of John Arrowsmith, for example, when, reading a mass of Puritan literature for another purpose, I suddenly passed from the plain goodness of Anthony Burgess to his delightful pages. The evangelical fervor of the writers of the great awakening, and the churchly flavor of the Anglican writers are naturally their most marked characteristics. Our task is to select from this varied literature just the books which will most feed our souls.[5]

Thinking that in the multitude of counselors there was likely to be strength, I made bold a few years ago to write to a number of religious teachers, each of them justly famous as a writer of books of devotional character, and asked their aid in making out a short list of "the best practical writers on the subject of religion" for the use of the students of the Seminary. I will give you one or two of the answers I received, and these may serve as preliminary guides to your practical reading. Dr. James Stalker, now a Professor in the United Free Church College, Aberdeen, thought the following, on the whole, the five most helpful books of practical religion: Thomas á Kempis' *Imitation of Christ,* Richard Baxter's *Reformed Pastor,* Jeremy Taylor's *Life of Christ,* John Owen's *Holy Spirit,* Adolph Monod's *Saint Paul.* The late Rev. Dr. William M. Taylor, of New York, gave the prefer-ence to the following five: Dean Goulburn's *Thoughts on Personal Religion,* Phelps' *Still Hour,* Tholuck's *Hours of Christian Devotion,* Alexander's *Thoughts on Religious Experience,* Faber's *Hymns.* Our own Dr. William M. Paxton recommends especially: Hodge's *Way of Life,* Bishop Ryle's *Holiness,* Doddridge's *Rise and Progress of Religion in the Soul,* Owen's *Spiritual Mindedness,* and Faber's *Thoughts on Great Mysteries.* These are all good books and would richly repay your loving study. A hundred others could be added just as good.

It would be useless, however, to draw out a long list of books to be especially recommended. I shall venture to set do 1 the titles of just a round dozen, which I look upon as indispensable. Each must be read for what it can give us: and in none of them shall we seek inspiration and instruction in vain. They come from every part of the Church and from every age, and they include representatives of every type of Christian thought, from the Mariolatrous Romanism of Thomas á Kempis or the bald Pelagianism of Sir Thomas Browne to the penetrating mysticism of the *Theologia Germanica* and the plain evangelicalism of John Newton. But they all are veritable devotional classics, and each of them has power in it to move and instruct the heart of whoever would live in the Spirit. Get at least these dozen booklets, keep them at your elbow, and sink yourselves in them with constant assiduity. They are:—Augustine's *Confessions;*[6] *The Imitation of Christ;*[7] the *Theologia Germanica;*[8] Bishop Andrewes' *Private Devotions;*[9] Jeremy Taylor's *Life of Christ;* [10] Richard Baxter's *The Saints' Everlasting Rest;*[11] Samuel Rutherford's *Letters;*[12] John Bunyan's *Pilgrim's Progress;* [13] Sir Thomas Browne's *Religio Medici;*[14] William Law's *Serious Call;*[15] John Newton's *Cardiphonia;*[16] Bishop Thomas Wilson's *Sacra Privata.* [17] To these twelve I should add two or three others which have peculiar interest to us as Princetonians, and which I am sure are worthy of association with them—Jonathan Edwards' *Treatise Concerning Religious Affections,* Archibald Alexander's *Thoughts on Religious Experience,* and Charles Hodge's *Way of Life.*

I have purposely omitted from this list collections of hymns and (in general) or prayers, in order that I might recommend the use of both to you in a separate category. I strongly advise you to make yourselves familiar with the best prayers to which saintly men have given permanent form. Faber's *Hymns* have a quality of intense adoration in them which recommends them to many as the best for such a purpose: Miss Rosetti's devotional poems are unsurpassed for elevation of feeling: many prefer the quieter note of Keble's *Christian Year:* others still love best the evangelical sobriety of *The Olney Hymns,* or the exotic flavor of Miss Winkworth's *Lyra Sacra Germanica:* others find more attractive the variety afforded by such a book as Dr. Schaff's *Christ in Song.* On the whole, I fancy most of you will find that Palgrave's *Treasury of Sacred Song* will meet your needs as well as any other single volume: it is a veritable treasurehouse of the best of English religious poetry. As to collections of prayers, nothing is more inspiring than Lancelot Andrewes' *Private Devotions,* which I have already named in the general list of recommended devotional books, unless it be Anselm's *Meditations and Prayers,*[18] which, despite the deforming hagiolatry which sometimes invades them, remain an example for all ages of how a great heart lifts itself up greatly to God.

There is yet another branch of religious reading which I think you will scarcely be able to neglect, if you would build yourself up into the full stature of manhood in Christ by the example of His saints. I refer to religious biography. Only let us remember that in selecting religious biographies to read with a view to our spiritual improvement, we must bear in mind that the adjective must be understood as qualifying the Life as well as the life: it must be the biographies themselves

that are religious. It must be confessed that many of the
greatest saints have been unfortunate in their biographers.
Not only are their lives often written without a particle of
literary skill, but equally often much of the religious impression of their holy walk has evaporated in the telling. Nevertheless from at least the time when the great Athanasius
himself edified the Church with a life of Anthony—written,
we fear, not without some imitation in form and content
alike of the popular romances of the time[19]—the Church has
never lacked a series of religious biographies which have in
them the promise and potency of religious life for their
readers. Dr. Stalker thinks the best of these for your use are
Augustine's *Confessions,* Baxter's *Reliques,* Hanna's *Life of
Chalmers,* Blaikie's *Life of Livingstone,* Witte's *Life of Tholuck,* and Brown's *Life of Rabbi Duncan.* The late Dr. William
M. Taylor recommended Bonar's *Memoirs of McCheyne,*
Hanna's *Life of Chalmers,* Arnot's *Memoir of James Hamil-
ton,* Guthrie's *Memoirs,* Blaikie's *Life of Livingstone,* J. G.
Paton's *Autobiography,* and Dr. Prentiss' *Life and Letters of
Mrs. Prentiss.* You will not fail to observe how Scotch Dr.
Taylor's list is. Tastes will differ: the late Dean Goulburn
wrote me simply that there were no religious biographies
equal to Isaac Walton's. I shall not undertake to add a list of
my own, which doubtless would have its peculiarities also. I
shall content myself with a bare hint that you must not miss
reading the great books. Such, for example, is Bunyan's
Grace Abounding—the seventeenth century replica of Augustine's *Confessions.* Such also is John Newton's *Authentic
Narrative.* Such also is Boston's *Memoirs* which can now be
had in a worthy form.[20] Such, also, is probably Doddridge's
account of James Gardiner's remarkable life. And such certainly is Edward's *Life of David Brainerd.* And if I am to
judge by my own experience of its religious impression, such
also is the *Life of Adolph Monod* by one of his daughters.
     Along with religious biography may I venture to men-

tion also religious fiction—the portrayal of the religious life under the cover of imagined actors? Take the *Chronicles of the Schoenberg-Cotta Family*. Take the *Heir of Redcliffe*. Who in the face of the experience of a generation can doubt the quickening influence of such books? A book that has played a part such as that played by the *Heir of Redcliffe* in the lives of men like Dr. A. Kuyper and Mr. William Morris is surely worthy of our serious attention as a religious force in the world. And speaking of these books brings to my lips the exclamation, What women the Church of Victorian England gave the world! Elizabeth Rundell Charles, Charlotte Mary Yonge, Frances Ridley Havergal, Dora Greenwell, Dora Pattison—the Lives of all of these are accessible to you as well as their writings—though some of them, I am sorry to say, are rather dully written. Put them by the side of the *Life of Mrs. Prentiss* recommended to us by Dr. Taylor, and learn from them what women Christianity is still making all around us.

Of *Sermons* I shall say nothing: they form a department of religious literature by themselves. But I have reserved for the last mention a class of religious literature which, for my own part, I esteem the very highest of all for spiritual impression. I refer to the great Creeds of the Church. He who wishes to grow strong in his religious life, let him, I say, next to the Bible, feed himself on the great Creeds of the Church. There is a force of religious inspiration in them which you will seek in vain elsewhere. And this for good reasons. First, because it is ever true that it is by the truth that sanctification is wrought. And next, because the truth is set forth in these Creeds with a clearness and richness with which it is set forth nowhere else. For these Creeds are not the products of metaphysical speculation, as many who know infinitesimally little about them are prone to assert, but are the compressed and weighted utterances of the Christian heart. I am not alone, of course, in so esteeming them. You will remember with what insistence Cardinal Newman warns us against "an untheological devotion," and with what force he expounds in his *Grammar of Assent* the spiritual import of the Creeds and Catechisms of the Church. For himself, he tells us, the Athanasian Creed has always seemed the most devotional formulary that Christianity has ever given birth to: and certainly readers of Dr. Gore's beautiful exposition of it as "the Battle-hymn of Christians" will not be slow to feel the truth of Dr. Newman's estimate. Dr. Alexander Whyte, in commenting on Andrewes' *Private Devotions*, takes up the theme afresh and remarks on the exemplification it receives in Andrewes' treatment of the Apostles' and Nicene Creeds. "When Andrewes takes up any of these things," he observes, "into his intellect, imagination and heart, he has already provided himself and his readers with another great prayer and another great psalm. So true is it that all true theology is directly and richly and evangelically devotional."

I do not think I go astray, therefore, when I say to you in all seriousness that the second and third volumes of Dr. Schaff's *Creeds of Christendom* have in them more food for your spiritual life—are "more directly, richly and evangelically devotional"—than any other book, apart from the Bible, in existence. Nor can I think myself wrong in directing you specifically to the Reformed Creeds as, above all others, charged with blessing to those who will read and meditate on their rich deposit of religious truth. Our Scotch forefathers turned for spiritual nourishment especially to "the Sum of Saving Knowledge and the Practical Use Thereof," which had come to be a stated portion of the current editions of the Confession of Faith, just because that volume circulated at first chiefly as a devotional book and a directory for practical religion. This treatise has never been a part of our "Church book." But in the Westminster Confession we have something even better. Read what Thornwell tells us of what the study of the Confession did for his soul,[21] and then ask yourselves whether it may not do the same for you too. By the side of the Westminster Confession put the Heidelberg Catechism: where will you find more faithful, more probing Christian teaching than this? I beg you, brethren, feed your souls on the Christian truth set forth with so much combined clearness of apprehension and depth of feeling in these great formularies.

And so we come around at the end to the point from which we took our start. Religious knowledge and religious living go hand in hand. "It might be instructive to inquire," writes good Dr. Andrew A. Bonar,[22] "why it is that whenever godliness is healthy and progressive we almost invariably find learning in the Church attendant on it: while, on the other hand, an illiterate state is attended sooner or later by decay of vital godliness." We deceive ourselves if we think we can give a portion of our being only to God. If we withhold the effort requisite to learn to know the truth, we cannot hope to succeed in any effort to do His will. Unknown truth cannot sanctify the soul; and it is by the truth that we are to be sanctified. Mind, heart and hand—true religious cultivation must embrace them all and carry on their training all together. We must indeed rebuke the lordly understanding if it essays to supersede the necessity of holy living. Our heart thrills responsively when the monk of Deventer, at the opening of his pungent book, asks us pointedly, How will it advantage you to know all things if you have no love?

"What is the profit," he demands, "of high argument on the Trinity if you lack humility and are offensive to the Trinity? Great words assuredly make no man holy and righteous; but by virtuous living he becomes dear to God. Far better feel compunction than have skill in defining it. Though you know the whole Bible and all the sayings of the philosophers, what would it all advantage you without God's love and grace? . . . . It is natural to man to desire knowledge; but knowledge without the fear of God—of what avail is it?"

Yes, yes, our hearts reply: it is all true, greatly true! But beneath our assent does there not lurk an underlying sense, as we read on deeper into the exhortation, that there is something of the narrowness of mysticism in the sharp "either—or" that is thrust upon us? If we must choose between knowledge and life, why of course give us life! But why put the alternative so sharply? Must it be knowledge *or* life? Must it not rather be knowledge *and* life? *Non comprehenditur Deus per investigationem sed per imitationem,* says Hugh of St. Cher. Ah, but "investigation" is the first step in "imitation;" for how shall I strive to be like God, except by first discovering what God is like? And "imitation" itself—is it after all the key-word of Christianity? It is, no doubt, a great word. But it is not the greatest. "Trust" is greater. And by the side of "trust" there stand but two others. "But now abideth," says Paul, "faith, hope, love, these three; and the greatest of these is love."

Happily we have not been left to ourselves to make the correction. The Church has had greater teachers than even Thomas á Kempis. And a greater than he begins a greater book than his with greater words than he could give us:

"Great art Thou, O Lord, and highly to be praised; great is Thy power and Thy understanding is infinite. Yet Thee would man praise—though but a little particle of Thy creation: even man, who bears about with him his mortality, bears about with him the proof of his sin, even the proof that Thou resistest the proud: yea, Thee still would man praise, this little particle of Thy creation. 'Tis Thou that dost excite us to delight in Thy praise; for Thou didst make us for Thyself and our heart is restless till it find its rest in Thee. Grant me, Lord, to know whether I should first call upon Thee or praise Thee; whether I should first know Thee or call upon Thee. . . . Alas! Alas! tell me for Thy mercies' sake, O Lord, my God, what Thou art unto me. Say unto my soul, 'I am thy salvation.' So speak that I may hear. Behold, the ears of my heart are before Thee, O Lord: open Thou them and say to my soul, 'I am thy salvation.' Make me to run after Thy voice and lay hold on Thee. Hide not Thy face from me. Let me die that I die not: only let me see Thy face. Narrow is my soul's house; enlarge Thou it, that Thou mayest enter in. It is fallen into ruins: repair Thou it. There is that within it which must offend Thine eyes: I confess, I know it. But who shall cleanse it? Or to whom but to Thee shall I cry?"

Here, I venture to say, is the essence of all true religion. Humility of spirit is here rather than depreciation of intellect: trust in the mercy of God to sinners rather than dependence on deeds of man. There is no such note struck here as this: "Even though I knew everything in all the world and were not in charity, what would it advantage me in the sight of God, who will judge me *ex facto.*" *Ex facto* indeed! Who that is judged by his works shall stand? It is not an antithesis of knowledge and works that Augustine draws. It is an antithesis of man and God: and its note is, "In Thee only do I put my trust, O Lord, for in Thee only is there salvation." *Dic 'Habeo,'* says he tersely, *sed, 'Ab Eo.'* It is an execrable word-play, but excellent theology, and the very quintessence of religion. And when we have learned this well,—learned it so that it sounds in all the chambers of our hearts and echoes down through all the aisles of our lives,—we shall have learned the great lesson of practical religion.

FOOTNOTES

[1] An address delivered to the incoming Students, Sabbath afternoon, September 20, 1903, in the Oratory of Stuart Hall, Princeton Theological Seminary.

[2] P. 43.

[3]*Life in Christ and for Christ,* p. 37.

[4]*Morning by Morning,* p. 256.

[5]We have no good history of edifying literature in English. The amazing diligence of Hermann Beck has given the Germans two admirable books in this department of knowledge: *Die Erbauungsliteratur der evang. Kirche Deutschlands* (Erlangen: Deichert, 1883, Part I) and *Die relig. Volksliteratur d. ev. Kirche Deutschlands in eine Abriss ihrer Geschichte* (Gotha: Perthes, 1892). A volume on *Books of Devotion,* by the Rev. Charles Bodington, has lately appeared in the series of practical treatises called *The Oxford Library of Practical Theology,* edited by the Rev. W. C. E. Newbold, M.A., and the Rev. Darwell Stone, M.A. (London and New York: Longmans, Green & Co., 1903). It is written from an extreme Anglican point of view: and I am afraid I shall have to add that it is high and dry to a degree and, beyond giving some account of the contents of a number of books of devotional tenor in English, largely of Romish origin, is of little value.

[6]The editions are numerous. The best Latin text is that of Pius Knöll, which is accessible in the Teubner series of Latin texts (Leipzig, 1898). Of the English translations of the whole work, Dr. Pusey's is best both for the translation and its admirable notes. Dr. Shedd's edition of Watt's version contains an interesting Introduction. An excellent new translation of the first nine books, with introduction and notes, by Dr. C. Bigg, was published by Methuen in 1898.

[7]The editions are numerous and easily accessible in both Latin and English. Much the best English translation is that by Dr. Charles Bigg, published in Methuen's series of Devotional Books. A new departure was made by the publication at Berlin in 1874, by Dr. C. Hirsche, of an edition the text of which is presented "metrice." The English version of this metrically arranged text, published by A. D. F. Randolph, New York, 1889, is somewhat diffuse but interesting.

[8]Get the edition in Macmillan's *Golden Treasury Series,* edited by Dr. Pfeiffer, and translated by Susanna Winkworth.

[9]There are many editions. The best is *The Preces Privatæ of Bishop Andrewes,* edited by F. E. Brightman, M.A. (London: Methuen, 1903). I recommend for the English reader also Dr. Alexander Whyte's edition (Edinburgh: Oliphant, Anderson & Ferrier, 1896), to which is prefixed an admirable "Biography" and still more admirable "Interpretation."

[10]Printed in Vol. 2 of Heber's edition of his *Works.*

[11]An edition is published by the Presbyterian Board of Publication, and another in Methuen's series of Devotional Books.

[12]Dr. Bonar's edition is the best (New York: Carter): cf. Dr. A. Whyte's *Samuel Rutherford and Some of His Correspondents.* The Messrs. Longmans publish an excellent selection from the letters, edited by Miss Lucy M. Soulsby, under the title of *Christ and His Cross.*

[13]A good edition is issued by the Presbyterian Board of Publication.

[14]*The Golden Treasury* edition (Macmillan) is particularly to be recommended.

[15]Get the edition in Dent's *Temple Classics.*

[16]An edition is printed by the Presbyterian Board of Publication.

[17]Keble's edition (Oxford, 1860) is the standard. A good edition is *Bishop Wilson's Sacra Privata,* edited by A. E. Burn, B.D. (London: Methuen, 1903).

[18]An English translation, with prefatory matter by Dr. Pusey, was published at Oxford in 1856. A good edition is that of London, 1872. The latest edition, *The Devotions of St. Anselm,* edited by C. C. J. Webb, M.A. (London: Methuen, 1903), contains only (along with the *Proslogion* and some letters) four each of the *Meditations* and *Prayers.*

[19]See a very interesting essay on "Greek and Early Christian Novels," pp. 357 *sqq.* of Mr. T. R. Glover's *Life and Letters in the Fourth Century* (Cambridge, 1901).

[20]Edited by Rev. G. H. Morrison (Edinburgh: Oliphant, Anderson & Ferrier, 1899).

[21]See Palmer's *Life of Thornwell,* pp. 162, 165.

[22]Introduction to his ed. of *Rutherford's Letters,* N. Y., 1851, p. xvi.

PAUL ON WOMEN SPEAKING IN CHURCH[1]

I have recently received a letter from a valued friend asking me to send him a "discussion of the Greek words *laleo* and *lego* in such passages as I Cor. 14:33-39, with special reference to the question: Does the thirty-fourth verse forbid all women everywhere to speak or preach publicly in Christian churches?" The matter is of universal interest, and I take the liberty of communicating my reply to the readers of *The Presbyterian.*

It requires to be said at once that there is no problem with reference to the relations of *laleo* and *lego.* Apart from niceties of merely philological interest, these words stand related to one another just as the English words *speak* and *say* do; that is to say, *laleo* expresses the *act of talking,* while *lego* refers to *what is said.* Wherever then the fact of speaking, without reference to the content of what is said, is to be indicated, *laleo* is used, and must be used. There is nothing disparaging in the intimation of the word, any more than there is in our word *talk;* although, of course, it can on occasion be used disparagingly as our word *talk* can also—as when some of the newspapers intimate that the Senate is given over to mere talk. This disparaging application of *laleo,* however, never occurs in the New Testament, although the word is used very frequently.

The word is in its right place in I Cor. 14:33ff, therefore, and necessarily bears there its simple and natural meaning. If we needed anything to fix its meaning, however, it would be supplied by its frequent use in the preceding part of the chapter, where it refers not only to speaking with tongues (which was a divine manifestation and unintelligible only because of the limitations of the hearers), but also to the prophetic speech, which is directly declared to be to edification and exhortation and comforting (verses 3–6). It would be supplied more pungently, however, by its contrasting term here—"let them be silent" (verse 34). Here we have *laleo* directly defined for us: "Let the women *keep silent,* for it is not permitted to them to *speak.*" Keep silent—speak: these are the two opposites; and the one defines the other.

It is important to observe, now, that the pivot on which the injunction of these verses turns, is not the prohibition of speaking so much as the command of silence. That is the main injunction. The prohibition of speech is introduced only to explain the meaning more fully. What Paul says is in brief: "Let the women keep silent in the churches." That surely is direct and specific enough for all needs. He then adds explanatorily: "For it is not permitted to them to speak." "It is not permitted" is an appeal to a general law, valid apart from Paul's personal command, and looks back to the opening phrase—"as in all the churches of the saints." He is only requiring the Corinthian women to conform to the general law of the churches. And that is the meaning of the almost bitter words which he adds in verse 36, in which, reproaching them for the innovation of permitting women to speak in the churches, he reminds them that they are not the authors of the gospel, nor are they its sole possessors—let them keep to the law that binds the whole body of churches and not be seeking some new-fangled way of their own.

The intermediate verses only make it plain that precisely what the apostle is doing is forbidding women to speak at all in the church. His injunction of silence he pushes so far that he forbids them even to ask questions; and adds with special reference to that, but through that to the general matter, the crisp declaration that "it is indecent"—for that is the meaning of the word—"for a woman to speak in church."

It would be impossible for the apostle to speak more directly or more emphatically than he has done here. He requires women to be silent at the church-meetings. For that is what "in the churches" means; there were no church buildings then. And he has not left us in doubt as to the nature of these church-meetings. He had just described them in verses 26ff. They were of the general character of our prayer-meetings. Note the words, "let him be silent in the church," in verse 30, and compare them with "let them be silent in the churches," in verse 34. The prohibition of women speaking covers thus all public church-meetings—it is the publicity, not the formality of it, which is the point. And he tells us repeatedly that this is the universal law of the church. He does more than that. He tells us that it is the commandment of the Lord, and emphasizes the word "Lord" (verse 37).

The passage in I Tim. 2:11ff. is just as strong, although it is more particularly directed to the specific case of public teaching or ruling in the church. The apostle had already in this context (verse 8, "the men," in contrast with "women" of verse 9) pointedly confined public praying to men, and now continues: "Let a woman learn in silence in all subjection; but I do not permit to the woman to teach, neither to rule over the man, but to be in silence." Neither the teaching nor the ruling function is permitted to woman. The apostle says here, "I do not permit," instead of as in I Cor. 14:33ff., "it is not permitted," because he is here giving his personal instructions to Timothy, his subordinate, while there he was announcing to the Corinthians the general law of the church. What he instructs Timothy, however, is the general law of the church. And so he goes on and grounds his prohibition in a universal reason which affects the entire race equally.

In the face of these two absolutely plain and emphatic passages, what is said in I Cor. 11:5 cannot be appealed to in mitigation or modification. Precisely what is meant in I Cor.

11:5, nobody quite knows. What is said there is that every woman praying or prophesying unveiled dishonors her head. It seems fair to infer that if she prays or prophesies veiled she does not dishonor her head. And it seems fair still further to infer that she may properly pray or prophesy if only she does it veiled. We are piling up a chain of inferences. And they have not carried us very far. We cannot infer that it would be proper for her to pray or prophesy *in church* if only she were veiled. There is nothing said about church in the passage or in the context. The word "church" does not occur until the 16th verse, and then not as ruling the reference of the passage, but only as supplying support for the injunction of the passage. There is no reason whatever for believing that "praying and prophesying" in church is meant. Neither was an exercise confined to the church. If, as in I Cor. 14:14, the "praying" spoken of was an ecstatic exercise—as its place by "prophesying" may suggest—then, there would be the divine inspiration superceding all ordinary laws, to be reckoned with. And there has already been occasion to observe that prayer in public is forbidden to women in I Tim. 2:8, 9. Unless mere *attendance* at prayer is meant, in which case this passage is a close parallel of I Tim. 2:9.

What then must be noted, in conclusion, is:

(1) That the prohibition of speaking in the church to women is precise, absolute, and all-inclusive. They are to keep silent in the churches—and that means in all the public meetings for worship; they are not even to ask questions; (2) that this prohibition is given especial point precisely for the two matters of teaching and ruling covering specifically the functions of preaching and ruling elders; (3) that the grounds on which the prohibition is put are universal, and turn on the difference in sex, and particularly on the relative places given to the sexes in creation and in the fundamental history of the race (the fall).

Perhaps it ought to be added in elucidation of the last

point just made, that the difference in conclusions between
Paul and the feminist movement of today is rooted in a
fundamental difference in their points of view relatively to
the constitution of the human race. To Paul, the human race
is made up of families, and every several organism, the church
included, is composed of families, united together by this or
that bond. The relation of the sexes in the family follows it
therefore into the church. To the feminist movement the
human race is made up of individuals; a woman is just
another individual by the side of the man; and it can see no
reason for any differences in dealing with the two. And,
indeed, if we can ignore the great fundamental natural difference of sex, and destroy the great fundamental social unit of
the family, in the interest of individualism, there does not
seem any reason why we should not wipe out the differences
established by Paul between the sexes in the church. Except,
of course, the authority of Paul. It all, in the end, comes back
to the authority of the apostles, as founders of the church.
We may like what Paul says, or we may not like it. We may
be willing to do what he commands, or we may not be willing
to do it. But there is no room for doubt of what he says. And
he certainly would say to us, what he said to the Corinthians:
"What? Was it from you that the word of God went forth? or
came it to you alone?" Is this Christianity ours—to do with as
we like? Or is it God's religion, receiving its laws from him
through the apostles?

---

[1] Reprinted from *The Presbyterian*, October 30, 1919.

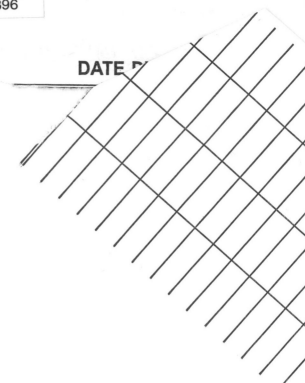

DATE D